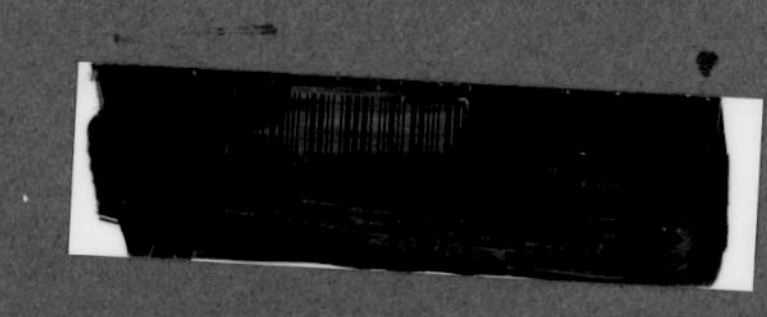

D0040946

Due To Circumstances Beyond Our Control . . .

Due To Circumstance

by FRED W. FRIENDLY

Beyond Our Control . . .

RANDOM HOUSE *New York*

First Printing

Published in New York by Random House, Inc., and simultaneously in Toronto, Canada, by Random House of Canada Limited.
Library of Congress Catalog Card Number: 67–13812
Manufactured in the United States of America
by H. Wolff, New York

For the professionals at CBS NEWS:

"I'd know—that's who'd know."

"I believe television is going to be the test of the modern world, and that in this new opportunity to see beyond the range of our vision we shall discover either a new and unbearable disturbance of the general peace or a saving radiance in the sky. We shall stand or fall by television—of that I am quite sure."

E. B. WHITE 1938

"This instrument can teach, it can illuminate; yes, and it can even inspire. But it can do so only to the extent that humans are determined to use it to those ends. Otherwise it is merely lights and wires in a box."

EDWARD R. MURROW 1958

"What the American people don't know can kill them."

DOROTHY GREENE FRIENDLY 1958

Contents

Introduction

> "Too often the machine runs away with itself . . . instead of keeping pace with the social needs it was created to serve."
>
> WILLIAM S. PALEY, 1936.

"All I'm trying to do is save the company some money."

"All I'm trying to do is save the company."

The first line was spoken by James Aubrey, president of the CBS Television Network, in the late spring of 1960, the second by me. As president, Aubrey's mission was to push the annual profits of the parent company, Columbia Broadcasting System, Inc., past the plateau where they had rested for several years—at about $23,000,000 after taxes. (Before he left he had doubled this figure.)

As the executive producer of a new project, *CBS Reports,* my job was to create a series of bold documentaries which would help restore the prestige of CBS and, indirectly, the broadcast industry recently tarred by the quiz scandals.

Our argument was over budgets and time availability—specifically a time period for the first Walter Lippmann conversation, for which we still had no air time. In the course of the conversation Aubrey, who had flair and never lacked candor, said something that stayed with me all the rest of my days at CBS.

"Look, Fred, I have regard for what Murrow and you have accomplished, but in this adversary system you and I are always going to be at each other's throats. They say to me [he meant the system, not any specific individual], 'Take your soiled little hands, get the ratings, and make as much money as you can'; they say to you, "Take your lily-white hands, do your best, go the high road and bring us prestige.' "

Jim Aubrey is no philosopher, but in that brief, cynical conservation he did spell out the dilemma and the contradiction that split personalities and the television screen itself. Because television can make so much money doing its worst, it often cannot afford to do its best. Aubrey's words could have been spoken by any of the five other presidents who preceded or succeeded him, or by any one of the presidents of the other networks.

I remembered Aubrey's words in August 1965 when space bulletins about the trouble in the fuel cell of Gemini-Titan V had to be superimposed on the bottom of Mighty Mouse and Quick Draw McGraw cartoons. I remembered those words in 1966 while the United Nations debated about Vietnam and all three networks stayed with their soap operas and game shows. I remembered those words when *Playhouse 90* died and when NBC took most of its fine documentaries out of their expensive evening-time periods.

Most of all I remembered Aubrey's words at 10 A.M. on February 10, 1966, when the Senate Foreign Relations Committee hearings on Vietnam began and CBS put an ancient rerun of *I Love Lucy* on its screen while NBC televised the testimony of Ambassador George F. Kennan. At that instant I wished that I could have superimposed an announcement saying: "Due to circumstances beyond our control, the broadcast originally intended for this time will not be seen"—and I said exactly that in my letter of resignation to CBS Board Chairman William S. Paley and President Frank Stanton.

So much of what is wrong with television is due to circumstances beyond somebody's control.

At that instant in February 1966, another memory also

flashed through my mind. On November 18, 1951, Murrow and I bought a $3,000 video line to San Francisco in order to show the Golden Gate Bridge and the Brooklyn Bridge simultaneously on a television tube at the beginning of the first *See It Now* broadcast. As this image appeared on the screen Murrow said: "For the first time in the history of man we are able to look out at both the Atlantic and Pacific coasts of this great country at the same time . . . no journalistic age was ever given a weapon for truth with quite the scope of this fledgling television."

Others had preceded us. Sometimes we Americans like to believe that freedom was invented in this country in 1776. But for all the wisdom of the Founding Fathers, it was due to the accident of chronology that at the very time when the idea of freedom and man's rights had to be broadcast to a wilderness people, pamphleteers like Thomas Paine appeared not only with a message but a medium. Long before the Declaration of Independence, Benjamin Franklin had helped bring about a better postal system and establish special rates and routes. Paine's *Common Sense* and *The Crisis*, and the rest of the Revolutionary literature as well, were available for a few cents and were disseminated through the Colonies by river boat and post road. Simultaneously, the freedom bonfires fed by the pamphleteers were being lit in France and Britain, and soon spread to other parts of the world.

The place of the printing press in this new common market of ideas was as decisive as that of the railroad and the industrial revolution. As the telegraph, the high-speed press and later the linotype accelerated the pace, newspapers and magazines became as indispensable as government. Horace Greeley, Joseph Pulitzer and Adolf Ochs added stature and depth; Hearst added color. From Tom Nast to Lincoln Steffens to Carr Van Anda to Walter Lippmann, practitioners brought meaning and interpretation to the medium, and as America turned from isolationism to world responsibility, the American journalist became the essential American.

With the abundance of foreign news prior to and during World War II, radio shrank the gap between continents and quickened public understanding of international affairs. H. V. Kaltenborn and Raymond Swing during the Munich crisis, William L. Shirer at Compiègne, Ed Murrow and Elmer Davis during the Blitz, George Hicks and Charles Collingwood on D-Day, Bob Trout on V-E Day made radio a reliable, swift and immediate sword.

Radio was more than just another competitive medium. So fast that it killed the newspaper extra, it provided the listener with an ear-witness seat at history in the making. The newspaper journalist now had to write many of his stories with the knowledge that his reader had shared the event at Nuremberg, No. 10 Downing Street or Yankee Stadium.

In the late thirties and early forties, such radio-documentary and news-oriented dramas as *They Fly Through the Air with the Greatest of Ease*, by Norman Corwin, and *The Fall of the City*, by Archibald MacLeish, had fused the art form of the theater and audio journalism. Radio's *March of Time* leaned heavily on re-creation with actors who mimicked Roosevelt, Hitler, Hirohito and Willkie with such skill that the listener was never quite sure who was speaking. The actor reading lines improvised by a writer who was guessing what Foreign Minister Eden might have said to Prime Minister Chamberlain was the order of the day, and the limit was reached on the night of Orson Welles's re-enactment of *The War of the Worlds*, when his Martian invasion so crossed the line into reality that a national panic resulted.

Still, the use of dramatization, phony sound effects and mood music was something the serious news commentators of the late thirties resisted. But in those early years, network policy prohibited the use of recordings lest the entire concept of chain broadcasting be destroyed; lowering the barriers on delayed-broadcast material might lead to such widespread syndication by records that there would be no need of a live interconnected network. It was the advent of lightweight wire and tape recorders that finally broke the ban on actual recording late in World War II. But though it was inevitable that technical wizardry and more honest journalism would make re-creation obsolete, the truth is that it was slow to die.

Another invention, the light valve, which permitted newsreels to carry sound, had provided one more dynamic dimension to journalism. There were pioneers here, too, who gave us a rich legacy. From a generation of newsreel editors like William "Mowgli" Montague, and cameramen such as Leo Rossi, Charlie Mack and Norman Alley, we learned that sound cameras could be a journalist's tool even if they weighed a thousand pounds. Some of the Signal Corps's work during World War II demonstrated what an art form news presented visually could be. Television journalism also owes much to such men as Louis de Rochemont of the *March of Time*, which brought serious reporting with a point of view into the theater.

Much of this book is the story of how television journalism found its way by beginning with actuality and never turning back. When World War II made radio come of age, Ed Murrow was its first authentic original. Elmer Davis once wrote that he was "painfully scandalized that such good reporting can be done by a man who never worked on a newspaper in his life." Murrow always professed a desire to edit a country newspaper someday, but the truth is that writing for print always was an ordeal for him, and if it had not been for the communications revolution he might have remained an educator. Instead, due to an accident of history, Murrow was at the end of a shortwave circuit when radio and World War II burst upon an isolationist America. Thus, more than a decade later, when radio, the newsreel and the motion picture documentary merged into a new form called television, a journalist was available who knew the grammar of electronics and the history of uninformed people. "We want you to know that we are aware of the electronic wonder entrusted to our fingers," Murrow said. "As human beings, we hope we are up to it; as reporters we hope that we never abuse it."

Edward Roscoe Murrow was born in North Carolina in 1908 and raised in the lumber country of the state of Washington. Coincidentally, he came to CBS in 1935 within a month of the time that Frank Stanton arrived, and his first position was that of director of talks and education. He was in Warsaw in March 1938 as European director of CBS at the time of the Anschluss, and chartered a plane to Vienna. There he got permission to go on the air to report the entry of German troops into Vienna—his first assignment as a broadcaster. Subsequently he went to London, where he set up the CBS European news staff which, besides William Shirer, was to include Charles Collingwood, Eric Sevareid, Howard K. Smith, Larry LeSueur, Bill Downs and Richard C. Hottelet.

Whether speaking from the rooftops of London during the Blitz or on a bombing raid over Berlin or from Buchenwald on the day it was liberated, Murrow became one of the most identifiable and trusted voices of the war. He seared the conscience of America with its stake in London's trial. As Archibald MacLeish said at the time: "You burned the city of London in our houses and we felt the flames that burned it. You laid the dead of London at our doors and we knew the dead were our dead—were all men's dead—were mankind's dead—and ours. Without rhetoric, without dramatics, without more emotion than needed be, you destroyed the superstition of distance and of time—of difference and of time."

Murrow was the only reporter with President Roosevelt on

the night of Pearl Harbor, and he was Churchill's occasional companion at Chartwell or in the Prime Minister's bomb-shelter command post deep under London. During this period he became extremely close to William S. Paley, who later was made deputy chief of psychological warfare at SHAEF. When peace was declared Murrow became a vice-president of CBS and director of public affairs.

As Murrow himself said, he failed in the job. An uncomfortable administrator, with "no stomach for the hiring and firing required," he returned to radio broadcasting in 1947 to do a nightly news series. It was then that I became his junior partner. Our relationship began with a promising idea and a collection of records, out of which emerged a best-selling record album, *I Can Hear It Now.*

From 1937 to 1941 I had been a local radio producer-reporter in Providence, Rhode Island. During the war I was a master sergeant in the Information and Education section of the China-Burma-India Theater, serving as a correspondent for the Army newspaper *CBI Roundup,* the Asian equivalent of *Stars and Stripes.*

I saw Hiroshima and Nagasaki from a low-level reconnaissance plane just a few days after the first two atomic bombs had been dropped. This, and the sight of the Bataan Death March survivors after their liberation from a prison camp in Mukden, Manchuria, and the liberation of the Mauthausen concentration camp in Austria are the only scars I bear from what was, for me, a relatively soft war.

Ed and I met in 1947 when J. G. Gude, who was Elmer Davis' and Raymond Swing's business manager and who handled some of Murrow's affairs, thought my idea for an album of recorded history of the years 1933 to 1945 might interest Ed.

Until that time there had never been a successful talk album, but in 1947 Goddard Lieberson, then a young executive in charge of Columbia Records' classical-music department, was faced with one of Jimmy Petrillo's perennial musicians' strikes, and for this reason he agreed, against others' advice, to take a chance on my idea. Also, Peter Goldmark, CBS's resident inventor, had developed the revolutionary long-playing record, and Lieberson wanted material to keep the idle recording facilities busy. We received a $1,000 advance for *I Can Hear It Now,* which Murrow and Gude insisted that I keep. Dorothy Greene, a *Time-Life* researcher, and I had just been married, and this generosity meant the difference between sticking it out in New York or having to go back to Providence. Still, the record album was a labor of love, and it took us almost eighteen months to complete it. Murrow insisted that it be a "Murrow-Friendly" production, as he did with every project on which we ever worked.

I Can Hear It Now was released at Thanksgiving time 1949, and by Christmas its sales were so spectacular that I went to the bank with a royalty check of $25,000. The Guaranty Trust Company, as it was then called, still remembers the day, because they were on the verge of politely suggesting that a balance which never went above a hundred dollars be transferred to a bank better suited to handle such accounts.

In the next few years there were several sequels to *I Can Hear It Now,* including a Churchill album authorized by the Prime Minister; though they all have had respectable sales, the first album is the staple, and has provided for the college educations of Andrew, Lisa and David Friendly.

In 1950, when we were producing Volume Two of *I Can Hear It Now,* Sig Mickelson, director of public affairs, and Hubbell Robinson, vice-president in charge of network programs, asked me to leave my job as producer at NBC to join the CBS news department. "The Quick and the Dead," a four-part NBC radio documentary about the birth of the atomic bomb which I had produced, convinced the CBS management that a permanent Murrow-Friendly partnership might be productive. Our first venture was *Hear It Now,* a weekly one-hour news-documentary series that had its premiere just as the Chinese Communists entered the Korean War.

After one season *Hear It Now* was replaced by its video equivalent, *See It Now,* which saw the light of day primarily because of a sponsor, the Aluminum Company of America. After the antimonopoly decisions of the federal courts, Alcoa had decided to embark on an advertising campaign designed more to improve its institutional image than its sales, and the idea of a Murrow television program interested the company. They bought it without a pilot program, and Ed and I agreed to produce the series without quite knowing what we would be doing, or even which end of a camera one looked into. We received lots of suggestions, but the only good advice came from Bosley Crowther, the motion picture critic, who refused to suggest the name of a motion picture director to help us get started. "If you do that," said Bosley, "you'll end up making all the mistakes they've made in the newsreels." We did hire Palmer Williams, a young documentary production man who knew a 16-in. lens from a Movieola, and who was our pathfinder as we ventured down an unmarked trail. "PW," who came to stay for four weeks, remained for the life of *See It Now* and *CBS Reports,* and in 1965 became executive producer of the latter. At a moment's notice Williams could not only tell you the time and flight number of the next plane from Karachi to New Delhi, he could also diagnose the editorial flaws of footage on Bertrand Russell or the Polaris submarine. In his way, he was as much my teacher as was Murrow.

One night after Palmer and I had shipped Murrow off to a foreign ministers conference on a midnight freight plane to Berlin, and Ed had to stay up all night in the cargo hatch feeding sleeping pills to the four barking dogs that were his only fellow passengers, we received a cable from him at the end of the journey saying only: THE THINGS WE DO FOR FRIENDLY! That phrase became a battle cry, for it was one of Murrow's ploys that it was I who called the shots and sent him into combat. In a book about television I was once erroneously identified as the man behind Murrow. The truth is that Murrow was the man behind Friendly—and always way ahead of him.

It is not false modesty for me to say that when Murrow left CBS, part of my guts went with him. It is also true that CBS was never the same again. On the day in 1965 when Murrow died, the victim of lung cancer, Bob Trout said in a broadcast: "Of course we shall miss him. The truth is, we have—for a long time."

I never promised Murrow that I would write this book someday, but from time to time he would send me memos from the company, or photostats of complimentary letters, with a note saying: "Here's something for your memoirs, Fritzel." He usually scoffed at any suggestion that he write his autobiography, though once he told me that he had refused to tell a friend who was a famous writer the substance of what happened at the White House on the night of Pearl Harbor. "I expect to send Casey through college with that kind of material," he said with a smile.

Because this book is a series of interconnected essays about broadcast journalism and an occupational memoir, and because it concerns the Columbia Broadcasting System—often the boldest and best of the three networks—it may be useful to sketch for the reader the two principal officers of the company.

In 1966 Chairman of the Board William Paley, sixty-five years old, and President Frank Stanton, fifty-eight, operate CBS much like father and son, with all the complexities and nuances of such a relationship. Paley loves show business and society, and his circle of friends ranges from Jock Whitney, who is also his brother-in-law, to Dwight Eisenhower, Frank

Sinatra, Truman Capote, Leland Hayward and Walter Thayer, president of the now-defunct New York *Herald Tribune.*

Stanton hates "show biz" and is upset when a news effort is referred to as a "good show." It is a news program—and even "news program" offends him; he prefers the term "news broadcast." The words "editorial decisions" and "commentator" are also anathema to him because they suggest a point of view. Stanton's friends include Frank Collbohm, former president of The RAND Corporation; Jesse Kellam, who operates the Austin television station; Philip Johnson, the architect; Elmo Roper, the pollster; and President Johnson (whose desk he redesigned). In the two years that I was president of CBS News, Stanton never took a day off; he was at his desk at eight o'clock in the morning, seven days a week. He was absent from his office only to attend a meeting of The RAND Corporation, the Rockefeller Foundation or The Business Council, or to fly to London to consult with Henry Moore on a statue for Lincoln Center, of which he is a trustee, or to fly to Vietnam on a government information mission.

Paley, on the other hand, spends more than a third of the year away from the office, usually at one of his retreats in Nassau or New Hampshire. Often he takes on a government assignment, such as a Presidential study of materials and resources, a subject on which he is an authority. He is currently chairman of Resources for the Future.

Stanton, always more interested in form rather than content, employed all his taste and sense of design in the new CBS building at 51 West 52 Street—the official name of the skyscraper—because he knew that he could place his mark on it. I believe that he despaired of the broadcast schedule about 1960; thereafter he did not bother to watch much of it except for news and special programs.

On one occasion the CBS advisory committee or board, including all division presidents, sat and listened for thirty-five minutes while Stanton expatiated on the directory in the main lobby of the building; once we discussed for half an hour the problem of how to keep sandwich and coffee deliveries out of the elevators. Another time Stanton consulted us about whether the sign on the men's room should have the simple letter M or MEN (the former prevailed). A division president, to his regret, ventured to suggest that the building was being overemphasized at the expense of the broadcast schedule, which more accurately reflects CBS's public image than any building ever could.

The thirty-six-floor tower of gray Canadian granite and tinted glass was designed by the late Eero Saarinen. It is an aesthetic masterpiece, but nowhere, except for some small panels of letters over the doors, is there a symbol to indicate that it is the home of a great television and radio network. The CBS eye is not to be found in the cathedral-like lobby; nor is there one television or network radio facility in the entire building, although WCBS, the New York radio station, does have studios there. 51 West 52 Street is, to quote Emerson, "the lengthened shadow of one man."

Stanton's office is as fastidious and as disciplined as he is; it resembles a small wing in a modern museum, complete with a large Henry Moore sculpture. There is nothing visible to suggest broadcasting. He is the only corporate president I know of who places all his own phone calls. I have never heard him identify himself as "Doctor," and I have never heard him referred to by any other title. A habitual critic of the quality of color television, he does not have a color set in his home. Occasionally he would call me to ask about the color values on a certain broadcast because he believed that the compromises made for a color production harmed visual qualities on a black-and-white set. Since I'm color-blind myself, some of our conversations sounded like the blind leading the blind.

Paley's suite, facing east and north on the thirty-fifth floor, is furnished with antiques and Picasso, Dubuffet and Rouault originals. The central piece of furniture is a round leather-topped desk which was once a Paris gaming table. On one wall hang the microphones of all the original CBS radio stations, and an authentic cigar-store Indian (a gift of Mrs. Paley) stands in a corner as a nostalgic reminder of Paley's early days with La Palina cigars. Paley is a gourmet who often stops at The Ground Floor, a restaurant in the CBS lobby, to sample a dish before ascending to his private dining room, where the poulet au pot and lamb stew are specialties of the house.

Murrow, who is as much a part of this book as its author, was, along with Paley and Stanton, one of the three most influential forces in the building of CBS. It has been said that Paley was responsible for its creation, that Stanton made it go and that Murrow gave it heart. But this is an oversimplification; each man gave the company more.

If it is true that Murrow can't help being the hero of what I write, it does not follow that others are the villains. No opprobrium is intended for anyone other than Senator McCarthy —certainly not for William Paley or Frank Stanton. I think I understand Murrow and Stanton better than I do Paley, and if that ambivalence is displayed in this book, it reflects my admiration as well as my reservations. Less disciplined than Stanton, less courageous than Murrow, less of a visionary than Sarnoff of RCA, more of an impresario than any of them, Paley is a man for all television seasons. When Marshal Joffre was asked who won the Battle of the Marne, he replied, "I don't know who won it, but if we had lost I know who would have been blamed." So it is with Paley, the richest and single most influential man in broadcast history. The fact that the industry may now be beyond even his control is perhaps as much the fault of the system as of anything else.

In spite of his influence CBS is not, as the trade press likes to call it, Paley's "candy store"—or even its forty-one thousand stockholders'. Television is no more a preserve set aside for any special-interest group than is a school board or draft board, or the Tennessee Valley Authority or Grand Canyon National Park. Nor are the three networks' plans and deliberations entitled to any more privacy. It can be argued that the decisions made in the board rooms of any one of these broadcasting companies are at least as vital to the public interest as our national education, as crucial as national defense, as far-reaching as those made by the Congress, and as relevant to beauty and aesthetics as all our museums and national parks. "Television," a British Member of Parliament recently proclaimed, "will determine what kind of people we are." And Archibald MacLeish has said that broadcasting "matters more over the long run . . . than what anybody else does because [it is] more persistently shaping the minds of more people than all the rest of us put together."

In spite of my desire to make this report as accurate and as comprehensive as decency allows, it is not intended as an exposé. Doubtless there is more in these pages about me than anyone cares to know, but I propose to tell the trials of broadcast journalism by sharing my sixteen-year experience at CBS without, I hope, revealing any privileged financial information which might bring comfort and aid to a rival of the company. Though I may be more generous to persons and principles I supported than to those I opposed, I have tried to be objective —but never so much, I hope, as to obscure my own point of view. Although CBS has in its records a file of their own generous statements about my objectivity as a journalist, it is my ability to be subjective which is on trial in these pages. I may be faulted by some for leaving too much out, but where I have done so it was because the incident or anecdote revealed more about the individual's foibles and weaknesses—my own included—than it did about the principle and issues involved.

My tenure as president of CBS News is a small documentary about that age of detergents when survival came in a giant economy package and security was something you put under your arms, when World War II movies were residual assets while the Senate's Vietnam hearings were a dead loss because the "opinion leaders are not at home during the daytime." Or, to quote a more reasonable position for those who may find the above too weighted: "There are times when responsible business judgments have to determine how much coverage of the Vietnam war one network and its shareholders can fiscally afford."

I lost my job over that choice, and though it may be the better part of humility to say that what happens to any one person isn't important, it would be out of character for me to say that. The stand I took was the most important act of my life, and whether it was I who lost my head or the television industry which has lost its way is something each reader may decide for himself. If it is the former, no action is required; if it is the latter, a possible course of action is outlined in the final chapter, "Circumstances Within Our Control."

Where I have no notes for the exact wording in a conversation, I have paraphrased it to the best of my ability. I have documented facts with the objective assistance of Tinka Nobbe, who is an experienced television researcher, and Martin Clancy, my teaching assistant at Columbia. Hazel Layton, who has been my secretary for eleven years and who was the only person I asked to leave CBS with me, has always been invaluable whether I had the support of hundreds or only of herself. Barbara Elliot retyped the manuscript and was extremely helpful throughout.

Those who encouraged me to write a book include former President Eisenhower, Raymond Swing, Edward P. Morgan, Blanche and Alfred Knopf, Robert Bernstein of Random House, Edward Barrett, dean of the Columbia School of Journalism, McGeorge Bundy, president of the Ford Foundation, Ed Fogel, Sam Standard, Harold Isaacs and J. G. Gude. Jimmy Breslin not only prodded me to write the book but sent me a hundred-pound crate of paper and carbons to help me get started. Carl Sandburg told me that being a writer is easy: "You write down one word and then another." It's not that simple.

As for the editing of this book, the best that can be said for it—and the worst—came from an eminent scholar of American journalism. After reading the manuscript he said, "Now, that sounds the way Friendly talks . . . don't let any Random House 'fancy Dan' editor change your style." Since the manuscript had already gone through the hands of Joe Fox, my editor at Random House, three times, this is the highest compliment I can pay him and my copyeditor, Barbara Willson.

All the above, plus a necessarily anonymous list of those who encouraged, helped and inspired me, deserve not only my gratitude but also the assurance that any errors of fact and judgment are mine alone. To paraphrase an oft-repeated disclaimer heard on television and radio—this book was "produced under the supervision and control of its author, who is solely responsible for its contents."

FRED W. FRIENDLY
Riverdale, N.Y.
October 30, 1966

Due To Circumstances Beyond Our Control . . .

Something of a Hero: Milo Radulovich

There is an indoor tennis court now where Studio 41 used to be, but on the third floor of that windowless labyrinth above the railroad tracks of Grand Central Station, some early television history was enacted. With his penchant for understatement, Ed Murrow referred to such broadcasts as "minor footnotes." I first heard him use the phrase on the day of the first *See It Now* program, in November 1951.

In the course of his introduction, Ed said to the television audience: "This is an old team trying to learn a new trade." It took us two years to learn that job. There was a one-hour report from Korea at Christmas 1952, which was the first combat report via television, but for the most part we were, as Ed said, just a bunch of old radio hands learning the hard way that cameras need something more than emulsion and light valves to create electronic journalism. The missing ingredients were conviction, controversy and a point of view. The industry found them on the night of October 20, 1953, when Murrow looked up at the television camera and said: "We propose to examine . . . the case of Lieutenant Radulovich . . ."

Just thirty seconds before air time Murrow took a final sip from the glass of Scotch at his feet, offered me my customary gulp and said, "I don't know whether we'll get away with this one or not, and things will never be the same around here after tonight, but this show may turn out to be a small footnote to history in the fight against the senator." He meant the junior senator from Wisconsin; the Radulovich program was television's first attempt to do something about the contagion of fear that had come to be known as McCarthyism, and when he said that things would never be the same again, he meant at 485 Madison Avenue, headquarters of the Columbia Broadcasting System. However, this was only a guess, since no one in the management ever discussed the Radulovich case with us, either before or after the show.

Ed was usually nervous before a broadcast, but on this night his involvement created a special empathy which everyone in the control room could sense. Though it was the first time a nationally televised news broadcast had engaged itself in controversy, Murrow always believed that we were six months late with such a program. Others had been critical of television's and Murrow's apparent unwillingness to cope with the problem of blacklisting and guilt by association. Murrow's personal courage in World War II was part of the legend of combat reporting, but that was against a common foe, his detractors argued. In 1953 the question was being asked whether—and when—Murrow would stand up and be counted. I remember one delegation of civil-liberty professionals admonishing him for hiding his conscience behind the neutrality of a camera. Ed and I argued that we weren't going to use our microphones and cameras as a monopolized pulpit from which to preach, but that when there was a news story that dramatized the problem of guilt by association we might be able to make our point legitimately.

We did not tell anyone at the time, but the thought of doing a half-hour study of McCarthy and his investigations had been considered as early as the spring of 1953, when we instructed our camera crews to begin compiling filmed records of all the senator's speeches and hearings. We had tried our hand at a series of live interviews in which McCarthy would appear on one program, and one of his earliest critics, Senator William Benton of Connecticut, on another. I failed to budget enough time for them, and the experiment got out of hand with the two senators hurling broadsides against each other.

When one visitor accused Murrow of not denouncing McCarthy, declaring that it was fear of upsetting his comfortable nest that prevented him from speaking out, Murrow politely replied, "You may be right." When a McCarthy supporter criticized Murrow for a radio report which he considered unfair, and proclaimed his faith in McCarthy's crusade against Communism in government ("His methods may be a little harsh but he's doing a nasty job that needs doing"), Ed took a long drag on a cigarette and again said, "You may be right." It was his way of conserving his convictions and energy for the proper foe. In the meantime we kept compiling the McCarthy record without a shooting budget while waiting for the right incident that would provide us with a "little picture"—our shorthand for a real situation which would illustrate a national issue.

I first heard of the Radulovich case in the CBS lobby one day in October 1953. Murrow was late for a lunch date, I was returning from the cutting room, and as we passed each other, he handed me a wrinkled newspaper clipping. "Here, read this," he said. "It may be our case history. I don't know how we missed it on the wires, but the Detroit *News* has been doing a hell of a job with it. It's the story of an Air Force lieutenant who is losing his commission because his father and his sister are supposed to be left-wing sympathizers. Let's have someone check it out."

That afternoon reporter-producer Joe Wershba left for Dexter, Michigan. By noon of the next day he had met Radulovich and read most of the transcript of the Air Force hearings.

First Lieutenant Milo J. Radulovich, aged twenty-six, a meteorologist in the Air Force Reserve and a student at the University of Michigan, had been asked to resign his commission because his sister and father were secretly accused of radical beliefs. When Radulovich refused to resign, an Air Force board at Selfridge Field ordered his separation as a security risk. According to Wershba, Radulovich was attractive, articulate and willing to participate in the broadcast. "He'll make a convincing witness and I'd like to get it on film before he changes his mind. I have a date to see his father, and I'm working on his sister, who lives in Detroit. The Air Force officials here won't talk, but I can film the air base and the town of Dexter. It's a big story here and the townspeople will talk. Can I have Charlie Mack and his camera crew out here tonight?"

Mack, a veteran of the newsreel business and Murrow's favorite cameraman, left Washington a few hours later; forty-eight hours after that, we were looking at the film.

Wershba's "dope sheets" were sometimes more comprehensive than the film they accompanied, but in the Radulovich case they were unnecessary, for after each interview he called to brief us. From the beginning the material seemed promising. When our reporters were doing well they would promote their stories with phrases like "first rate" or "pretty good stuff." But when the material was truly exciting, there was often a note of restraint. "Fred," Wershba said now, "please try to see this film tonight. I don't want to try to evaluate it from this end, but if there is any sound on the track and the picture is as good as Mack thinks it is, we may have something here." His last words were: "And tell the lab not to scratch the film." When a reporter says that, you know he has something.

On the way home that night I went by the screening room which, with our cutting room, was located in a loft at 550 Fifth Avenue. After watching and listening to five minutes of Lieutenant Radulovich ("The [Air] Force does not question my loyalty in the least . . . They have presented me with allegations against my sister and father . . . to the effect that . . .

[they] have read what are now called subversive newspapers, and that my sister and father's activities are questionable . . . The actual charge against me is that I had maintained a close and continuing relationship with my dad and my sister over the years") I called Murrow, and after apologizing for bothering him just before his nightly radio broadcast, I suggested that he see the Radulovich film that night. He said that he'd go home for dinner and then meet me in the cutting room.

Before Ed arrived, Wershba had called again. "I don't want to prejudice you before you see it, but we just interviewed Radulovich's father. He's a Serb, has been in this country for forty years, is a veteran of World War I, and works at the Hudson automobile factory. He's written a letter to President Eisenhower about his son." Wershba read me the text, which concluded: "Mr. President . . . they are doing a bad thing to Milo . . . He has given all his growing years to his country . . . I am an old man. I have spent my life in this coal mine and auto furnaces. I ask nothing for myself. [All] I ask is justice for my boy. Mr. President, I ask your help." Wershba's last words were: "We are shipping the film tonight, but let me know first thing what Ed thinks of the interview with Milo."

When Murrow saw the film, he was jarred. Whenever someone appearing on one of our programs spoke with great conviction and force, Ed would say, "The guy has a fire in his belly." He said that now about Radulovich, but he was also impressed with the young officer's control.

"What about the sister?" he asked me. "Will the Air Force talk?"

"No."

"Will the townspeople talk?"

"Yes. Wershba says a former American Legion head who runs a gas station will speak up for the lieutenant, and here's the transcript of the trial."

Radulovich had not been allowed to face his accusers, or

even to read the specific allegations against him. I told Ed that I was sure there was a broadcast here. He agreed but said, "We can't cover this in ten minutes. What would you think of our doing an entire half-hour on it?" I said that I was for it, but that we should make the decision after we had seen the footage of Radulovich's father.

The next afternoon we watched the old Serb speak in his halting accent. We saw the sister, unwilling to talk about her own political beliefs, but angry that they should be the criteria for her brother's loyalty. Radulovich's counsel, a Detroit lawyer, was eloquent and persuasive, and so were the legionnaire and the officer of the UAW local to which the elder Radulovich belonged. But the star was Milo. "If I am being judged by my relatives," he said, "are my children going to be asked to denounce me? Are they going to be asked what their father was labeled? Are they going to have to explain to their friends why their father's a security risk? . . . This is a chain reaction if the thing is let stand . . . I see a chain reaction that has no end . . ."

"Let's do an entire half-hour on Tuesday night," said Ed. "Let's see if we can get the Pentagon to comment. You try to get CBS to give the broadcast some promotion and I'll work on the ending."

The next morning we informed the Air Force at the Pentagon that we were pursuing the Radulovich story and that we would like to have comments from a high-ranking spokesman. The public-information officer I spoke to expressed surprise that we were doing such a program, but he said he would check. Did Murrow himself know about it? I told the officer that it had been Ed's idea.

When I informed the news management about the broadcast, the only reaction was a kind of quick, silent gasp.

"Ed and I haven't put it together yet, but would you like to see parts of it?" I said.

"No," the vice-president I had called said, "I think we'd prefer to watch it on the air on Tuesday night."

It must be remembered that in 1953 *See It Now* enjoyed something close to autonomy. Our mandate came from William S. Paley and Irving W. Wilson, the president of Alcoa. Actually, *See It Now* had been created and given a place in the night-time schedule because the sponsor wanted just such a broadcast and was willing to pay for it. Sig Mickelson, director of news and public affairs for CBS Television, with administrative control over the *See It Now* operation, knew that Murrow was not going to let him or anyone else tell him how to edit a broadcast, and he naturally did not want to be involved in a program over which he had no editorial authority. In those days our operation had the same independence granted a columnist such as Walter Lippmann or Arthur Krock. We were notifying the CBS management about the Radulovich broadcast only because the issue was highly volatile; we felt the company had a right to know that by next Wednesday morning it would probably be engulfed in criticism.

Two days later Murrow called me on the private line connecting our two offices to say that a general and a lieutenant colonel from the Air Force were coming in to see him, and could I be available at three that afternoon. I was.

The dialogue with the officers was restrained, and there was a minimum of discussion of Milo Radulovich himself. They were "not members of the security panel, of course," and knew only the barest details. But there was this thorny problem of security during the Cold War and "in cases such as this the military has to bend over backwards." Murrow kept insisting that we wanted to do a fair, balanced job of reporting, but that it would be impossible if the Air Force did not comment. The general was sympathetic but seemed unconvinced that the broadcast would ever get on the air. I remember Ed's face when he was not too subtly reminded of his close relationship with the Air Force over the years and the fact that he had won the Distinguished Service to Airpower Award. The general ended by saying, "You have always gotten complete co-operation from us, and we know you won't do anything to alter that." Murrow simply let that last sentence hang there against his quiet stare. I expect the general remembers that moment thirteen years later.

After our visitor had left, Ed predicted that we would have no official spokesman, nor even a written comment on the case, and added wryly that now we couldn't postpone the program even if we wanted to. I had never seen him display quite such an appetite for a broadcast.

By now Wershba and Mack had shot some thirty thousand feet of film—about five hours' worth—on the Radulovich story. We had begun to edit this down to air length, and Murrow asked that we be sure to leave him three or four minutes for a "tailpiece." "Leave me enough time because we are going to live or die by our ending. Management is going to howl, and we may blow ourselves right out of the water, but we simply can't do an 'on the other hand' ending for this."

We were both mindful of an old CBS news adage laid down by Paul White, the dynamic wartime head of the CBS news department: "Ideally, in the case of controversial issues, the audience should be left with no impression as to which side the analyst himself actually favors." In the case of Milo Radulovich, Murrow doubted that such an attitude was possible. "We can't make the Air Force's case if they won't help us. Besides, some issues aren't equally balanced. We can't sit there every Tuesday night and give the impression that for every argument on one side there is an equal one on the other side."

Ed did not mean that it was our job to televise an editorial advocating a course of action, but just the fact that we were doing such a broadcast gave it a built-in point of view. Then Murrow made the only reference I ever heard about his brief, unhappy tenure as director of the public affairs programs. "I failed in that opportunity," he said, referring to a plan about an editorial policy for news broadcasts. He and a staff had spent more than six months on such a prospectus, but it had been rejected by the management. "We can't fail with *See It Now,* and this broadcast may give us the chance to stake out an important claim that broadcast journalism could occupy."

Of course Murrow was aware of pressures from the company. He would speak bitterly about a radio broadcast on Korea that he had prepared in Japan a year earlier, only to have it censored by the management. Ed Chester, then the head of the "hard news" operation, had not used it because it was critical of General MacArthur's war strategy at Pusan. Murrow had come home from Korea in anger, and in his first major rift with Paley, had thought of resigning. He suspected that now there would be pressure on CBS and the sponsor—Alcoa, after all, was a supplier of aluminum for the Air Force—and he believed that we were risking our sponsorship and probably the future of *See It Now*.

We had urged Bill Golden, the gifted and independent creative director of advertising, to place an advertisement about the program in the New York newspapers, but the twentieth floor—the executive floor—turned it down. There was to be no promotion for this broadcast. We had told the sponsor, the Aluminum Company of America, that we thought we had something special, and asked them to drop the middle commercial and to buy an ad announcing the program. They agreed to drop the commercial but said no to the advertisement.

Ed and I decided that the Radulovich program was too important and too good not to be publicized, so we raided our family tills to provide $1,500 for a display ad in the *New York Times*. It was a simple layout in bold graphic type that said: "The Case Against Milo Radulovich, A0589839," and listed the time and station. Instead of using the CBS eye and the corporate logo, it was signed "Ed Murrow and Fred Friendly." On the morning of the broadcast an embarrassed Golden called to ask for the cash because the company would not advance the money to the newspaper on its regular account.

Meanwhile, work in the cutting room continued over the weekend. Wershba had finished his filming in Michigan and joined us late on Friday to help in the editing. Murrow wanted to read all the transcripts of the hearings that were not classified; he would write an ending over the weekend.

There is nothing as stimulating and hectic as putting together a weekly or daily half-hour news broadcast. In those early days, with facilities nowhere near as good as today, and those that existed stretching over half of Manhattan, we were constantly living on the edge of our nerves. The journalistic headquarters of *See It Now* were then at 485 Madison Avenue. The film, shot in Dexter, Michigan, was developed and printed in a laboratory on Ninth Avenue. The screening and editing were done at the Fifth Avenue facilities near Forty-fifth Street. The Murrow off-camera narration was recorded in a studio at CBS Radio near his office, piped over to the mixing facility (transferring several audio tracks to a common tape) on Fifth Avenue and thence went by telephone circuit to the control studios and Master Control at Grand Central. Also involved were four or five incompatible unions, which had contact only by remote control. Often the final "mix" was not completed until an hour before a broadcast.

The Radulovich broadcast was conceived, produced and edited in less than a week in this pressure-cooker atmosphere. Under such tension the stopwatch kept one from wavering, and in the last forty hours the clock always seemed to move at double time.

By Sunday evening we had cut the film down to forty-five minutes. Murrow came in to look at the editing and was impressed, but he was preoccupied with his task, for he felt that the entire half-hour would be wasted if there wasn't a strong conclusion.

On Monday morning, when I got to the office, Murrow was already there dictating his "tailpiece"—his third attempt, he said. A few minutes later he brought it in and kept pacing while I read it. When I had finished I think I did something awkward, like shaking his hand. "You know, Ed, this language is so precise and eloquent that I hate to see you ad-lib it."

"Why don't I just read it?" he said. "I despise those damn prompters."

I shared his feeling; we both believed that prompters created a kind of invisible wall between the reporter and his audience. The viewer may not be aware that the broadcaster is reading, but there is a lack of communication.

The cutting room worked all through Monday night, and through the day of the show until an hour before broadcast time. We had difficulty cutting it all down. Though Ed had viewed all the material, he did not see the final edit until dress rehearsal, which began at 9:40 in Studio 41 at Grand Central. It was here that his live, on-camera commentary was to be combined with the documentary film material. When we began the final rehearsal, the second reel was still being carried across Forty-fifth Street. We never did get to rehearse the entire program, for we had to interrupt the final run-through to rerack the film so that it would be ready for the broadcast.

Murrow read his ending on camera twice before the show. Don Hewitt, an executive producer today but in those days our on-air director, sat just inches away from Ed because the control room was also our studio, and he had to cue his camera and projectors in hushed tones. When he heard Ed's ending, I remember that he raised his eyebrows and whistled. In those days the film and the audio tape ran on different machines held in synchronization by an electric pulse and a prayer. Hewitt told the crew he'd murder someone if we lost "sync" that night, as we had a few weeks before.

The broadcast went off without a hitch. It was the shortest half-hour in television history. Radulovich himself seemed even more alive in the intimacy of the small tube than on the big movie screen of the projection room. Murrow read his closing exactly as he had written it:

> We have told the Air Force that we will provide facilities for any comments, criticism or correction it may wish to make in regard to the case of Milo Radulovich. The case must go through two more Air Force boards routine and channels before it reaches Secretary Talbott, who will make the final decision. We are unable to judge the charges against the father or the lieutenant's sister because neither we nor you nor the lieutenant nor the lawyers know precisely what was contained in that manila envelope. Was it hearsay, rumor, gossip, or hard, provable fact backed by creditable witnesses? We do not know.
>
> There is a distinct difference between a loyalty and a security risk. A man may be entirely loyal, but at the same time be subjected to coercion, influence or pressure, which may cause him to act contrary to the best interests of national security. In the case of Lieutenant Radulovich, the board found that there was no question of his loyalty, but that he was regarded as a security risk. The security officers will tell you that a man who has a sister in Warsaw might be entirely loyal, but would be subjected to pressure as a result of threats that might be made against his sister's security or well-being. They contend that a man who has a sister in the Communist Party in this country might be subjected to the same kind of pressure, but here again, no evidence was adduced to prove that Radulovich's sister was a member of the Party, and the case against his father certainly was not made.
>
> We believe that "the son shall not bear the iniquity of the father," even though that iniquity be proved beyond all doubt, which in this case it was not. But we believe too that this case illustrates

> the urgent need for the Armed Forces to communicate more fully than they have so far done the procedures and regulations to be followed in attempting to protect the national security and the rights of the individual at the same time.
>
> Whatever happens in this whole area of the relationship between the individual and the state, we will do ourselves; it cannot be blamed upon Malenkov, Mao Tse-tung or even our allies. It seems to us—that is, to Fred Friendly and myself—that it is a subject that should be argued about endlessly . . .

With that, the tension finally broke. If twenty men in a control room can figuratively lift a man on their shoulders, it happened in Studio 41 that night. Technicians and stagehands came over to Murrow, who was bathed in sweat and smoke, and shook his hand. Some had tears in their eyes.

The television audience is a silent ghost whose reaction is usually a time-delayed reflex, but that night it had an ignition all its own. The telephone lines to the control room, to the reception desk down the hall and to Master Control were lit up in an instant. Elmer Davis of ABC and several of the CBS correspondents got through on company lines to talk to Ed. There were calls from all over the East and South. The program was not shown in Detroit that night, so we did not hear from Radulovich or from anyone in Dexter. The advertising manager of Alcoa called to say they were proud to have been a part of the broadcast. Though there was no word from anyone in the CBS management, we felt that this might be because the circuits were tied up.

The calls were still coming in when Ed and I and some of our exhausted colleagues left the studio for our Tuesday evening ritual at the Pentagon bar on Vanderbilt Avenue. As Murrow entered, still in his make-up, the proprietor, the bartender and several of the patrons came over to shake his hand. The CBS operators kept phoning to say that the switchboard was still clogged and that they had stopped counting after about a thousand calls. The studios in Washington and Philadelphia were also flooded with messages. Night operations reported that they too were receiving hundreds of telephone calls, most of them favorable, but some of them bitter denunciations of Murrow and CBS.

The press reaction was overwhelming. There were news stories reporting the telephone response and telegrams; but more important, there was a realization that television could be more than another arm of show business. In the *New York Times,* Jack Gould wrote:

> Edward R. Murrow's presentation of the case of Lieut. Milo Radulovich, who is threatened with dismissal from the Air Force because of anonymous charges of pro-Communist sympathies against his father and sister, was not just a superb and fighting documentary . . . It was a long step forward in television journalism.
>
> The program marked perhaps the first time that a major network, the Columbia Broadcasting System, and one of the country's most important industrial sponsors, the Aluminum Company of America, consented to a program taking a vigorous editorial stand in a matter of national importance and controversy.

One right-wing publication called the Radulovich broadcast a "very cleverly slanted program that produced no evidence that Radulovich had been judged wrongly," and criticized Murrow for having done a program that pleased the Communist Party.

The Providence *Evening Bulletin* said exactly what Ed and I had hoped the broadcast would achieve:

> By permitting a defense of Radulovich to appear on the air, not only by the man himself, and his father, his sister, his wife and the people of the town of Dexter, Michigan, who knew him (in other words, his peers), but also in the form of a spoken editorial by Murrow himself, the broadcaster allowed the accused opportunity for a direct defense of his personal and legal rights before millions of people.

Several days after the broadcast the Secretary of the Air Force, Harold E. Talbott, invited Murrow down for a chat. Ed later reported that the atmosphere had been gracious but that the substance of the talk was just a reiteration of the Air Force policy concerning security risks. He did add that he detected unhappiness, and perhaps a note of uncertainty, in the Secretary's stand on the ouster of Lieutenant Radulovich. When I asked Murrow if he thought there was a chance of a reversal, he replied quickly, "Not a chance," but I was not sure he meant it.

As for CBS, it remained silent. I never heard a word from any company executives about the Radulovich broadcast other than about the mail count, which continued to run in Murrow's favor. Some of the affiliated stations complained, and I know that there was uneasiness in the CBS high command—the feeling being that if there was to be a broadcast as controversial as the one about Radulovich, it ought to be the decision of the management and not simply of Murrow and Friendly. The friction was aggravated by the fact that all the praise was heaped on Murrow and his partner, but that those who were angered had enough animosity left over to include CBS. This pattern was repeated over and over again. For example, after another of our controversial broadcasts, Jack O'Brian of the New York *Journal-American* wrote: "It is interesting . . . to note that Murrow and his partner in port-sided reporting, Mr. Friendly, made it clear they alone were responsible for last night's show in a quick credit at the start. CBS can't duck responsibility that easily." Obviously the company's anguish was complicated by the press; the liberals castigated them for not supporting us, the McCarthyites for not stopping us.

Alcoa received a few threats of order cancellations, but several viewers wrote asking how they could thank the company with their patronage; one woman even wanted to purchase an ingot of aluminum as a gesture of gratitude. Murrow and I had our annual Pittsburgh luncheon with Mr. Wilson and the

Alcoa management several weeks after the Radulovich broadcast. After praising the broadcast, Mr. Wilson said that it was still his company's position that they would make the aluminum and that we would produce the programs; at the same time, he hoped that *See It Now* would not now devote itself to "civil-liberty broadcasts" to the exclusion of all else.

The Radulovich broadcast may have been a "footnote to history," but there was a postscript to the program which took us all by surprise and established for the first time the enormous impact of television reporting. On November 24, 1953, we were doing another *See It Now,* called "Argument in Indianapolis," whose substance was the old argument over the right to hire a hall. Some Indianapolis citizens had rented the Indiana War Memorial, a civil auditorium, to form a local chapter of the American Civil Liberties Union. Arthur Garfield Hays, a prominent crusader for civil liberties, had agreed to be the guest speaker. When the American Legion and the Minutewomen protested, however, the managers of the hall caved in and permission to use the auditorium was denied.

We filmed both the American Legion, in a meeting condemning the Civil Liberties Union, and the Civil Liberties Union, in a meeting to protest the ban. It was the first time we had edited such conflicting views in juxtaposition, and the film was most effective. The climax of the broadcast was the offer of a Roman Catholic priest, Father Victor Goosens, to lend the ACLU the meeting hall of his church. He was not a member of the organization, but on the program he said: "You know . . . all of us at some time or other are going to find ourselves in a minority group . . . and [if] it is possible for any group outside of the legally constituted branches of government to restrain another from peaceful assembly . . . then all our liberties are in danger . . ."

At eight o'clock in the morning of the "Argument in Indianapolis" broadcast I had just arrived home to change and was taking a shower when my wife came in to say that Ed was on the telephone. I asked if I might call back in ten minutes. When she returned shaking her head, I rushed to the phone soaking wet. Murrow apologized; his own face was covered with lather, he said, but he had just received an emergency call from the Secretary of the Air Force, and "could Charlie Mack and his camera crew get over to the Pentagon by nine o'clock."

I didn't have to ask whether the summons concerned Radulovich. The Secretary of the Air Force would not have called Murrow at home to tell him that the decision to oust Milo had been confirmed, and Murrow wouldn't have called me to rush a crew over if he didn't believe that we had won our point.

That night Murrow delayed the start of "Argument in Indianapolis" by making an announcement:

> Good evening. Five weeks ago tonight, this program devoted considerable time to the case of Lieutenant Milo Radulovich, an Air Force Reserve officer who a Security Review Board felt was a security risk . . . The case had been under the consideration of the Air Force ever since . . . Today, the decision was reached . . .

Ed then looked up at a monitor on which the Secretary's face appeared, and introduced Harold E. Talbott.

> Mr. Murrow, as Secretary of the Air Force it is my sworn duty to uphold and protect the security of the United States. I am also keenly aware of my responsibility to protect the individual rights and privileges of each man and woman in the United States Air Force. The preservation of our American way of life requires that we must be alert to safeguard our individual liberties. I have given the case of First Lieutenant Milo J. Radulovich the most serious consideration. I have decided that it is consistent with the interests of the national security to retain Lieutenant Radulovich in the United States Air Force. He is not, in my opinion, a security risk . . . I am also convinced that the record does

> not support the conclusion that Lieutenant Radulovich's father has engaged in activities of such a type as to bear upon the decision in this case. The question raised as to security has thus been resolved in Lieutenant Radulovich's favor, and I have, therefore, directed that Radulovich be retained in his present status in the United States Air Force.

The Radulovich verdict, combined with the Indianapolis broadcast that followed, was a triumph for Murrow and for television. *Newsweek* quoted an admirer of Ed Murrow and Fred Friendly as saying: "[They] have become the eyes of conscience." The American Legion and others attacked the Indianapolis broadcast, claiming that it was slanted. (The feud over the right to hire that hall festered for over a decade, until 1965, when the courts dissolved the restraining order that prevented the ACLU from meeting in the War Memorial auditorium.)

The assault on Murrow accelerated after "Indianapolis." Both CBS and Alcoa felt much more pressure than after the Radulovich show.

One of our reporters informed us that a few days after the Radulovich reversal Don Surine, an investigator for McCarthy, had asked him, "What's Murrow trying to do with that fellow Radvich, or whatever his name is?" Surine then lowered his voice and said, "Your Mr. Murrow better be careful. What would you say if I told you that we have definite proof that Murrow is a paid agent of the Soviet Union?"

"I wouldn't believe it," said our man.

"Then come up to the committee office and I'll show you."

There Surine pulled out a "document," a photostatic copy of the Pittsburgh *Sun-Telegraph*, a Hearst newspaper, dated February 18, 1935. The bold headline proclaimed: "AMERICAN PROFESSORS TRAINED BY SOVIETS TEACH IN U.S. SCHOOLS." The article contained a list of American educators, an advisory group to the Moscow University Summer Session. Among the "conspirators" were John Dewey, professor emeritus at Columbia

University; William Neilsen, president of Smith College; Frank Graham, president of the University of North Carolina; and Robert Hutchins, president of the University of Chicago—as well as an obscure assistant director of the Institute of International Education named Edward R. Murrow. The institute had sponsored the exchange program with the financial backing of the Rockefeller and Carnegie foundations.

Our reporter asked Surine if he might show this document to Murrow. When Ed saw it, his only quotable comment was: "You know, we never got over there. The Russians canceled the program before it ever got going." Today that photostatic "documentary evidence" is still in my files, a grim relic of the times.

On Thanksgiving Day, Lieutenant Radulovich wrote Murrow to thank him for the broadcast:

> Your commentary on my case with the USAF had the effect [of focusing] the real significance and danger of guilt by association and relationship, of state vs. individual, onto the screen of the American people. The resulting reaction from the people I will always cherish and will think of it as the real reason for Mr. Talbott's reversal of his own opinion on my case.

As we left Studio 41 on the night of the Indianapolis broadcast and walked to the elevator down the long corridor crowded with all the false props of show business that spilled out from the cramped studios—a papier-mâché tree, a submarine panel from a *Studio One* drama, a set of French windows—Ed asked how much film we had shot on McCarthy. I told him that we had about fifty thousand feet. Had anyone shot McCarthy's speech in Wheeling, West Virginia, on the night in 1950 when the senator claimed to have definite proof that there were two hundred and five Communists in the State Department? I said that I did not think so. Ed emphasized that we ought to use this even if we could only find an audio tape of it.

The Murrow-Friendly partnership was not one that lived on memos, as Ed liked to say, but after that conversation I began to receive little notes from him about McCarthy's scheduled speeches, to remind me that we ought to cover them.

The real hero of the Radulovich broadcast was, of course, Milo. There is a line from Santayana: ". . . the common citizen must be something of a saint and something of a hero." Milo Radulovich had been told by the Air Force that if he resigned his obscure commission in the Reserve without a fuss, nothing would ever be said about his "association" with his sister and father. He stood his ground because his conviction was so firm, and because he could not abide the image he would have seen in the mirror every morning if he had compromised. As it turned out, millions of his countrymen, including the Secretary of the Air Force, were strengthened by what they saw in the electronic mirror. And those who held up the mirror on that night many years ago will never forget the powerful light that glowed from the screen. As much as any other single factor, the Radulovich program encouraged us to attempt the McCarthy broadcast. Milo, now a meteorologist for the United States Weather Bureau in California, ought to know that.

The McCarthy Broadcast

"When the record is finally written, as it will be one day, it will answer the question, Who has helped the Communist cause and who has served his country better, Senator McCarthy or I? I would like to be remembered by the answer to that question."

EDWARD R. MURROW, April 6, 1954.

To say that the Murrow broadcast of March 9, 1954, was the decisive blow against Senator McCarthy's power is as inaccurate as it is to say that Joseph R. McCarthy, Republican, Wisconsin, single-handedly gave birth to McCarthyism. The disease was here long before he exploited it. Elmer Davis compared it to malaria and prescribed courage as the only antidote. What Murrow did was to administer a strong dose of that medicine, then in such short supply, and it was fitting that he did it on television, where the disease had reached epidemic proportions long before McCarthy became its chief carrier.

By the early fifties the central nervous system of the vast broadcast industry was so conditioned that it responded to self-appointed policemen and blacklists as though they were part of the constitutional process. For me, one scene, enacted in an office on the fourteenth floor of CBS, still retains all of the noxious atmosphere of the period.

Murrow and I never believed in background or mood music for documentaries, but we did want to commission an original composition for the opening and closing titles and credits of our broadcasts. I had gone to see the vice-president in charge of programs who at that time had administrative control over *Hear It Now,* and later *See It Now,* to explain the project and request special funds for it. When the vice-president asked me what composer we had in mind, I handed him the names of three well-known modern composers listed in order of our preference. He glanced at the top name and asked, "Is he in the book?"

"I don't know," I said, "but I'm sure 'Music Clearance' has his number."

"I know," said the vice-president, "but is he in the book?"

I started to ask a secretary for a telephone directory when the vice-president pulled open a drawer of his desk and said, "This is the book we live by." It was a pamphlet called "Red Channels."

Even today I can recall every item in that desk drawer: the "Red Channels" blacklist, a rating book beside it, some paper clips, pencils, an eraser, an extra set of cuff links, a small Civil War memento. Luckily, the "book" did not contain the name of our first choice, though both of the other composers were listed.

"Red Channels" and its weekly companion piece, "Counterattack," the bible for broadcast companies, sponsors, advertising agencies and motion picture studios, among others, was a catalogue of quarter-truths, gossip, and confessions of ex-Communists and other informers of questionable credentials. In the fifties it was the death warrant for the careers of hundreds of talented actors, playwrights, directors, composers, authors and editors. Some of the most valued and loyal news broadcasters were rendered unemployable by "Red Channels." Raymond Swing, one of the innovators of radio journalism in serious interpretation of foreign affairs, who chose to fight "Red Channels" publicly by debating its publisher, suffered grievous personal loss because of his stand. His career was never the same again, and for a time his employment with Voice of America was jeopardized. Called before the McCarthy committee, which of course could not prove any of its allegations, Swing stayed with

Voice of America until he was reconfirmed, and then resigned in protest at the State Department's failure to defend its own agency. Later Swing joined CBS in a nonbroadcast capacity to assist Murrow with his nightly radio series. Even the great Elmer Davis, who even earlier than Winston Churchill had alerted Americans to the Cold War and warned of Stalin's aggression, was attacked by "Counterattack" as a "smearer of anti-Communists . . ."

"Red Channels" was not the only blacklister at that time, however. Sponsors, who in those days exerted much more control over program content than they do today, had their own little dark books. When I was at NBC in 1949, producing a news quiz broadcast called *Who Said That?*, the sponsor, an oil company, dictated a blacklist of its own which NBC accepted. The list of objectionable guests included Norman Thomas, Al Capp, Oscar Levant, Henry Morgan and several prominent senators and congressmen—not because they were necessarily part of the Communist conspiracy, which they weren't, but because in a live, ad-lib broadcast "they just might say something." Perhaps the classic example of this kind of dreaded spontaneity occurred at Christmas of 1952 when on a CBS broadcast, *This Is Show Business,* George S. Kaufman said: "Let's make this one program on which no one sings 'Silent Night.'" Though this was a wish shared by others, the advertising agency decided to banish Kaufman from the show even before the program was over.

The case of Jean Muir, the actress, barred from playing the mother of Henry Aldrich on an NBC situation comedy because of a "Red Channels" blacklisting which disturbed the sponsor, was to have its echo as late as 1966 when ABC deleted a reference to this incident during an interview with Miss Muir.

The flat Indiana twang of Elmer Davis kept pleading, "Don't let them scare you," but the industry *was* scared, and by winter of 1954 much of Washington was so terrorized by McCarthy that national policy was often made in reaction to his tirades. Dean Acheson, whom the New York *Daily News,* a McCarthy supporter, later called a strong Secretary of State, was dubbed the "Red Dean" by the senator, and his last years in office were ineffective partly because of this monstrous slander. General Marshall, whom Harry Truman called the "greatest living American," was denounced in the Senate as virtually a traitor by the junior senator from Wisconsin: "A man steeped in falsehood [and part of] a conspiracy so immense and an infamy so black as to dwarf any previous venture in the history of man . . ." The Eisenhower Administration fared little better. By 1953 it was "twenty years of treason," and the guilt included the Republicans, the State Department, the U. S. High Commissioner for Germany James Conant, the ambassador to the U.S.S.R. Charles Bohlen and Mutual Security Administrator Harold Stassen.

In January 1954 the Eisenhower Administration, or rather the executive branch, was under attack from another quarter, one unrelated to McCarthyism. Republican Senator John Bricker of Ohio was the author of a constitutional amendment designed to limit the treaty-making powers of the President. Many of his colleagues supported the bill, and Eisenhower, among others, feared that Bricker might get it through the Senate.

On January 12 we did a broadcast called "The Bricker Amendment." With Murrow as moderator, Senators John Bricker and Estes Kefauver debated the amendment live from their respective offices. There were also interviews with former Supreme Court Justice Owen Roberts, Professor George Finch of Georgetown Law School and Dean Erwin Griswold of Harvard Law School. After the broadcast Senator Bricker was furious. He said that it had been his understanding that the entire half-hour was to involve only him and Kefauver; actually, he had been told otherwise. In spite of the fact that Professor Finch pleaded most effectively for limiting the President's power,

Bricker felt that the broadcast was slanted against him. He threatened an investigation and issued the two hostile Bricker reports on network practices, which were believed to have been stimulated by his irritation at our broadcast. Under severe attack from President Eisenhower and Secretary Dulles, the Bricker amendment eventually died, but Bricker and his supporters never forgave Murrow for the *See It Now* broadcast.

The CBS management was upset about the broadcast, since it was one of the factors that unleashed a harassing investigation designed to punish the networks. Our Washington lobby, its delicate sensory attachments imbedded in the congressional skin, gave off all kinds of warning signals. For an industry that has always needed all its friends, we were collecting a formidable list of enemies.

When Murrow went to Europe the following month to do a *See It Now* program on the Big Four foreign ministers meeting in Berlin, he reported that State Department officials and other Americans were kept busy trying to convince our allies that the United States was not bent on a fascist course similar to Hitler's Reich. The morale and effectiveness of Voice of America was seriously damaged when McCarthy sent his two "junketeering gumshoes," Roy Cohn and David Schine, to investigate the Communist underground in the United States Information Agency. These two "experts," both in their twenties and unfamiliar with the nuances of propaganda, became the jest of Europe; journalists taunted them and the nation they represented by chanting, "Positively, Mr. Cohn–absolutely, Mr. Schine."

"The perilous night," as Elmer Davis called it, was perhaps blackest during the winter of 1954, when 50 percent of the American people, according to public-opinion polls, approved of such McCarthy investigations as "Who promoted Major Peress?" On February 18, at a closed hearing in the courthouse at Foley Square in New York City, McCarthy assaulted Brigadier General Ralph Zwicker, a hero of Normandy and the Bulge, in whose Camp Kilmer command Peress had been an obscure dentist.

Peress had taken the Fifth Amendment rather than answer questions of alleged Communist affiliations, and then resigned, receiving an honorable discharge after his automatic promotion to major. Because Zwicker, under orders, refused to reveal details and the names of the officers involved in the Peress promotion and separation, the senator humiliated him. "Then, General," said the senator, "you should be removed from any command. Any man who has been given the honor of being promoted to general and who says, 'I will protect another general who protects Communists,' is not fit to wear that uniform, General. I think it is a tremendous disgrace to the Army to have to bring these facts before the public, but I intend to give it to the public."

On his daily radio program on February 24, Murrow quoted CBS News Paris correspondent David Schoenbrun's report on the reaction of our European allies to the senator's attack on Zwicker and the Army: "It is a case of burning down the barn to catch a rat, one French editor told me. Our allies don't think a line can be drawn between objectives and methods, particularly when methods, as in the McCarthy case, are so spectacular and destructive. Hitler's methods may have been to eradicate Communism in Germany and destroy the Soviet Union, but what his methods did in fact accomplish was to eradicate democracy in Germany and destroy France, not Russia."

Other CBS correspondents, notably Howard K. Smith and Eric Sevareid, made sharp comments about McCarthy, but these were primarily on radio, and though the voices were loud and clear, radio's effect had already been diminished by the growth of television. When H. V. Kaltenborn of NBC, an early defender of McCarthy, attacked him after the Zwicker affair, calling him "egotistical, arrogant, reckless, irresponsible, corrupted by power," it created hardly a ripple, because it was heard but not seen.

On the afternoon when Ed went through the transcript of the McCarthy attack on Zwicker, he asked me to put together all the McCarthy material on a few big reels so that we could screen it. The next morning we ran the film for almost three hours. Some of the footage we had seen before. The testimony of Reed Harris, of the State Department's information agency, who appeared before the McCarthy subcommittee to defend a book he had written "exposing" football in 1932 while a student at Columbia, had been shown on an early *See It Now.* Still, the sequence we had selected was a chilling experience; the challenge was whether we could maintain that mood in distilling it to a half-hour.

We decided to try. We never did find any film or tape of McCarthy's famous 1950 Wheeling speech; one station reported that they had such a tape and would send it to us, but it turned out that it had been "accidentally" wiped. Ed and I knew that we had no scoop, no exclusively new material on the senator. The only hope for such a program was that by capturing the pure essence of McCarthyism and comparing his accusations with the record, we might create an atmosphere that would justify a strong editorial by Ed at the conclusion of the broadcast.

As with Radulovich, Murrow would concentrate on the ending. Joe Wershba, who had supervised most of the filming of the senator in action, would be pulled off his other assignments to work on the connecting narrative with me. All our editors and assistants would also work on the film. Jack Beck, our West Coast producer who had just arrived in New York with thirty thousand feet of film on the Navajo Indians, provisionally scheduled for March 9, would have to wait. (We never did get the Indian film on the air, but Beck became a useful associate editor and critic for the McCarthy project.)

The *See It Now* show for March 2 was what we called a "let-up piece"—a profile of the New York Philharmonic. We had photographed and recorded Conductor Mitropoulos and the orchestra over a period of weeks, and the editing process was near completion, thus providing us with more than ten days to prepare the McCarthy program. Our target date was March 9.

Ed and I knew that the timing on this broadcast was crucial. If we waited much longer, history or McCarthy—or both—might run us down. On the morning of March 1 we looked at a rough cut of the selected material. It was pretty thin; though Murrow found it encouraging, some of us felt slightly let down, mostly because we didn't have film of the Wheeling speech or his attack on General Marshall. Nevertheless, on Tuesday morning we committed ourselves to the McCarthy broadcast with the ending we wrote for the Philharmonic show that evening: "We . . . desired to do one report that has nothing whatever to do with the cold war, with current crises, or with the retreat into unreasoning fear that seems to be part of the climate in which we live. We shall try to deal with one aspect of that fear next week." It was curious that of all the millions of viewers supposedly watching, no one, not even a newspaper editor or critic or a single CBS executive, asked what the program next week was to be about. Had anyone taken the trouble, he would have had a scoop on what became the most controversial broadcast of its time.

The cutting-room staff in that loft on Fifth Avenue assembled on the morning after the Philharmonic show and worked straight through the next six days. Everyone went home for one or two short nights, but the Movieola lights were on all the time and our projectionist did not have a single day or night off.

In that one week our chief editor, a "McKinley conservative" who had come to the project with some sympathy for what McCarthy was trying to accomplish, became convinced by our film that the senator was a menace.

On Thursday, March 4, we informed the company that next week's *See It Now* would deal with McCarthy. Whether the news ever reached the twentieth floor I am not certain. We did ask Bill Golden to run an advertisement on the morning of the ninth, and when he said that the management had again turned down his request, Murrow and I once more came up with some money of our own—part of it award money we had put aside for just such a purpose. The ad was scheduled to appear in the *Times* on Tuesday, but we still had not made a final decision whether to run the program. The point of no return, a decision to go or scrub, would be made on Sunday night.

It was fortunate that we had made a reference to the McCarthy project on our previous broadcast, because of a strange series of events that clouded the weekend. In a Miami speech Adlai Stevenson made a strong political attack on the Republican Party, including several critical references to McCarthy. CBS and NBC televised the speech and McCarthy demanded equal time to answer, which was denied. McCarthy supporters protested vehemently, and when the Murrow broadcast was officially announced a few days later, the cry was heard that this was CBS's way of getting even with its critics. Nothing could have been further from the truth, and our mention of the program on March 2 was evidence. (The networks finally did provide the Republican Party with time, and Vice-President Nixon answered Stevenson.)

At 9 o'clock that Sunday evening we viewed the next-to-the-last edit of the film. It was still seven minutes long, and Ed and I had our usual tug of war over the cuts. We had to drop four minutes from the McCarthy-Reed Harris inquisition, but even when cut, it still held much of its original impact. No network or newsreel service had had cameras running during McCarthy's castigation of Zwicker because it was a closed session, but by rare good luck Mack and Wershba had been present in Philadelphia when the senator restaged the entire episode—including the verbatim reading of the transcript—for a Washington's Birthday celebration. The scene, enacted under a huge mural of the first President, took on additional terror because of McCarthy's obvious delight in reliving it all—the unbridled bravado and rage were interspersed with the famous McCarthy giggle.

We had also extracted from the Philadelphia speech the senator's savage attack on Secretary of the Army Robert T. Stevens, the bland, naïve defender of the Army's position. Of Secretary Stevens, McCarthy intoned: "'On what meat does this our Caesar feed . . .'"

We moved the Philadelphia re-enactment up near the beginning of the show in order to establish the senator's violent streaks early, and placed the Reed Harris sequence toward the end as a lead-in to Ed's final comments. In between there was a variety of the McCarthy techniques; after each one, Murrow would point out the misuse of the facts. There was also a glowing tribute to the senator by one of his ardent supporters at a testimonial banquet, and McCarthy's emotion-choked reply. There were some McCarthy quotes on Eisenhower, on the Democratic Party's twenty years of treason, and on the Republicans' share of the guilt from another West Virginia speech.

After the cutters had taken the reels back to their editing tables, we sent out for coffee and ran a final critique on our footage. I had sensed a certain uneasiness on the part of some members in the unit. I was not sure whether this was timidity over our confrontation with the senator or whether there was something in their own background which might make us vulnerable. Looking back on it now, I suppose it was my own uncertainty and fear that made me decide that it would not be fair to Ed or CBS to enter into this battle if we had an Achilles heel. Also, I wanted all hands to share in a decision that would obviously involve everyone's future.

Ed agreed, and so a meeting of the unit was called. We asked each member, first, whether he thought our analysis of the senator's technique was effective enough to make the points we were striving for; second, whether anyone knew of any reason why we should not do the broadcast. Was there, in other words, anything in their own backgrounds that would give the senator a club to beat us with, because if this broadcast was successful, he and his supporters would certainly be looking for one. Although this was a team effort, we all knew from the aftermath of the Radulovich and Indianapolis shows that Murrow would be the target of all the attacks. But if there was anything in any of our lives that might make us vulnerable, we had to know now. Ed reminded everyone that we were not referring to "Red Channels" or any other such blacklist.

We moved around the room from editor to cameraman to reporter to field producer, and each indicated his position. Two or three of our colleagues were unhappy that we did not have the Wheeling speech and that the material was not as dramatic or cohesive as the Radulovich or Indianapolis programs. Perhaps we should wait another few weeks and assemble more McCarthy material; the senator had some speeches scheduled for the following week, and there would undoubtedly be more hearings in Washington. I said that I disagreed; if we were going to do the program at all, this was the time, and I was convinced that if we could sustain the proper mood for the first twenty-five minutes, Ed's ending would more than justify our stand.

Then each person talked for a few minutes about himself; no one had any personal reservation or indicated any vulnerability. One man told us that his first wife had been a Communist Party member but that their marriage had been dissolved years before.

At the end we all turned to Ed. In a characteristic pose, his elbows on his knees, his eyes on the floor, he was silent for about ten seconds. At last he said, "We, like everyone in this business, are going to be judged by what we put on the air; but we also shall be judged by what we don't broadcast. If we pull back on this we'll have it with us always." He snuffed out what was probably his sixtieth cigarette of the day and said he would have his summation on my desk by morning.

When I got up on Monday and went to work, it was the beginning of a grueling but stimulating weekly routine; few of us would see a bed or get home until early Wednesday morning. In the meantime, the life of the broadcast took over. We told Bill Golden to give final confirmation to the advertisement in the *Times*. The copy read simply: "Tonight at 10:30 on *See It Now*, a report on Senator Joseph R. McCarthy over Channel 2"; again there was no CBS eye or other trademark, and it was signed "Fred W. Friendly and Edward R. Murrow, Co-producers."

We were tempted to tell Alcoa that because of the importance and nature of the broadcast we wanted to run their commercials at the begining and end, thus eliminating a middle break, but decided that rather than involve them in any of the decision-making, we would simply exercise our prerogative and do it on our own. We tried to persuade CBS to do some air promotion, but there was little interest. Shortly before noon, Murrow showed me his closing piece, and I asked him to rewrite the opening I had drafted. He changed a few words and inserted the sentence: "If the senator believes we have done violence to his words or pictures and desires to speak, to answer himself, an opportunity will be afforded him on this program."

Ed's conclusion, the product of six or seven rewrites, was tight and forceful. There was no doubt in his mind that this ending crossed the line into editorial comment, but we both knew that that line had to be crossed again. To do a half-hour on so volatile and important a matter and then end with a balanced "on the other hand" summation would be to dilute and destroy the effect of the broadcast.

Briefly we debated sending a copy of the ending to Sig Mickelson, but again decided against it. It would be unfair to him to involve him in the editing process in this isolated instance, when we were not inclined to accept any major changes. Of course, if Mickelson asked to see the script, it was available.

On Tuesday morning Paley called Ed, as he occasionally did on the day of an important broadcast, and wished us well. "I'll be with you tonight, Ed, and I'll be with you tomorrow as well." Murrow was moved by the implication and tone of the message.

This was one broadcast we wanted time to rehearse so that there would be no chance of being run over by the stopwatch. We determined to go into triple-pay overtime in the cutting room and Studio 41 in order to start our final run-throughs by 8:30. Ed could have a quick sandwich after his 7:45 radio program and we would still have time for two complete rehearsals. But we ran late in the cutting room with the "mix," though we had started early on Tuesday afternoon, and it was almost 9 o'clock before Murrow and I and all the film and tape were in the studio.

Because the control room was also our studio, we had standing orders that there were to be no visitors, no company brass or sponsors. But on this night I asked the security department of CBS to furnish uniformed guards at the Grand Central elevator and just outside the studio. By this time Murrow was getting crank telephone calls, and emotions on the senator ran so high that conceivably some fanatic would try to crash the studio while we were on the air.

Fifteen minutes before broadcast time we finished the final run-through. Don Hewitt, our control-room director, told us that it was thirty seconds long, and we decided to kill the closing credits if we needed the time. The test-pattern easel was pulled away from camera #1 as Ed settled into his chair. At 10:28 the assistant director whispered that we had one minute. Hewitt picked up the private line to Master Control and asked them not to cut us off if we ran long; there might not be time for credits and we needed every second we could squeeze. "Give us till 10:59:26," he pleaded. One of the outside lines rang and Don smothered it. "No, this is not the eleven o'clock news. Try Forty-four. Operator, I tell you every week to shut off these phones. Now, *please,* no calls until eleven o'clock."

Murrow was usually "unflappable," but as broadcasters go, he was a much more tense performer than Walter Cronkite or Robert Trout. When he was emotionally involved in a story it usually showed. At the close of one of our Korean reports about a wounded G.I. fighting for his life, Ed's voice broke ever so slightly. It was because he always cared so much, and also because he had a trace of camera fright which he never completely lost. But this was one night when he wanted a steady hand, when he did not want to be accused of an emotional attack.

The preceding program ended; it was followed by what is known as "system" and thirty seconds of blackout, when local stations identify themselves and insert their local commercials. During this seemingly endless void, I leaned over to Ed and whispered, "This is going to be a tough one." His answer was: "Yes, and after this one they're all going to be tough."

Suddenly the hands on the clock pointed straight up and the red light came on. Ed leaned into the camera. "Good evening. Tonight *See It Now* devotes its entire half-hour to a report on Senator Joseph R. McCarthy, told mainly in his own words and pictures." Looking up at the long bank of monitors, I knew that Murrow was in complete control of the air and of himself; in contrast, my right hand was shaking so that when I tried to start my stopwatch I missed the button completely and had to compensate by two seconds all through the half-hour.

For the next thirty minutes that control room was like a submarine during an emergency dive; fourteen technicians and a director were all responding to Murrow's cues and he to theirs. Murrow into a 1952 film of McCarthy . . . Murrow to radio tape of the senator . . . Murrow to Eisenhower . . . Murrow live in the studio reading from a stack of American newspapers, most of them critical of the senator's attack on the Army . . . Murrow introducing film of the senator laughing and scoffing at Eisenhower . . . the Zwicker affair . . . the senator attacking "Alger, I mean Adlai," which was how McCarthy referred to Stevenson.

Finally we came to the Reed Harris hearing. Somebody in the control room started to talk while the mikes were closed during this footage. Murrow shut him up quickly; he wanted to hear every word of the questioning, almost as though he were listening to it for the first time instead of the tenth. I suspect that subconsciously he wanted no one in the entire nation to miss a single word or nuance of the questioning.

MURROW: Now a sample investigation. The witness was Reed Harris, for many years a civil servant in the State Department directing the Information Service. Harris was accused of helping the Communistic cause by curtailing some broadcasts to Israel. Senator McCarthy summoned him and questioned him about a book he had written in 1932.

MCCARTHY: Mr. Reed Harris, your name is Reed Harris?
HARRIS: That's right.
MCCARTHY: You wrote a book in '32, is that correct?
HARRIS: Yes, I wrote a book, and as I testified in executive session—
MCCARTHY: At the time you wrote the book—pardon me, go ahead, I'm sorry, proceed.
HARRIS: —at the time I wrote the book the atmosphere in the universities of the United States was greatly affected by the great de-

pression then in existence. The attitudes of students, the attitudes of the general public were considerably different than they are at this moment, and for one thing there certainly was no awareness to the degree that there is today of the way the Communist Party works.

McCarthy: You attended Columbia University in the early thirties, is that right?

Harris: I did, Mr. Chairman.

McCarthy: Will you speak a little louder, sir?

Harris: I did, Mr. Chairman.

McCarthy: And you were expelled from Columbia?

Harris: I was suspended from classes on April 1, 1932. I was later reinstated and I resigned from the university.

McCarthy: You resigned from the university. Did the Civil Liberties Union provide you with an attorney at that time?

Harris: I had many offers of attorneys and one of those was from the American Civil Liberties Union, yes.

McCarthy: The question is did the Civil Liberties Union supply you with an attorney?

Harris: They did supply an attorney.

McCarthy: The answer is yes?

Harris: The answer is yes.

McCarthy: You know the Civil Liberties Union has been listed as a front for and doing the work of the Communist Party?

Harris: Mr. Chairman, this was 1932.

McCarthy: I know it was 1932. Do you know they since have been listed as a front for and doing the work of the Communist Party?

Harris: I do not know that they have been listed so, sir.

McCarthy: You don't know they have been listed?

Harris: I have heard that mentioned or read that mentioned.

McCarthy: You wrote a book in 1932. I'm going to ask you again: at the time you wrote this book, did you feel that professors should be given the right to teach sophomores that marriage "should be cast off of our civilization as antiquated and stupid religious phenomena"? Was that your feeling at that time?

Harris: My feeling was that professors should have the right to express their considered opinions on any subject, whatever they were, sir.

McCARTHY: I'm going to ask you this question again.

HARRIS: That includes that quotation, they should have the right to teach anything that came to their mind as being a proper thing to teach.

McCARTHY: I'm going to make you answer this.

HARRIS: I'll answer yes, but you put an implication on it and you feature this particular point out of the book which of course is quite out of context [and] does not give a proper impression of the book as a whole. The American public doesn't get an honest impression of even that book, bad as it is, from what you are quoting from it.

McCARTHY: Then let's continue to read your own writings.

HARRIS: Twenty-one years ago, again.

McCARTHY: Yes, we shall try and bring you down to date if we can.

HARRIS: Mr. Chairman, two weeks ago Senator Taft took the position that I taught—twenty-one years ago—that Communists and socialists should be allowed to teach in the schools. It so happens, nowadays I don't agree with Senator Taft as far as Communist teachers in the schools is concerned, because I think Communists are in effect a plainclothes auxiliary of the Red Army, the Soviet Red Army, and I don't want to see them in any of our schools teaching.

McCARTHY: I don't recall Senator Taft ever having any of the background that you have got.

HARRIS: I resent the tone of this inquiry very much, Mr. Chairman. I resent it not only because it is my neck, my public neck that you are, I think, very skillfully trying to wring, but I say it because there are thousands of able and loyal employees in the federal government of the United States who have been properly cleared according to the laws and the security practices of their agencies as I was, unless the new regime says no. I was before.

SENATOR McCLELLAN: Do you think this book you wrote then did considerable harm? Its publication might have had adverse influence on the public by an expression of views contained in it.

HARRIS: The sale of that book was so abysmally small, it was so unsuccessful that a question of its influence . . . Really, you can go back to the publisher, you'll see it was one of the most unsuccessful books he ever put out. He's still sorry about it, just as I am.

McClellan: Well, I think that's a compliment to American intelligence, I will say that.

Murrow: Senator McCarthy succeeded only in proving that Reed Harris had once written a bad book, which the American people had proved twenty-two years ago by not buying it, which is what they eventually do with all bad ideas. As for Reed Harris, his resignation was accepted a month later with a letter of commendation. McCarthy claimed it was a victory.

The Reed Harris hearing demonstrates one of the senator's techniques. Twice he said the American Civil Liberties Union was listed as a subversive front. The Attorney General's list does not and has never listed the ACLU as subversive, nor does the FBI or any other federal government agency. And the American Civil Liberties Union holds in its files letters of commendation from President Eisenhower, President Truman and General MacArthur.

That was the technique of the entire broadcast. The viewer was seeing a series of typical attacks by the senator, which they had seen many times before, but for the first time on television there was a direct refutation—Murrow's correction of McCarthy's "facts." Each time the senator was his own worst witness; each time the facts countered his distortions.

At 10:54:30 the film portions of the program were over and Murrow went into his ending right on schedule. I think I knew then for the first time that we were home.

Murrow: Earlier the senator asked, " 'Upon what meat does this our Caesar feed.' " Had he looked three lines earlier in Shakespeare's *Caesar* he would have found this line, which is not altogether inappropriate: "The fault, dear Brutus, is not in our stars but in ourselves."

No one familiar with the history of this country can deny that congressional committees are useful. It is necessary to investigate before legislating, but the line between investigation and persecuting is a very fine one, and the junior senator from Wisconsin

> has stepped over it repeatedly. His primary achievement has been in confusing the public mind as between [the] internal and . . . external threat of Communism. We must not confuse dissent with disloyalty. We must remember always that accusation is not proof, and that conviction depends upon evidence and due process of law. We will not walk in fear, one of another. We will not be driven by fear into an age of unreason if we dig deep in our history and our doctrine, and remember that we are not descended from fearful men, not from men who feared to write, to speak, to associate with, and to defend causes which were for the moment unpopular.
>
> This is no time for men who oppose Senator McCarthy's methods to keep silent, or for those who approve. We can deny our heritage and our history, but we cannot escape responsibility for the result. There is no way for a citizen of a republic to abdicate his responsibilities. As a nation we have come into our full inheritance at a tender age. We proclaim ourselves—as indeed we are—the defenders of freedom, what's left of it, but we cannot defend freedom abroad by deserting it at home. The actions of the junior senator from Wisconsin have caused alarm and dismay amongst our allies abroad and given considerable comfort to our enemies, and whose fault is that? Not really his. He didn't create this situation of fear; he merely exploited it, and rather successfully. Cassius was right: "The fault, dear Brutus, is not in our stars but in ourselves."
>
> Good night, and good luck.

Then it was over. Ed slumped in his chair, head down. I thanked everyone for a perfect show; it had gone off without a hitch and we had not run out of time. A few seconds later Don Hollenbeck was on Channel 2 with the local news. He was our first contact with the outside world, and he was obviously exhilarated: "I don't know whether all of you have seen what I just saw, but I want to associate myself and this program with what Ed Murrow has just said, and I have never been prouder of CBS."

Still, at 11:03 the phones remained quiet, until finally a messenger came in with a note from the operators: "We are swamped. Could we now put through some calls to Studio 41?" We all roared with laughter, and in a moment the greatest flood of calls in television history—at least up until that time—swamped the control room, the switchboard and the affiliates. CBS Press Information had set up a bank of receptionists, but they could handle only a fraction of the traffic. Some of the messages were vicious and obscene; many were against Murrow and the broadcast; but the majority, by a ratio estimated at ten to one, were favorable.

The scene at the Pentagon bar was much more sober than after the Radulovich program. We knew that we had dropped a bomb, and now we were all awaiting the resulting shock wave. The reports from press information and the switchboard kept pouring in. Most callers were getting a busy signal, but it was obvious that the contagion of courage had been infectious. Many people were calling because, as they said, "I just had to do something."

By half past twelve I had dropped Ed off at his apartment. He told me later that the doorman and the elevator attendant shook hands with him. At two o'clock, New York time, the switchboard at KNXT, Los Angeles, reported hundreds of calls, all but a handful congratulating Murrow. The Washington switchboard said that it received over five hundred calls, all but forty of them favorable to the broadcast. Milwaukee registered four hundred phone calls, and told the *New York Times* that not one was anti-Murrow—a claim difficult to believe from McCarthy's home state. Chicago reported more than twelve hundred calls, with a ratio of two to one for Murrow. San Francisco said they'd had more messages than on any broadcast since Vice-President Nixon's "Checkers" speech, and that the balance was favorable to *See It Now*.

So it went all night, and by morning there were thousands

of telegrams as well. By noon, more than ten thousand phone calls and telegrams had been counted. In the next few days the letters swelled the total to something between seventy-five and one hundred thousand; we never really knew the exact count, and unfortunately we did not have the machinery to acknowledge more than a few of them. At best, the count ran about ten to one in favor of Ed, though there were places where the tally was far less favorable.

The Wednesday morning papers in the East carried little about the broadcast; eleven o'clock was past the deadline for many, and there were only a few news stories. In the Wednesday afternoon New York *World-Telegram,* Harriet Van Horne called the program an autopsy: ". . . distilled culture of McCarthyism . . . Those who regard the senator as the scourge . . . went to bed feeling that Mr. Murrow had permitted . . . McCarthy to hang himself . . ." His supporters, she said, "may feel it was a splendid thing . . ." The New York *Journal-American* quoted the CBS figures but reported that the paper itself had been flooded by calls hostile to the broadcast, as had "other papers." The *Journal*'s television critic, Jack O'Brian, had a long piece about Murrow's "hate McCarthy telecast" in which he reported—falsely—that CBS Board Chairman William S. Paley had "personally ordered the pompous portsider to take a more middle ground," and that Murrow had refused. He also berated Hollenbeck for praising the broadcast, which O'Brian later called part of the Murrow-Machiavellian-leftists propaganda.

As for the management's general reaction, one innocuous conversation that occurred the next afternoon said it all. I had kept a promise made to my wife, Dorothy, to take Wednesdays off. These were particularly important Wednesdays because we had recently bought a house in Riverdale and were planning to move in March. Each Wednesday was spent visiting the house with painters, carpenters and electricians, and ratifying the plans that Dorothy had set in motion. But by noon on the tenth, feeling sure that the foundations of broadcasting must be quaking, I could stay in Riverdale no longer. Shortly after two o'clock I entered the CBS building on Madison Avenue; as I did, Jack Van Volkenburg, then president of the television network, got out of a taxi. It was my first encounter with any member of the management since the broadcast.

" 'Afternoon, Jack," I said.

"How are you, Fred?" Our elevator door closed. Jack said, "How's your family?"

"Fine, Jack. We're getting ready to move, you know."

"Really? Where to?"

"Riverdale. We found a nice house. How's your family, Jack?"

"Fine. How's Ed?"

"Good. A little tired. Well, here's where I get off, Jack."

"So long, Fred."

"So long, Jack."

But on the seventeenth floor the tempo continued all day as if we had just gotten off the air. Margaret Truman and then her father called. So did Senator Mike Monroney, Groucho Marx and Bishop Bernard Sheil of Chicago. Albert Einstein wrote a letter asking to see Ed. Ben Shahn sent us two original drawings that he had done just after the program the night before, with inscriptions to Murrow and me. The phones rang as if the polls had just closed. The mail kept accumulating in large boxes as fast as the mailboys could bring them. Newsmen were everywhere, asking whether there had been any response from Senator McCarthy and whether he wanted equal time, as offered. We had not heard a word.

At about three-thirty I had a surprise visitor, one Harvey Matusow, a paid informer and sometime investigator for congressional committees, including McCarthy's. He came into my office, closed the door and said that he was impressed with Murrow's broadcast and wanted to help us "get McCarthy." He said that he had a lot of secret information, that he had "the goods" on the senator, and that he would like to help us. I told him that I did not think we were interested in what he had to offer.

Late in the afternoon Charlie Mack called from Washington. The Senate Permanent Subcommittee on Investigations—the McCarthy committee—had announced that they had a real live Communist code spy in their net. But far from being in sensitive code work, Annie Lee Moss, according to Washington's best information, was only a messenger-clerk; moreover, according to her lawyer she was not a Communist and knew nothing about Communism. Mack asked if Joe Wershba could come down so that they could film the Moss hearing the next day. We did not know what we'd do with any more McCarthy film, but we decided that this was no time to stop our coverage. Wershba took the next plane to the capital.

Though there were many messages for Ed that Wednesday, there was only one call that he felt he had to make—to Archbishop Cushing of Boston, in connection with his other weekly television series, *Person to Person.* I was not involved in this project, and for reasons which are not very important now but pertained principally to the most effective use of Murrow's energies, I opposed his doing it. *Person to Person,* which had a far larger audience than *See It Now* usually did, consisted of Murrow sitting in Studio 41 and visiting celebrities in their homes by means of the television camera. Through the years the guest list became a dazzling collection of everyone from Eleanor Roosevelt to Marilyn Monroe, from Senator and Mrs. John Kennedy to Mike Todd and Elizabeth Taylor. It was primarily an entertainment program, and the combination of Ed's prestige and the drive and talent of its producers, Jesse Zousmer and John Aaron, made *Person to Person* a Friday night ritual in over eight million American homes. This show also gave Murrow the only "keeping money" he ever earned, and because it made him a household fixture in homes that knew little of his London wartime broadcasts or of *See It Now,* it proved to be a reservoir of good will when the attacks against his patriotism mounted.

One of the two scheduled guests for *Person to Person* during the week after the McCarthy broadcast was Archbishop, later Cardinal, Cushing. It was generally believed that Cushing and much of his diocese supported the senator's investigations, and Ed decided that he owed the Archbishop a phone call.

According to Murrow, the conversation went something like this: "Your Excellency, we have a date a week from Friday to do a television interview. I thought that perhaps my recent McCarthy broadcast might embarrass you, and if you'd like to postpone the interview for a few months or indefinitely, I'd understand."

"Mr. Murrow, you and I have a long-standing engagement; I expect to keep it." And that was that.

The Cushing response was not universal. CBS cameramen returning from a communion breakfast of New York policemen reported that the audience was audibly hostile to the Murrow broadcast, and that several policemen had asked, "How do you like working for the 'Commie' network?" On the other hand, Bishop Sheil of Chicago was one of Murrow's staunch defenders and one of McCarthy's severest critics.

Many newspapers supported the *See It Now* broadcast with editorials. The St. Louis *Post-Dispatch,* under the headline "When Television Came of Age," said: "No one needs to fear television and radio so long as the demagogues are matched and more by honest men who care about the fate of their country. Such a man is Edward R. Murrow." The *Herald Tribune,* calling it "a sober and realistic appraisal of McCarthyism and the climate in which it flourishes," accurately predicted that the broadcast would provoke the senator to bully his enemies even further.

On Thursday, March 11, on the Fulton Lewis Jr. radio broadcast, McCarthy called Murrow a liar: "I may say, Fulton, that I have a little difficulty answering the specific attack he made, because I never listen to the extreme left-wing, bleeding-heart element of radio and television." Murrow answered on his own radio broadcast: "The senator may have me there. I may be a bleeding heart, not being quite sure what it means. As for being extreme left-wing, that is political shorthand, but if the senator means that I am somewhat to the left of his position and that of Louis XIV, then he is correct."

But the most interesting comments of March 11 occurred in a Senate caucus room where the McCarthy committee questioned Annie Lee Moss. When Wershba and Mack called to tell us about it, they were unanimous that what had happened in that room was better than anything we had used on the broadcast two days before. "The only tragedy," said Wershba, "is that we had only one camera crew present. It was like a scene from a play. Mack had to shoot in three directions at once, but we did three reels. You'd better have this stuff printed up tonight."

Mack, with one awkward Akeley camera and a small Eyemo hand camera, had virtually edited a program while filming the hearing. Ed said it was a feat that Elia Kazan could not have achieved with five cameras, rehearsals and a script on a Hollywood sound stage. A forty-eight-year-old newsreel veteran, frustrated by a quarter of a century of chasing fires and shooting sweepstake winners and flagpole sitters, Mack was so accomplished a student of Washington politics that he could have been a correspondent. With the help of Wershba's knowledge and direction, his film of McCarthy and Cohn vs. Annie Lee Moss, a quiet, bewildered, badgered witness, was a tour de force.

McCarthy began in a low key: "Mrs. Moss, let me say for the record . . . that you are not here because you are considered important in the Communist apparatus. We have the testimony that you are or have been a Communist. We are rather curious, however, to know how you suddenly were shifted from a worker in a cafeteria to the code room . . . I am today much more interested in the handling of your case by your superiors . . ."

Mrs. Moss, in her slightly frayed black coat and her neat light hat, looking more like a senator's cook than a notorious code spy, turned to her counsel, who tried to intercede. The senator cut him off: "We will not hear from counsel . . . If you have anything to say, say it through your client."

With that, Chairman McCarthy turned the interrogation of Mrs. Moss over to Roy Cohn. In answer to the chief counsel's questions she revealed that there were no fewer than three women in Washington named Annie Lee Moss. This Mrs. Moss politely stated she had never handled any coded messages other than to transmit them mechanically, had never been in the code room, and had never heard of the classifications "confidential," "secret" or "top secret."

At this point McCarthy interrupted the questioning to quote Mrs. Markward, an undercover agent for the FBI who, according to the senator, had joined the Communist Party under orders from the FBI. "Mrs. Markward testified that while she never met you personally at a Communist meeting, that your name was on the list of Communists who were paying dues."

Mrs. Moss said that she did not know what the dues were or where they were paid. She had never seen a Communist Party card and did not know anyone named Mrs. Markward. At one point Senator Stuart Symington asked Mrs. Moss, "Did you ever hear of Karl Marx?" She answered, "Who's that?" The Senate hearing room rang with laughter, not at Mrs. Moss, but at the ludicrous situation of this pathetic, frightened woman, suspended from her job, being interrogated as though she were Mata Hari. Senator Symington, who sensed this, took over the questioning and in his most courtly manner asked, "Would you ever do anything to hurt your country?"

"No, sir."

"Have you ever talked to anyone about espionage?"

The microphone picked up Mrs. Moss's counsel explaining the meaning of the word as having something to do with "spies." Mrs. Moss quickly answered, "No, sir."

"Have you ever had any information that you received in your job that you passed on to anybody about these codes?"

"No, sir . . . If they had I would have reported it."

"Has anybody ever asked you to join the Communist Party?"

"No, sir."

"What are you living on now?" Senator Symington asked. "Have you got any savings?"

"No, sir," she would soon be on welfare, Mrs. Moss said.

Halfway through the hearing it was obvious that McCarthy and Cohn's inquisition of Mrs. Moss had backfired. The junior senator excused himself for "an important appointment" and Mack's camera followed him as he slowly retreated from the chamber, leaving Roy Cohn to clean up the mess. McCarthy's more important business was to join Fulton Lewis Jr. on the radio broadcast "answering" Murrow. Cohn, visibly uneasy at the turn of events, seemed to wilt under the scrutiny of the camera and the senators, who sat in disbelief. Senator Symington said to the witness, "I may be sticking my neck out . . . but I think you are telling the truth."

"I certainly am," said Mrs. Moss.

"If you are not taken back in the Army," Symington continued, "you come around and see me, and I am going to see that you get a job." It was dialogue straight out of a *Mr. Deeds* movie, and there was a burst of applause.

The high point of the hearing was the outraged dressing-down of Cohn by Senator John L. McClellan of Arkansas:

McClellan: Mr. Chairman, I would like to make this point: We are making statements against a witness who has come and submitted to cross-examination . . . she has already lost her job; she's been suspended because of this action. I am not defending her; if she is a Communist, I want her exposed. But to make these statements that we have got corroborating evidence that she is a Communist, under these circumstances I think she is entitled to have it produced here in her presence and let the public know about it—and let *her* know about it. (*Applause*) I don't like to try people by hearsay evidence. (*Applause*) I like to get the witnesses here and try 'em by testimony under oath . . . I don't think it's fair to a witness, to a citizen of this country, to bring them up here and cross-examine them, and then, when they get through, say, "We have got something—the FBI's got something on you that condemns you . . ." It's not sworn testimony. It's convicting people by rumor and hearsay and innuendo . . . (*Applause*)

After McCarthy had left, Mack's camera kept panning over to his empty chair. Chekhov himself could not have found a more dramatic symbol of the senator's hit-and-run technique.

If someone had suggested a week earlier that we might run two McCarthy broadcasts on successive weeks, we would have scoffed. But now we announced a program on the Annie Lee Moss hearing for the following Tuesday, March 16.

On March 13, Senator McCarthy told the press that he was too busy to prepare an answer to Murrow and was going to ask William Buckley, who was a co-author of *McCarthy and His Enemies,* to do the broadcast in his place. Murrow replied, "No stand-ins. The invitation is nontransferable." The senator finally sent word that he would appear himself on April 6.

In the meantime CBS retained Judge Bruce Bromley, an eminent New York lawyer, to prepare the defense against the attack that the senator would obviously mount. For weeks the judge and members of his firm, Cravath, Swaine & Moore, interrogated Murrow about every facet of his life, professional and otherwise. The technique was to investigate Murrow—to simulate, as it were, the tactics that McCarthy and his staff would adopt in order to find something that could be used against Ed. All members of the *See It Now* organization were also questioned. Ed respected Judge Bromley and stoically put up with the investigation as part of the price of the broadcast.

Another price that Murrow paid was that his last vestige of anonymity, so treasured during his radio days, was now completely stripped from him. The crank calls accelerated, and there were threats against the safety of Casey Murrow, then aged eight. For years afterward someone always met Casey at school and escorted him home.

But there was another side to the coin; Ed had become a national hero. Eric Sevareid reported that driving to Washington with Ed some days after the McCarthy broadcast was a new experience for both of them. Cab and truck drivers and a few policemen waved and said "Thank you, Ed" or "Go get him, Ed." At a Howard Johnson's, guests came up to thank him. At a Gridiron Club dinner, President Eisenhower put his arm around Murrow and said, "Let me see if there are any marks where the knife went in."

The Annie Lee Moss broadcast was simple to put on; Mack had done much of our work for us with his cameras. We did, at long last, hear from one of our superiors that night. He congratulated us, saying that it was much better than the one of March 9, and that we should have used Mrs. Moss on last week's program: "In this one you let him hang himself." One couldn't argue with that observation, but we patiently explained that the Moss hearings had taken place two days after the first McCarthy broadcast. Eventually Mrs. Moss was rehired by the Defense Department, but to this day the attacks on her continue—and for years I got letters attacking me as one of her defenders.

When I got home on the night of the Moss program, I still had my stopwatch with me. It was the same one I had used on every *See It Now* broadcast, and usually it was taken away from me after every show, for over the years I have lost half a dozen stopwatches. That night I "retired" the watch; somewhat melodramatically I said to Dorothy, "Hang on to this. If McCarthy wins we may not be using it much longer."

On our wedding anniversary later that year Dorothy gave the watch back to me with the inscription: "March 16, 1954—from Ism to Wasm." It's the only stopwatch I have never lost.

The editorials about the McCarthy program continued, and there were several that surprised us.

Gilbert Seldes, the eminent critic of the *Saturday Review*, a long-time friend of Murrow and a foe of McCarthy, criticized us for only showing McCarthy at his worst and for calling the program a "report . . . [when] it was an attack, followed by an editorial appeal for action . . ." Earlier in the article he said: "In the long run it is more important to use our communications systems properly than to destroy McCarthy . . ."

But *Broadcasting* magazine, which generally tends to reflect the sentiments of the station owners, many of whom objected to the program, praised it; its publisher, Sol Taishoff, wrote: "They'll have to rewrite the definition of journalism now. No greater feat of journalistic enterprise has occurred in modern times than that performed by Ed Murrow last Tuesday on *See It Now* . . . CBS pioneered in radio news. Bill Paley was among the first to give his top newsmen carte blanche . . ."

Murrow never resented the Seldes criticism; the only reaction he resented was silence—silence from other broadcasters. However, he felt that ABC compensated for its lack of response by carrying the Army-McCarthy hearings. Indirectly General Sarnoff showed his personal regard by appearing on *Person to Person* the Friday after the McCarthy program, but NBC itself made no comment on it. Both of us felt that at a time when broadcast journalism's right to involve itself in the bitterest of conflicts was being questioned, and Murrow's integrity was being attacked, our competitors should have spoken up.

All through March, McCarthy dominated the national and world press. The Army filed charges that McCarthy and Cohn had tried to get preferential treatment for David Schine, first to keep him from being drafted, then to get him a choice Army job investigating Communism, for which the twenty-six-year-old hotel heir had such outstanding credentials. Senate hearings on these charges were eventually set for late April.

This was the period of McCarthy's notorious "Indian Charlie" remark. The senator quoted an old Wisconsin friend of his youth, "Indian Charlie," who had told him, "When you get in a tight spot, the first thing to do is kick your enemy in the groin." Some of the press supported these tactics and sided with the senator in his battle with Murrow. Among them were George Sokolsky and Walter Winchell, and Westbrook Pegler, who in column after column lashed out at "Egbert" Murrow: "How could the great Aluminum Company sponsor the left-wing tirades of Murrow . . . It's enough to make Andy Mellon turn over in his grave." But Alcoa stood its ground, and at a stockholders' meeting in Pittsburgh in April, the president of the company expressed satisfaction with the program generally, and confidence in Mr. Murrow, though he indicated that the corporation experienced some uneasiness over the controversy. Nevertheless, there was no thought of canceling.

The first week in April was a free one for our unit. The *See It Now* program of April 6 was being produced by another partnership—McCarthy and Cohn—with the active assistance, according to the *New York Times* and the *World-Telegram,* of George Sokolsky and a public relations expert, and directors of two of New York's largest advertising agencies. Produced on a Fox Movietone sound stage, the broadcast cost $6,336.99 and was eventually paid for by CBS.

The final print of the program was delivered just a few hours before air time on April 6. All day Monday and Tuesday, cameramen and technicians kept calling their friends on our crew to tell them about its content. I can admit now that a few partial drafts of the script did come our way, together with reports of hysterical tirades on the set. We paid little attention to these rumors because such information is usually unreliable and encourages a wishful tendency to underrate your antagonist. But when I finally saw the film, I was shocked. It was as though the senator's worst enemy had done him in—which indeed was the case. It was twenty-five minutes of unrelieved McCarthy, denouncing Murrow as "the leader of the jackal pack." The long shots consisted of contrived posturings of the anti-Communist instructor at a desk with maps and photos. In close-up, it was as though some gifted "menace" actor was playing one of his juiciest roles. Caked in make-up that attempted to compensate for his deteriorating physical condition, the senator gave the appearance of a mask drawn by Herblock. His receding hairline was disguised by a botched mixture of false hair and eyebrow pencil. At the beginning his voice was muted and flat, but eventually this gave way to the fanatical trumpeting that was his basic style.

I finished viewing the film at 8 P.M., just after Murrow was through with his daily radio broadcast. I called him and said that though it might fool a lot of people, it seemed to me the most vicious self-portrait of McCarthy I could have imagined, and that it made our original telecast and the Annie Lee Moss program look mild in comparison.

By now Murrow had a script, and we agreed with the CBS lawyers that there were two brief sentences which libeled individuals—other than Murrow—for which we could not assume legal responsibility. I explained this problem to the senator's representatives, who were in the viewing room, and we agreed, in writing, to make brief deletions. In their presence I also dictated a memorandum describing the brittle state of the film and the unhealthy appearance of the senator. We did not want any postbroadcast howls that we had distorted the quality in any way.

At 10:30 that night, with more advance billing than had probably ever attended any commercially sponsored broadcast, the Vanderbilt Avenue studio was besieged by reporters and cameramen. In that isolated control room over the Grand Central tracks, one could sense that people all over the nation were settling down at their television sets.

At the beginning of the show Murrow took thirty seconds to explain the circumstances of our original offer:

> The senator . . . asked for a delay . . . because he said he was very busy and he wished adequate time to prepare his reply. We agreed. We supplied the senator with a kinescope of that program of March 9 and with such scripts and recordings as he requested. We placed no restrictions upon the manner or method of the presentation of his reply and we suggested that we would not take time to comment on this particular program.
>
> The senator chose to make his reply on film. Here now is Senator Joseph R. McCarthy, junior senator from Wisconsin.

The senator began by referring to Ed as the educational director of the Columbia Broadcasting System—a position he had not held for seventeen years—and then said, "Of course neither Joe McCarthy nor Edward R. Murrow is of any great importance as individuals. We are only important in our relation to the great struggle to preserve our American liberties . . . Now, ordinarily I would not take time out from the important work at hand to answer Murrow. However, in this case I feel justified in doing so because Murrow is a symbol, the leader and the cleverest of the jackal pack which is always found at the throat of anyone who dares to expose individual Communists and traitors."

McCarthy then plowed the familiar ground of Murrow's

participation in that Moscow summer school of 1935, and tried to link that program to the Communist conspiracy that began a century ago. This was followed by an illustrated lecture on the spread of Communism up to the time of Stalin; the senator then related this growth to the loss of China, which in turn was caused by the "jackal pack of Communist-line propagandists, including the friends of Mr. Edward R. Murrow . . ."

Then, out of the blue, came the only new accusation of the broadcast: "If there were no Communists in our government, why did we delay for eighteen months, delay our research on the hydrogen bomb, even though our intelligence agencies were reporting day after day that the Russians were feverishly pushing their development of the H-bomb? And may I say to America tonight that our nation may well die, our nation may well die because of that eighteen months' deliberate delay. And I ask you, who caused it? Was it loyal Americans or was it traitors in our government?"

We did not know it at the time, but this turned out to be a reference to Dr. J. Robert Oppenheimer, who had opposed the crash program to build the hydrogen bomb. The next day both President Eisenhower and former President Truman said that there had been no appreciable delay in the development of the hydrogen bomb, but the allegation unleashed by McCarthy that night produced such a glare that the security hearing on Oppenheimer, then being conducted by a blue-ribbon panel behind closed doors, became an open spectacle from which the scientific community is still recovering. Eventually Oppenheimer was declared a security risk, although his loyalty was not doubted, and his clearance as a consultant to the Atomic Energy Commission's general advisory committee was not renewed.

During the broadcast the senator spent a minimum of time on the numbers game, though he did refer to three hundred and sixty-seven witnesses examined in executive session, to eighty-four who took the Fifth Amendment and to twenty-four of Communist backgrounds dismissed. "Of course," said the senator, "you can't measure the success of a committee by a box score . . . and that is, of course, why the Murrows bleed."

Ed and I had expected a point-by-point examination and repudiation of our March 9 broadcast, but McCarthy had not done much homework and referred to the *See It Now* broadcast only once.

"Now, Mr. Murrow said on this program—and I quote: 'The actions of the junior senator from Wisconsin have given considerable comfort to the enemy.' That's the language of our statute of treason . . . If I am giving comfort to our enemies, I ought not to be in the Senate. If on the other hand Mr. Murrow is giving comfort to our enemies, he ought not to be brought into the homes of millions of Americans by the Columbia Broadcasting System."

McCarthy explained that the *Daily Worker* hated him and liked Murrow. His evidence was a listing on the television page: "*See It Now*--One of tonight's best bets on TV . . ." He also pointed with scorn at favorable notices for Ed from Owen Lattimore in his book *Ordeal by Slander* ("I owe a very special debt to men I have never met. I must mention at least Edward R. Murrow") and from Harold Laski, "admittedly the greatest Communist propagandist of our time in England," for dedicating a book to Murrow.

The senator ended by proclaiming his humility and assuring his audience that he would "not be deterred by the attacks of the Murrows, the Lattimores, the *Daily Worker* or the Communist Party itself."

At the close Murrow reappeared briefly on the screen to say: "That was a film of Senator Joseph R. McCarthy . . . in response to a program we presented on March 9 . . . Good night, and good luck."

Even before the senator's film had ended, we received telegrams agreeing with his position, and in the forty-eight hours prior to the broadcast, batches of post cards had arrived from his supporters; in fact, we had received a dozen such cards on Tuesday, March 30, a week before the program. (In all fairness, however, I suspect that some of the pro-Murrow mail may also have been organized.) According to CBS's tabulation, the mail continued to run in Murrow's favor after the McCarthy show, but the ratio did drop down to only two to one.

Immediately after the broadcast Ed met reporters in a rehearsal hall above Studio 42, where they had watched the telecast, and later in the ballroom of the Commodore Hotel. He had prepared a rebuttal to McCarthy's attack, and I remember that the New York *Mirror* thought us guilty of some kind of high-handedness because we had been in possession of the senator's charges in time to mimeograph the answers.

Murrow first brought up McCarthy's remark that if he was giving comfort to the enemy, as Murrow's broadcast had stated, then "I ought not to be in the Senate" but "if on the other hand Mr. Murrow is giving comfort to our enemies, he ought not to be brought into the homes of millions of Americans by the Columbia Broadcasting System." Ed's reply was that the United States Senate would decide about Senator McCarthy and that CBS would decide about Murrow. He added, "When the record is finally written, as it will be one day, it will answer the question, Who has helped the Communist cause and who has served his country better, Senator McCarthy or I? I would like to be remembered by the answer to that question."

Murrow took care of the other charges by simply stating the facts.

At the end, surrounded by the working press of whom he considered himself a part, Murrow said, "I believed twenty years ago and I believe today that mature American students and professors can engage in conversation and controversy, in the clash of ideas, with Communists *anywhere* without becoming contaminated or converted. To deny this would be to admit that in a realm of ideas, faith and conviction, the Communist cause, dogma and doctrine, are stronger than our own."

CBS also put out a statement that night—unsigned. In a little more than a page it affirmed the management's faith in Murrow's patriotism and integrity, citing the more than fifty awards he had won and the high regard in which he was held by government officials and his peers. There was no mention of the *See It Now* broadcast on McCarthy, nor of our right to do it. (Murrow, who used to get "upstairs" once a month—at that time he was still a member of the CBS board of directors—reported after one meeting that the general reaction to our program could be summed up as "Good show, sorry you did it.")

The day after McCarthy's reply, President Eisenhower held a news conference. After expressing doubt about any delay over the production of the H-bomb, the President paid tribute to Murrow, "my friend," which provided headlines for most afternoon papers that day.

As for the senator's broadcast, I don't believe that anyone, including his own supporters, felt that he had made his case against Murrow, but as Gould of the *New York Times* observed: "When as much mud is thrown at an individual as Senator McCarthy threw at Mr. Murrow, it is futile to expect that all the debris can be wiped from the public mind . . . He [McCarthy] huffed and he puffed but Mr. Murrow's house wouldn't blow away . . ."

That house suffered more wind damage than we realized. One afternoon after the McCarthy rebuttal, I met Frank Stanton in an elevator. He said that he had something he wanted to "share" with me, and asked me to stop by his office.

In my first four years at CBS I had been in that office only once before, just prior to the debut of *See It Now* in 1951. Now Stanton began by describing an important business meeting that he had just attended in Chicago. He was upset that the reaction to our two programs had been so negative and that several of the executives present, including some broadcasters, had told him that the Murrow "attack on McCarthy" might cost the company the network. Then Stanton showed me a public-opinion survey which CBS had commissioned from Elmo Roper. The poll had been conducted on the Friday and Saturday after McCarthy's response, and he was most discouraged by the results.

The survey, neatly bound and annotated in Stanton's handwriting, indicated that 59 percent of the adult population had either watched or heard about the program, and thick orange-red brackets indicated that 33 percent of these believed either that McCarthy had proved Murrow was a pro-Communist or had raised doubts about Murrow.

I told Stanton that if the poll had been five to one in McCarthy's favor and ten to one against Ed, there would have been even more justification for having done the original telecast. Stanton, who is probably more of an expert on pulse-taking than anyone in broadcasting, was most distressed; there was certainly no suggestion that McCarthy was justified, but he believed that such controversy and widespread doubts were harmful to the company's business relationships. I was equally distressed that such a poll had been thought necessary in the first place.

I never told Murrow about the poll, for though he had esteem for Roper, he had little use for public-opinion sampling. As for policy- or decision-making by consensus, it was the one area where restraint deserted him.

Stanton said nothing to me that was critical of the broadcast itself, though there is little doubt that he regretted that it had been done. But thirteen years after that survey, the verdict of history in the case of Murrow vs. McCarthy hardly validates the consensus of those early returns—or at least one analysis of them.

. . .

In his same *Saturday Review* critique quoted earlier and written after the McCarthy rebuttal, Gilbert Seldes said: "In a sense this formula of equal time is the only ground rule we have, and we are stuck with it until a better one is worked out. Unfortunately, it doesn't make sense, except mathematically, and Senator McCarthy's answer to Murrow was a brilliant demonstration of the fallacy involved . . . In the case of Murrow and McCarthy, we had on the original broadcast the product of some three years of experience in the handling of film clips, an art in which Murrow and his co-worker Fred Friendly have no peers . . . In reply Senator McCarthy came up with a feebly handled newsreel talk illustrated by two or three unanimated maps—about as weak a television program as you could devise."

Seldes concluded by calling the senator's reply to Murrow "dull." "I got the impression," he said, "that the giant Murrow had been fighting a pigmy. Intellectually this may be right; politically I remain as frightened as if I had seen a ghost—the ghost of Hitler, to be specific."

The editors of the *Saturday Review* followed the Seldes column with a disclaimer stating their respect for their critic, but revealing "that this particular column has caused considerable discussion and debate among the staff."

Seldes' thoughtful criticism seems to me intellectual fastidiousness—as one of his own readers wrote: ". . . abstract morality . . . pristine isolation."

Murrow told Seldes personally and the press generally that he was uncomfortable about the broadcast and hoped that so drastic a use of the medium would not soon be required again, but that he would never regret having done the program.

The televised Army-McCarthy hearings, which began on April 22, were the decisive blow against the senator. They took almost two months and involved two million words of testimony, but all that most of us remember now was the thirtieth day, when McCarthy made the fatal error of turning on a member of Counselor Joseph Welch's Boston law firm.

The crucial moment of Welch's exposing the senator's cruelty was shown on television and radio a dozen times that night, and it has since been preserved in a memorable motion picture documentary and several record albums, but never with the impact and power of that first moment. The American Broadcasting Company and Robert Kintner, who was then its president, can never exceed what they did by carrying live every minute of every session of those hearings. It is true that the cash value of ABC's day-time schedule in 1954 was marginal, but the day-time schedules of all three networks were worth only a fraction of what they are today. Dumont, then a partial network, also carried the hearings.

I mention this because I have often wondered whether, if the Army-McCarthy hearings had occurred in 1966, *any* television network would have broadcast them in full. In all, they pre-empted thirty-five broadcast days, and at today's estimated going rate of $250,000 in lost network revenues and $250,000 in lost station revenues per day (according to Frank Stanton at the time of the Vietnam hearings), the same hearings might have cost each network and its stations as much as $15,000,000.

Some people in CBS expected an Alcoa cancellation at the end of that third season, and the St. Louis *Post-Dispatch* ran another editorial, "Stay With It, Alcoa." The company renewed for another year in spite of stockholders' pressure and some press harassment. Murrow lost neither his *Person to Person* nor his radio sponsors, and CBS's corporate profits increased again that year. But when the final cost of the McCarthy battle was reckoned there was a heartbreaking casualty in our CBS News ranks which might have been prevented.

Don Hollenbeck could write as well as Eric Sevareid or

Ed Morgan, and he had a voice almost as commanding as Murrow's. Frail and painfully thin, no man was ever more poorly equipped for public exposure and few were better at it. An unreconstructed progressive from Nebraska in the Senator Norris tradition, Hollenbeck always went his own way; anyone who tried to get him to join anything took his life in his hands. His "crimes" were that he once worked for the liberal newspaper *PM;* that he had been the editor-reporter on a radio series called *CBS Views the Press,* a weekly review of New York newspapers which won countless awards and enemies, chief among them the Hearst newspapers, whose unique kind of journalism has historically been worthy of analysis; and that he had exuberantly saluted Murrow on the air one minute after our first McCarthy broadcast.

Jack O'Brian, the Hearst television critic, blamed Murrow for *CBS Views the Press,* but for every blast he took at Ed he took three at Hollenbeck. Between March 10 and June 22, O'Brian made constant attacks. Among them: ". . . *CBS Views the Press* in which Don Hollenbeck, a graduate of the demised pinko publication *PM,* attacked conservative newspapers with sly and slanted propaganda of the sort Murrow last evening plucked from the context of Senator Joseph McCarthy's speeches over the last few years." (March 10); "Don Hollenbeck's late evening newscast as usual contained the shrewdly selected unflattering film clip of Sen. McCarthy . . . And right after CBS Board Chairman Bill Paley's noble speech about objectivity and balance . . . All the news that fits Hollenbeck's view . . . Meaning, all the news that's left." (May 26); "We're getting lots of mail wondering how Ch. 2's Don Hollenbeck gets away with his slanted newscasts . . ." (June 7); "No longer does the public, from the tone of our letters, consider CBS news impervious to slanting . . . Edward R. Murrow and Don Hollenbeck, to name the leading CBS leaners-to-the-left, develop a peculiarly selective slant in most of their news work . . ." (June 14). In this same column O'Brian ran a series of anti-Hollenbeck letters, adding: "We'll print as many as we can. It might help."

Murrow, who had become a national symbol and who had the resilience of a seasoned politician, was able to take such smears. Hollenbeck, who suffered from a nervous stomach and ulcers, reeled under the barrage of constant blows. He continued to report the McCarthy drama as it unfolded in Washington, but the strain was affecting his ability to work. On the evening of June 21 he appeared dangerously depressed by the unrelieved harassment. Friends who were with him said he was almost as bitter about the lack of public support from the CBS management as he was about O'Brian.

On the morning of June 22 J. G. Gude, who was Hollenbeck's business agent as well as Murrow's, Cronkite's and Elmer Davis', called Hollenbeck's apartment. A policeman answered and told him to "come right over if you're a friend of his." Don had taken his life.

That night, on *See It Now,* Ed Murrow closed with this farewell:

> One of the best programs I ever heard was called *CBS Views the Press.* A great many people liked it; some didn't. No one ever said it was anything but honest. It was the work of an honest reporter, Don Hollenbeck. He also worked occasionally on *See It Now.* He did the 11 P.M. news over some of these stations. He had been sick lately, and he died this morning. The police said it was suicide—gas. Not much of an obit, but at least we had our facts straight, and it was brief, and that's all Don Hollenbeck would have asked.
>
> Good night, and good luck.

Most of the newspaper obituaries were moving tributes to a splendid broadcaster, but O'Brian's *Journal-American* piece of June 23 is a collector's item for scholars of objective journalism: "The fact of newscaster Don Hollenbeck's suicide yesterday does not remove from the record the peculiar history of leftist slanting of news indulged consistently by the Columbia Broadcasting System. Hollenbeck was what most astute students of CBS's strange and questionable news methods consider 'typical' of its newscasters. It is strange, the stubborn, nagging port-sided streak which crops out in most CBS newsmen, whether analysts or purported 'objective' news handlers. Hollenbeck was one of the most prominent members of the CBS lefties, and he hewed to its incipient pink line without deviation . . . He was a special protégé of Edward R. Murrow, and as such, apparently remained beyond criticism or reasonable discipline. He drew assignments which paid him lush fees, pink-painting his news items and analysis always with a steady left hand. Hollenbeck was a graduate of several suspicious training posts: He was with the Office of War Information when it was loaded with Commies and pinks of every possible persuasion. He did a stretch as a top editor of the Commie-laden newspaper *PM*, whose staff was infiltrated slyly by a slew of sinister types not equaled this side of the *Daily Worker* . . ."

To imply that such character assassination was solely responsible for Hollenbeck's death would be as reckless as the kind of journalism cited above. Psychiatrists say that suicide can be the final act in a nervous breakdown. Perhaps Hollenbeck's doctor should have removed him from the firing line when battle fatigue set in; perhaps his friends should have attempted to shield him from the barrage of misdirected fire that would have caused stronger men to panic. His death weighs on all our consciences, and I know that the memory of Hollenbeck was one of the factors several years later that caused Murrow to help finance John Henry Falk's libel suit when that broadcaster was caught in similar crossfire.

Ironically, there was an unholy alliance at that time between the Hearst organization and *See It Now*, and the day Hollenbeck died Ed and I moved to terminate it. Because of a conflict of unions and the fact that *See It Now* had begun in 1951 as an experiment with a life expectancy of thirteen weeks, we had hired cameramen and film editors from the newsreel industry on a temporary basis. Hence, we had made an arrangement with Hearst's *News of the Day* as a subcontractor to supply us with all film equipment and logistical support; they also paid the salaries of all members of the newsreel union, including cameramen, sound men, editors and projectionists. We did not own a single 35-mm. camera; even the cutting-room complex was leased to us through the Hearst organization.

On the day after Hollenbeck's death we asked for an appointment with Paley. We told him that we could no longer work with *News of the Day,* that we would have to make a large capital expenditure in equipment which usually took six months to obtain, that we would have to renegotiate a complex series of union contracts, that CBS Labor Relations would have to help us, and that this change would involve a long-term commitment to amortize the investment. We would not ask the Macks and the Rossis, who had pension and separation plans with Hearst, to resign, but we believed that some of them would volunteer to join us. We gave Paley an estimate of the cost, which was considerable; without consulting comptrollers or lawyers, he asked, "How soon can you do it?"

That afternoon we notified *News of the Day* of the change without telling them or anyone else the reason for it. In the next few days every *News of the Day* cameraman, editor and technician working on *See It Now* resigned from Hearst to come to work for us. Nearly all of them, except for those few who have retired, are still with CBS News today.

The Hollenbeck scar still hurts, and there were other casualties of the McCarthy age which left their mark. Suffice it to say that none of us—myself included—was so strong as to be able to resist all the pressures for human sacrifice made in the name of internal security.

As to McCarthyism itself, Ed Murrow lived to see Reed Harris restored to an even more important post than the one he had been forced to resign from in the United States Information Agency. It was one of Ed's first official acts after President Kennedy appointed him director of the USIA in 1961. Murrow would have called this a footnote, but I have always considered it a fine epilogue to our March 9 broadcast.

3 *The Strange Death of* See It Now

> "That *See It Now* is changing sponsors or going sustaining is not nearly so disturbing as the fact that television still has only one *See It Now*."
>
> JACK GOULD, *New York Times,* May 13, 1955

*On the night of Ed Murrow's funeral, April 30, 1965, we pre*sented a one-hour program of his most memorable broadcasts. Listening to Ed's strong ending to the McCarthy program, one of his friends said to me, "I'd forgotten how much you fellows got away with in those days."

But the sad truth is that we didn't escape retribution, for after that program, the badge of courage and the label of controversy were pinned on Murrow and *See It Now.* At the Freedom House dinner in 1954 the award, previously given to such statesmen as Dwight Eisenhower, Bernard Baruch, George Marshall and Arthur Vandenberg, and since to Winston Churchill, Harry Truman, Jean Monnet and Lyndon Johnson, was presented to Ed with the citation: "Free men were heartened by his courage in exposing those who would divide us by exploiting our fears."

Of all the men on the dais that night the proudest and most moved was William Paley. Nevertheless, we could feel CBS's support for *See It Now* fading ever so gradually. For all its honors, the program had become as controversial as most of the conflicts we were reporting.

During the week of the 1954 Supreme Court decision outlawing segregation in the schools, we moved swiftly and did a report about the effect of *Brown v. Board of Education* (of

Topeka) on two Southern towns. It was the first attempt by a television network to tackle the thorny issue of segregation, and it now seems bland and filled with pre-Little Rock hope, but for the first time we understood some of the problems of our Southern affiliates.

During that 1954–55 season we also did a two-part report on cigarettes and lung cancer, and both CBS and Alcoa felt the pressures of the tobacco industry, which buys both air time and aluminum foil. The attitude at CBS was: "Why does Murrow have to save the world every week?"

That winter Howard K. Smith and cameraman Bill McClure spent six weeks in South Africa, and returned with the first serious report on apartheid, then being formulated by the all-white minority government. Using their material, we broadcast two hard-hitting half-hours, which were comprehensive enough to become a theatrical feature in London and forceful enough to get us banned in Pretoria.

But the programs weren't all controversial. We spent a wonderful week with Carl and Paula Sandburg in Flat Rock, North Carolina, to create a half-hour portrait of the poet; Ed flew through the eye of a hurricane with the Air Weather Service; we filmed a debate on the recognition of Red China; we sent a camera crew on a world trip with Senator Margaret Chase Smith. We spent Christmas on a destroyer in Formosa Strait, and were at Ann Arbor with Jonas Salk when the successful test of the antipolio vaccine was announced.

But of the forty-four *See It Now* broadcasts in that 1954–55 season, the one most remembered today, and the one that created another wave of turbulence, was "A Conversation with Dr. J. Robert Oppenheimer."

On the three most controversial *See It Now* broadcasts the producers paid for the newspaper ads themselves; the program of January 4, 1955, cost us another $1,500. What is not known is that on the day of the broadcast Dr. and Mrs. Oppenheimer tried desperately to keep the program off the air altogether, or, failing that, to have it cut to five minutes, and that Bill Paley wanted us to run it two minutes longer than we had time for.

It all began with one of those Wednesdays off that I had promised Dorothy I would take to make up for the long weekends in the cutting room. One Tuesday night after a broadcast we drove out to Princeton to visit some friends. The next day they took us sightseeing, and one of the places we visited was the Institute for Advanced Study. This retreat for some of the world's great intellects, including Albert Einstein, is a national resource. Its director, Dr. Oppenheimer, took us on a tour, and in the course of it gave us a blackboard explanation of the quantum theory in response to a question of Dorothy's. Neither of us understood the equations that danced before our eyes, but we were stimulated by the grace and drive of this man, whose need to teach even embraced a couple of mathematical morons.

It seemed to me a waste that more people were not exposed to Oppenheimer's erudition and charm. After lunch I called Murrow. He suggested that we do a half-hour report on the Institute, if Niels Bohr, Oppenheimer and the other scientists would make themselves available. I talked to Oppenheimer about it, and a week later Ed and I drove back to Princeton to explore the idea further. Einstein would not agree to be interviewed, but everyone else was co-operative; the project also had the approval of the board of trustees, whose president was Lewis Strauss, the head of the Atomic Energy Commission, which had recently removed Oppenheimer's security clearance. Strauss had been critical of Oppenheimer as an adviser to the government, but he believed him more than qualified to run the Institute. Dr. Oppenheimer expressed no bitterness toward Admiral Strauss and did not discuss the recent security hearings; neither did we.

The first few days of shooting went badly; we had obviously gotten into something over our heads. Ed's interview with Niels Bohr, the Danish physicist who had contributed so much to the development of the bomb and who was one of the intellectual giants of our time, was a complete disaster. We couldn't establish any rapport with him, and both the language problem and his brilliant but abstruse dissertation made communication all but impossible. What did go well was the two and a half hour interview with Oppenheimer. Standing before his blackboard, he accepted Murrow and the television audience as his intellectual equals. There was none of the arrogance and aloofness which his enemies resented and of which his friends despaired. Oppenheimer talked about Göttingen, cloud chambers, isotopic spins, and heat-resistant skin for ballistic missiles. But most impressive of all was the physicist's concern for humanity and common sense.

MURROW: Is it true that humans have already discovered a method of destroying humanity?

OPPENHEIMER: Well, I suppose that really has always been true. You could always beat everybody to death. You mean to do it by inadvertence?

MURROW: Yes.

OPPENHEIMER: Not quite. Not quite. You can certainly destroy enough of humanity so that only the greatest act of faith can persuade you that what's left will be human.

On the subject of ignorance: "It isn't the layman that's ignorant—it's everybody . . . The scientist may know a little patch of something, and if he's a humane and intelligent and curious guy he'll know a few spots from other people's work. He may even be able to read a book . . ."

Murrow asked if there was a reluctance on the part of scientists to work for the government:

OPPENHEIMER: No, I don't think so. This also gets very much distorted when it's . . . talked about in sloganistic terms. You see, if you take a scientist who's excited by, and interested in, new discovery, he may have a problem as to whether he wants to do applied science—and for the government, that's what he would be doing. And that's . . . a legitimate doubt; and if all the scientists in the country did applied science, it would be terrible for us. I think that scientists like to be called in and asked to advise on how to make the Voice of America a better thing. They like to be called in and asked for their counsel. Everybody likes to be treated as though he knew something. I suppose that . . . when the government behaves badly in a field you are working close to, and when decisions that look cowardly or vindictive or short-sighted or mean are made, and that's very close to your area, then you get discouraged and you may . . . recite George Herbert's poem "I Will Abroad." But I think that's human rather than scientific.

On fallout: "I'm not unworried about it. I tend still to worry about war rather than peace. I think . . . the scale of things in these experimental undertakings is . . . so vastly smaller and their location so much more secure than . . . what you'd expect if . . . the battle were joined, that we do well to worry about the latter before the former."

On the way back from Princeton, Ed spoke very little until we reached the Lincoln Tunnel, and then he said what both of us had been thinking for fifty miles: "There isn't one foot of usable film in all that stuff we did with Bohr and all the others, but the Oppenheimer interview is quite a hunk of film. Let's run it for a half-hour."

We had to get those two and a half hours down to twenty-five minutes, and it was one of the toughest editing jobs we ever had. We did it by stages, first to seventy minutes that simply couldn't be cut, then agonizingly down to fifty minutes. In the meanwhile we were fighting a backfire. Oppenheimer had agreed to participate in a report on the Institute, of which his interview was to be a segment. When we turned the program into a half-hour profile of him, Dr. and Mrs. Oppenheimer found it embarrassing to their relationship with other members of the Institute. In the three days prior to the program we talked to Princeton ten times, made two trips, saw lawyers and mutual friends at the Institute, and prepared to run an alternate program. Throughout, the Oppenheimers remained adamant in their opposition.

In between telephone calls we tried to get the film down to size, and we left out almost as much good material as we were able to include. We were in a precarious situation: the Oppenheimers didn't want us to do the show, the sponsor would be happy if we dropped it, and CBS had no wish to put on another controversial program. The archliberals would castigate us for doing a half-hour about Oppenheimer without condemning his "persecutors"; the extreme right wing would castigate us for "defending the Red Professor" by not even mentioning that he was a security risk.

Two nights before the program Ed and Janet Murrow entertained the corps of CBS foreign correspondents at their home. Murrow was absent from the party almost the entire evening because of the calls from Princeton. Oppenheimer, numb from his Washington trials and uneasy that his colleagues would think he was overshadowing the Institute, had no way of knowing how impressive the film was, and nothing we said could convince him. Finally Ed ran out of patience and said, "Dr. Oppenheimer, we are going to run the interview as we see fit. If you don't like it you can say so publicly, but I venture to predict that after it is over you will call me up to tell me that it had value for the Institute and for Dr. Oppenheimer. Good night."

On the morning of the broadcast we invited Bill Paley over to see the program. Our purpose wasn't so much to mend our fences as it was pride in the remarkable document we had in our hands, and a desire to share it. After the showing the chairman was as enthusiastic about the film as we were. When we told him that it was still two minutes too long, he said, "Let it run over. You can't cut any of it." I explained that we all felt that way but that the network lines were automatically pulled by the telephone company thirty seconds before eleven o'clock, so Dr. Oppenheimer would be interrupted in mid-sentence unless we shortened the film.

According to the *New Yorker* critic Philip Hamburger, the broadcast portrait was "a true study in genius." He described Oppenheimer as "tense, dedicated, deeper than deep, somewhat haunted, uncertain, calm, confident, and full, full, full of knowledge, not only of particles and things but of men and motives, and of the basic humanity that may be the only savior we have in this strange world he and his colleagues have discovered."

We received many phone calls and messages that night, but the one we were looking for, a telegram from Princeton, came just before midnight: "You were right as often. Robert."

The response to the broadcast amazed us. All of Oppenheimer's fragile, sensitive quality had been transmitted over the television tube. In the scientific community, it was as though a stuck window had been opened. As someone said, too optimistically, "Egghead is no longer a dirty word." There were so many requests for prints of the Oppenheimer interview that we put together a special forty-eight-minute version of it, using some of the footage we had left on the cutting-room floor. The Fund for the Republic, which financed and distributed the prints, arranged to make hundreds of them available to universities and colleges.

As was our practice, we had not permitted Oppenheimer to see or sanction the program itself, but we did invite him in to approve the longer version. Carl Sandburg was in town that day and insisted on meeting the physicist, whom he greatly admired, and viewing the film with him. Afterward we took the professor and the poet across the city for a special luncheon with Bill Paley. I think each of us found it a fascinating experience—no one more so than the chairman.

Yet in a strange, disquieting way, the company that Paley ran found the broadcast disturbing. The pressure groups, which never reflect the sum total of public opinion, called CBS the "Red Network" for putting this "traitor" on the air. There was even more commotion about the forty-eight-minute film for universities than there was about the telecast itself. George Sokolsky wrote that the program "was an opportunity for Dr. Oppenheimer to state his side and his side alone of a vexed question" (a reference to the security case, which the program had not dealt with), and demanded equal time for Lewis Strauss. He also pointed out that the Fund for the Republic is not entitled to use tax-free money to engage in propaganda, professional or amateur.

The pressure and the embarrassment for CBS were so severe that two years later, at the time of the Sputnik crisis, when a *Where We Stand* program was put together by the news division, an interview by Howard Smith with Dr. Oppenheimer was cut by orders of the management. It was not until the early sixties that the climate had changed enough for Dr. Oppenheimer to be invited to appear on a CBS program.

The pressure on Alcoa also mounted. Aluminum salesmen had difficulty explaining to irate customers why their company felt it necessary to sponsor programs *against* McCarthy and *for* Oppenheimer, *against* cigarettes and *for* "socialized medicine"—which is what some doctors thought our program on the Salk vaccine advocated. In addition, Alcoa's market was changing. The short supply of aluminum caused by the Korean War was ending; increased competition demanded more of a hard sell. The job that *See It Now* had been purchased to achieve had been done; for many the name Alcoa had become a symbol of enlightened corporate leadership.

In any case, whatever chance there was of a renewal for the 1956 season by this loyal sponsor ended with our broadcast on May 3, 1955. It started out as a program about a small Texas weekly newspaper and the power of the press, but turned into the story of how the newspaper exposed a gigantic Texas land scandal involving high members of the state government. Our reporter, Ed Scott, was so much on top of the story that on the first Monday in May we had a camera on hand at the moment the editor of the Cuero *Record,* Ken Towery, received a phone call notifying him that he had won a Pulitzer Prize. It was a remarkable coup and it made exciting television, but the fact that we had given ventilation to the land scandal angered certain state officials.

At that time Alcoa was enlarging its installations in Texas, and the feedback to Pittsburgh was instantaneous. The pressure was just enough to tip the scales. On May 4 Alcoa's vice-president in charge of advertising asked Murrow to have lunch with him the next day. On May 5 we learned that after four remarkable years and almost two hundred controversial broadcasts, Alcoa's sponsorship of *See It Now* had come to an end. The program of July 7 would be the last. Under the glaring headline: "TV's SEE IT NOW SPONSORLESS; TO BE SEEN ONLY NOW AND THEN," the *New York Times* reported that *See It Now* was terminating its weekly half-hour scheduled broadcast and being replaced by a series of at least six one-hour documentaries.

In a requiem "to a courageous sponsor," Jack Gould of the *New York Times* wrote: "That *See It Now* is changing sponsors or going sustaining is not nearly so disturbing as the fact that television still has only one *See It Now.*"

It is almost certain that if Alcoa had renewed in May, *See It Now* would have stayed on the schedule for at least another year, but an event that occurred on the night of June 7 really had more to do with the future of *See It Now* as a weekly series than any decision made in Pittsburgh. That evening, a half-hour before we went on the air with Part Two of the report on cigarettes and lung cancer, Hal March stood for the first time before an "isolation booth" and announced: "This is *The $64,000 Question.*" Murrow, who seldom watched any show preceding ours, was riveted and horrified by what he saw. His instincts, accurate as usual, made him realize before the half-hour was over that the carny, midway atmosphere heralded by the big-money quizzes would soon be dominating the airwaves. By our next program he was even more sure; the newspapers, which were to do so much to glamorize and merchandise the quizzes, were already on the bandwagon. That night Ed leaned over to me in the control room and asked, "Any bets on how long we'll keep this time period now?"

Murrow was not a businessman; he knew little of ratings or the value of time periods. But in less than a month *The $64,000 Question* greatly increased the sales value of its half-hour, and hence of what is called its "adjacencies"—the shows preceding and following it. Alcoa had been paying some $50,000 for *See It Now* at 10:30 P.M.; now Revlon was paying $80,000 for the quiz and would be paying more than that a year later. Our time slot was now infinitely more valuable than it had been a month before. It was as though a highly successful amusement park had gone up across the street from a school; suddenly the property values had changed. I was not as pessimistic as Ed; naïvely I believed that *The $64,000 Question* would so increase the size of our lead-in audience that a new sponsor would think it an attractive buy. As it turned out, no sponsor came forward—though I doubt that *See It Now* was even offered for that time period once *The $64,000 Question* became an instant hit.

A day or two after the last *See It Now* of the 1954–55 season Murrow and I were summoned to a meeting in Paley's office.

The chairman commended us for our fine season just ended, but wondered whether a half-hour wasn't "too confining" for the type of documentaries we were now doing so well. What did we think of changing the format and doing a series of eight or ten one-hour *See It Now* reports? Wouldn't this be a more satisfying way of doing things? We asked what the time periods would be. They would be at night, Paley said, and added that sponsorship could probably be obtained. We asked what the alternative was; could we continue in the half-hour time period? The word "no" was never used, but it was obvious that the decision had already been made. It turned out to be the wrong decision, but I must admit that we didn't protest very vigorously. Our resistance was at an all-time low, and the idea of doing one-hour programs did have appeal.

What we were giving up, of course, was the invaluable regular weekly exposure of *See It Now*. Moreover, the new arrangement took long- and short-range scheduling out of our hands and made it a joint responsibility of the sales department, management and sponsors. No longer could we alone decide to do a McCarthy broadcast or a program on South Africa or a report on lung cancer.

For all of *See It Now*'s abrasive quality, I don't believe that there was any determined plot on the part of Bill Paley to whittle Murrow's influence and independence. I believe that the decision to change to irregular programing was primarily a business calculation to create more financial yield from the time period. That others in the company hoped that the weekly headaches would be eased to monthly ones was strictly their dividend.

Whatever the motivation, however, the independence of the *See It Now* unit had been altered by an elaborate decision-making process in which a variety of factors inside and outside CBS had to be weighed before we could get a program scheduled. This didn't mean that sponsors or sales executives would be telling us what to do—quite the contrary—but it did mean that each *See It Now* would now cost in excess of $150,000 for time and production, and that life was no longer as simple as it was in the days when Murrow could say, "Let's do Radulovich."

Indications of how awkward the new format would be came sooner than expected. In late July we were surprised and delighted to hear that General Motors had agreed to sponsor six and perhaps eight *See It Now* programs. The price they had agreed to encouraged our sales people, and other sponsors were nibbling. Then, in August, we announced the first *See It Now* for the new season: "The Vice-Presidency—The Great American Lottery," an examination of the office that gave our Founding Fathers such difficulty and whose concept has plagued us through the years. We were way ahead of events at that time, for President Eisenhower had suffered neither a heart attack nor ileitis.

When the President was stricken in Denver in September, the problems regarding succession, the nature of the Vice-Presidency and the President's disability became an acute national issue, and we were ahead of everyone with a comprehensive one-hour study scheduled for October. Mr. Eisenhower's illness made it a good news program—but as it turned out, not very good business. The sponsor was convinced that the Vice-Presidency program had been conceived by Murrow as an attack on Nixon, and their sponsorship was canceled for the entire series. Murrow and I couldn't believe that CBS would agree to the cancellation of a written contract, but it was approved. No new sponsor could be found for the broadcast, and in the days just prior to its showing on October 26, the salesmen were out on the street "fire-saling" it, as it is called in the trade, to anyone who would buy minutes. Two companies—one of them Columbia Records, a captive sponsor—brought a total of five minutes in spot ads.

The *See It Now* on the Vice-Presidency was well received, though several newspapers did accuse us of trying to do a hatchet job on Nixon. To my certain knowledge, the Vice-President did not share this opinion, and in 1964 he and former President Eisenhower were themselves active participants on a *CBS Reports* program called "The Crisis of Presidential Succession." In 1965 the Twenty-fifth Amendment was approved by Congress and the broadcast concept that had panicked a sponsor became part of the Constitution—or will, when ratified by the states.

There were six other *See It Now* broadcasts in the 1955–56 season. The most controversial of them, "The Farm Problem: A Crisis of Abundance," not only created a public storm, but started a dispute within CBS which, when coupled with a similarly needless row over a broadcast on statehood for Alaska and Hawaii, signaled the end of *See It Now*.

The night "Crisis of Abundance" went on the air Murrow was in Johnstown, Pennsylvania, where he had gone to watch the program with Secretary of Agriculture Ezra Taft Benson, who would comment during the last five minutes of the telecast. Though parts of the program came from the states of Washington (wheat) and Wisconsin (dairy products), a major portion of the broadcast was filmed in Iowa (corn and hogs), where one of our reporters had spent more than a month, and Murrow and I a few days. What Secretary Benson objected to most in the film was a ten-minute segment on the auction of a farm whose proprietor had made $2,500 in his best year and was forced to sell out. Perhaps the narration did echo *The Grapes of Wrath* too much, but government statistics revealed that in Iowa alone three thousand small farmers had quit, and that in the nation six hundred thousand had given up in the past four years. Murrow introduced the father of the farmer who was quitting, and the old man said it all: "I just kind of go by my bank account. It just don't add up, and it seemed like every year that bank account's getting a little less and our prices of machinery has gone up. Our expenses has gone up, and with these falling prices we can't replace any of that stuff and we're losing money . . ."

What we didn't know—and should have found out—was that though this farmer did auction off his equipment and furniture, his brother had then rented the farm. But our point was that there was one small farmer less in the United States.

The other fifty minutes of the broadcast gave what we hoped was a balanced evaluation of the problem of the small landowner competing with the large supermechanized giant farm in an age of overabundance in the United States, in contrast to near-famine conditions in many other parts of the world. A broad spectrum—farm agents, big and small farmers, lobbyists, politicians and other experts—was heard. Certainly the main thesis of the program—that the small farmer was in terrible trouble—was valid.

When Murrow finally turned the program over to Benson, the Secretary of Agriculture said: ". . . most interesting. . . . No one questions that agriculture is in a serious squeeze between rising prices for things farmers buy, and declining prices for products they sell . . . [but] I want to dispel once and for all any impression . . . that thousands of farmers in Iowa and elsewhere are being driven off their farms. . . . Farm foreclosures are at or near their record low." Then Mr. Benson looked Ed and the camera in the eye and proclaimed: "Any attempt . . . to persuade the American people that the small farmer is dying in Iowa or anywhere else is a perversion of the truth, and I think it's demagoguery at its worst." The Secretary said he was confident that the programs of the Eisenhower Administration would preserve the family farm, and then concluded by telling Murrow how much he had enjoyed the evening.

Murrow and Benson said good night, and as I watched them on our monitor after we were off the air, there was so much camaraderie between these two gentlemen farmers that the implications of the program were difficult to foresee. But the next day Fulton Lewis Jr. was after us again. The Farm Bureau, a lobby representing many of the larger farmers, as much as called the program dishonest. *Time,* under the heading "See It Now?," implied that the auction was a hoax. Still, many newspapers in and out of the Farm Belt gave us good marks, and most of the mail from the farmers of Iowa was favorable.

The evening after the broadcast, Murrow and I flew to the Middle East to prepare a broadcast on the Egypt-Israel dispute. Before we left we ran into Sig Mickelson in a corridor. With a smile he told us about a telegram that CBS had received from Benson and the Republican National Committee, denouncing "Crisis of Abundance" and demanding equal time. We discussed the matter for all of two minutes, and Ed's parting words were: "You're not going to give them that time, are you, Sig?" And Sig replied, "Are you kidding? Not a chance."

One week later, having driven back to Tel Aviv from an all-night session of filming Israeli fishermen under Arab guns on the Sea of Galilee (an Israeli newspaper's account of how we lit up the fishermen's boats with jeep headlights on a barge at the spot where once Jesus walked is a testimony to my arrogance, Murrow's bravery and the Hebrews' imperturbability), we walked into our hotel to find a series of cables telling us that CBS had announced they were giving a half-hour of television time to Secretary Benson for rebuttal. As Ed stood there in the lobby, grimy with the grit of the road and a two-day growth of beard, he didn't seem able to believe what he was reading. Granted that communications with Israel were difficult, nevertheless the company owed us consultation on such a reversal. In the case of the McCarthy program the idea of granting equal time had been Ed's idea, but with "Crisis of Abundance" there had been an honest attempt to do a balanced report. Though it may have had its imperfections, there was nothing in the broadcast to warrant giving anyone a free half-hour for what Ed predicted would be a political speech on the farm problem.

Murrow went to his room to shower before a late supper. When he came down he had with him the draft of a cable addressed to Paley and Stanton which was a bitter denunciation of the decision and announced his resignation. But after consultation we decided to do nothing until the next morning, and then at breakfast we decided that Ed should wait until we got back to New York.

It never became necessary for Ed to make his stand because the aftermath to CBS's concession made a joke of the whole affair. If anyone was more surprised than Murrow by the granting of equal time, it was Benson and the Republicans. At the 1956 Republican Convention, Jim Hagerty, the White House News Secretary, told Ed that they had never expected to get the time, and that "after we did we really didn't know how to use it." Finally they had decided to use most of the program for an address by Secretary Benson, and Senator Martin of Iowa would talk about how good things were for the small farmer.

Benson's speech was not so much an answer to Murrow as one more attack on the Democratic farm policies of the past. The consequences were an Art Buchwald parody: the equal-time concept escalated to triple time when the Democrats asked for time to answer Benson, and the public witnessed the spectacle of Senators Hubert Humphrey and Clinton Anderson attacking Secretary Benson's reply. After it was all over, the head of the Soil Conservation Service for southwest Iowa wrote us to say that Secretary Benson's had been a fine political speech blaming all the surpluses on the Democrats, but that the "Ed Murrow farm show" was "educational and informative."

As for the small farmer, those who talked about his decline in 1956 could not be accused, a few years later, of what Mr. Benson called "perversion of the truth" and "demagoguery." The platforms of the Republican and Democratic parties in 1960 and 1964 unanimously recommended that action be taken to save the small farmers.

The Benson dispute left its scars. It dramatized the problem of irregularly scheduled news documentaries which provided no suitable vehicle for handling an alleged breach of objectivity or error of fact. In a weekly series it would have been a simple matter to invite Mr. Benson back to continue his criticism—though a rereading of the transcript shows that he did pretty well by his position in those last five minutes. The bitter aftermath of the Benson affair was that the gulf between the policymakers and the program-makers at CBS had now become so wide that they could grant equal time without consulting us. Even more disturbing was the obvious bowing to political pressure.

At the time of the McCarthy broadcast there had been speculation, particularly in the Hearst press, that Murrow was an embarrassment to the CBS board of directors and would be asked to resign. Two years later, on October 10, 1956, it finally happened. Though there was an uneasy truce between Murrow and the management, neither side had much understanding of the other's actions. Murrow was becoming more and more openly critical of broadcasting, and the company was more and more apprehensive about the fact that Murrow's journalistic position on certain matters might be construed as the voice of CBS. Since Ed dreaded those monthly board meetings, it was decided by mutual consent that he resign as a director.

. . .

During the 1956–57 season there were nine irregularly scheduled *See It Now* programs, but by now we had been moved to Sunday afternoon at 5 P.M. The price of an hour of air time at night was up to $98,805, excluding production costs; more important, advertisers of regularly scheduled shows did not want their time periods and adjacencies "depressed"—again the rating man's phrase.

The most important program we did that season from the standpoint of *See It Now*'s survival was a special, *The Secret Life of Danny Kaye*. When the comedian went on a trip around the world for UNICEF, we sent along two full camera crews to film a one-hour report of his travels. They came back with so much good footage that we scheduled the show for ninety minutes, on December 2, 1956. The hitch came when the sales department couldn't find a sponsor, and in November they began "fire-saling" it to spot advertisers. I felt that if Danny Kaye wasn't salable, nothing was, so I asked for forty-eight hours to try my luck. My first call, to Pan American World Airways, paid off. We broke our strict rule not to let a sponsor see a broadcast in advance by showing the Pan American sales people ten minutes of the film. They were as enchanted as we were, and at my suggestion they agreed to sponsor our nine other shows as well.

On the night of the Kaye show Ed and I had a party for all concerned with the broadcast, and for those who had worked on *See It Now* through the years. Among others there were Danny and Sylvia Kaye, Dr. Oppenheimer and his wife, Carl Sandburg, Ben Shahn, Ralph Bunche, Bill Paley, Eric Sevareid and Bill Golden. Louis Armstrong and Jonas Salk couldn't come, but they called from out of town and everyone talked to them. All our producers, reporters, cameramen and editors were there, together with our new sponsors. Kaye did imitations of Paley, Murrow, Sandburg and myself; Bill Paley made a wonderfully simple and generous speech that no one will ever forget;

Sandburg sang; and I was photographed doing an imitation of Danny Kaye from the top of an upright piano. The evening ended with an all-night poker game at which Murrow lost an obscene amount of money.

See It Now had two extra programs that season which were unsponsored. In a six-month period between December 1956 and June 1957, Murrow scored two journalistic beats that one newspaper called "an all-time coup." Through the good offices of the Premier of Burma, U Nu, Ed arranged to do the first and only full-length television interview with Chou En-lai, Premier of Communist China, and traveled to Rangoon during Christmas week to film it. Then in June he flew to Brioni, Yugoslavia, to interview Marshal Tito. CBS, embarrassed by these exclusives, tolerated them reluctantly.

To view the Chou En-lai and Tito interviews in perspective, it must be remembered that they were shown within the same six-month period as the CBS interview with Nikita Khrushchev, which Dan Schorr, Stuart Novins and B. J. Cutler of the New York *Herald Tribune* had filmed inside the walls of the Kremlin, and which stands even today as the journalistic scoop of the television age. Murrow, who played no part in the Khrushchev broadcast, considered it a triumph, and in a speech to the Radio-Televison News Directors Association he said: "When my employer, CBS, through a combination of enterprise and good luck, did an interview with Nikita Khrushchev, the President of the United States uttered a few ill-chosen, uninformed words on the subject, and the network practically apologized. This produced a rarity. Many newspapers defended CBS's right to produce the program and commended it for initiative. But the other networks remained silent."

Earlier the CBS management had bent over backward to make certain that any propagandizing on the part of Chou En-lai be neutralized by a panel discussion immediately afterward. Ed was on his way back from Rangoon when, at a stop-off in Rome, I had to call to tell him of the plan for a rebuttal. He agreed, but reluctantly, both because he felt that such a technique underestimated the ability of the American audience to judge the Chinese position for themselves, and because it was not part of our agreement with the Chinese leader. We were further irritated when several of the China experts Murrow recommended as participants, including Teddy White, were not deemed acceptable to the management. We ended up with Ambassador Carlos Romulo of the Philippines and Nationalist China's Permanent Representative to the United Nations, Tingfu Tsiang, one of Chou En-lai's bitter enemies.

The Tito interview was also followed by a live rebuttal—this time by Clare Boothe Luce, Hamilton Fish Armstrong and Bill Lawrence, then of the *New York Times.*

I would think that today broadcast journalism has matured sufficiently so that if any network was enterprising and lucky enough to arrange an interview with, say, Premier Kosygin of the U.S.S.R., the program could appear without an immediate and defensive rebuttal.

Pan American dropped *See It Now* in November 1957. They were happy about our programs and their association with Murrow, but they were not pleased about the Sunday afternoon time period, particularly in the spring and fall when few intercontinental travel customers were at home. The airline did not have the budget for night-time exposure even if *See It Now* had been given a monthly evening schedule; the rising cost of television made such a move prohibitive. As it was, Pan American's money purchased little more than the air time, much of which went to the stations; what was left compensated CBS for only a part of our production costs. Our budget was a source of constant irritation to the business-affairs managers, who claimed that we were reckless and irresponsible, and there were all kinds of cost studies to indicate how we were affecting corporate earnings. The fact that CBS's profits were at an all-time high of over $16,000,000 after taxes; that *See It Now*'s out-of-pocket costs were comparatively favorable to those of an hour's entertainment program; that the series was the single most prestigious project in all television, the winner of every conceivable award; that it was the standard against which all news and documentary broadcasts were measured—all these factors made little dent on those who believed that the burden exceeded the glory.

That year not even an inspiring program about Marian Anderson's State Department tour to Asia could get us an hour at night—until Murrow assumed the salesman's burden. After sending Gene DePoris and a camera crew with Miss Anderson to India, Thailand, Vietnam, Korea and other points East, we were faced with the task of telling the singer and her manager, Sol Hurok, that we had no sponsor and no place for this remarkable hour other than Sunday afternoon. Ed muttered, "If Friendly can sell Danny Kaye, I can sell the Lady from Philadelphia." This, his own personal term of affection for Miss Anderson had become the title of the broadcast. He made the sale to IT&T for $150,000, and that's how "The Lady from Philadelphia" made prime time.

There were to be eight *See It Now* programs in 1958, and the one we expected to get us into most difficulty was a two-part study, "Atomic Timetable," dealing with fallout and peacetime uses of atomic energy, which Arthur Morse had put together. But the program that "blew us out of the water," to use Murrow's expression, was a placid and undramatic treatment of "Statehood for Alaska and Hawaii," a subject so tame that some members of our unit did not consider it enough of an issue for an hour-long *See It Now.* For years, statehood for Alaska and Hawaii had been unopposed but unimplemented planks in the Republican and Democratic platforms, and our broadcast was designed to create a sense of urgency about the issue. We made no attempt to influence the viewers on anything other than to recommend that the matter be brought to the floors of the Senate and House for a vote, and Murrow's last line was: "We have presented this report in the hope of [causing] a small argument about it." We certainly did!

On the program the most violent denunciation against statehood was made by Republican Senator Malone of Nevada, who said: "So you get two senators from Alaska, then you get two from Hawaii. Then Puerto Rico comes in, then . . . Formosa . . . the Philippines. First thing you know you got ten or fifteen . . . sixteen new senators on that Senate floor. What are you going to do with Canada . . . [what about] Mexico?"

There were other, slightly more rational arguments by Senators Stennis and Eastland, who were worried about the "complexion of the Senate." Eastland said: "Ed . . . the Communist Party controls the politics of the Islands [a reference to Harry Bridges, the leader of the International Longshoremen's Union], and if Hawaii were admitted to statehood, we would have in the American Congress two senators and a representative who, in my judgment, would be influenced by the Communist Party."

To answer these charges there were some advocates of Hawaiian statehood: Dan Inouye, a much-decorated hero of World War II who later became a Democratic congressman and United States senator; and Patsy Mink, who was elected to Congress in 1964. Defending his own position was Harry Bridges, who was given the opportunity to answer the charges against himself and Hawaii. The claim of a New York Republican, John Pillion, who, like Eastland, had argued that statehood would guarantee Harry Bridges two seats in the Senate and two in the House, was briefly quoted; Bridges laughed at this, said that he wished it was true and called his adversary "crazy."

I think that any serious student of television must have observed that, if anything, the broadcast was too evenly balanced. In an effort to be fair to both sides, we almost made it appear that for every point made for statehood there was an equal argument against it, when the facts clearly indicated that an overwhelming majority of leaders in both parties, including all living Presidents, the press and public opinion, favored immediate admission of the two territories.

"Statehood for Alaska and Hawaii" was broadcast on a Sunday afternoon in March 1958. There was little public comment on it, and very little mail—except for one crucial letter. Congressman Pillion of Lackawanna, New York, wrote to Stanton demanding equal time on the basis that "the opponents of statehood were all elderly gentlemen. By the trick of association, the implication was willfully created that only 'old fuddy-duddies' oppose statehood . . . the youth, the farmers, the disabled veterans, the veterans who were not disabled, the middle-age people, the intelligence of the universities, exemplified by the universities of Hawaii and Alaska, and the Communist fellow travelers, were all solidly behind statehood." Moreover, Harry Bridges, in referring to Pillion on the program, had said, "I think he's crazy," when replying to charges that the union leader would control Hawaii's congressional delegation. The result was the Benson story all over again.

In the beginning Ed and I hardly took it seriously. Obviously every congressman and politician who is mentioned derogatorily can't be given equal time—particularly when the name-calling is in response to equal abuse. Bridges had been answering charges made against him by Malone, Eastland and Pillion; giving equal time to the latter would load the issue even more against Hawaii.

We thought that the Hawaiians themselves were justified in requesting equal time; they could legitimately have argued that the quoted charges of Congressman Howard W. Smith of Virginia that "one Chinaman in Hawaii would have the same power in the election of senators as thirty-one American citizens of the great state of New York" deserved a reply. But I strongly suspect that even if the entire population of Hawaii and Alaska had cried foul on that broadcast, the only response would have been a polite letter. The congressman from Lackawanna, however, was awarded fifteen minutes on a Sunday afternoon—because he asked for it, because he was a United States congressman and because, as someone high in the CBS management told me, he was "a scholar on Communism."

When we heard that Pillion was being given an opportunity to reply over our protests and without the recommendation of any of the executives of CBS News, I wrote to Mickelson: "If Representative Pillion uses this time to attack Murrow, then my usefulness to CBS News will be at an end." Ed wrote a much stronger letter, perhaps too strong, saying that the decision made without consultation with him (I had been notified but my opinions disregarded) had undermined his relationship with the company and made continuation of *See It Now* doubtful under such conditions.

Mr. Pillion's television appearance was not an interview, but an unchallenged political speech in which he condemned statehood for Hawaii as "a major objective of the Soviet conspiracy." Senate advocates of statehood were outraged by the broadcast and asked for equal time, but their requests were denied.

When our confrontation over this issue did take place in Chairman Paley's office, the words were about Alaska and Hawaii and Congressman Pillion, but the meeting was really about the future of *See It Now*. The only participants—Paley, Murrow and myself—were the same three who had been present at almost every meeting dealing with the future of *See It Now*.

Murrow began by reviewing the Pillion affair, stating that

a situation in which the management of CBS had more of a say in granting equal time than he did put him in an untenable situation. He then proposed a plan in which he or I could participate in such deliberations, through the corporate editorial board, when they involved *See It Now.*

At this point Paley quietly said, "But I thought that you and Fred didn't want to do *See It Now* any more."

"Bill, what I am proposing is a procedure by which we share in the decision about equal time and under which we could continue to do *See It Now*," Murrow said. "Of course we want the program to continue."

The chairman replied with the firmness that goes with final authority. "I thought we'd already decided about *See It Now*," he said flatly.

Whereupon enforced calm vanished, and a forty-five minute scene ensued in which these two commanding figures, the industry's foremost reporter and its top executive, who had been intimate friends for twenty years, faced each other in a blazing showdown with all guns firing.

One brief burst of dialogue told it all.

"Bill," Murrow pleaded at one point, "are you going to destroy all this? Don't you want an instrument like the *See It Now* organization, which you have poured so much into for so long, to continue?"

"Yes," said Paley, "but I don't want this constant stomach ache every time you do a controversial subject."

"I'm afraid that's a price you have to be willing to pay. It goes with the job."

Nothing else that was said mattered. After seven years and almost two hundred broadcasts, *See It Now* was dead.

Murrow did talk about Stanton, the first and only time I ever heard him mention his name to Paley. "Frank is probably the most capable administrator in American industry, but he doesn't know anything about news," he said, in an effort to make the point that the Pillion decision had been an administrative one. But as always, Paley was loyal to his staff; he would allow no debate over Stanton or other members of the management.

It would be inaccurate to say that I was silent during the Paley-Murrow encounter, but I was out of my class in more respects than one.

There was another unfortunate meeting that summer when, in Ed's absence, I was summoned to discuss the terminal plans for *See It Now* with Paley. I permitted myself the emotional luxury of making what must have impressed the chairman as sophomoric statements, in which I berated him for killing off *See It Now*, the only consistently good program on the schedule with the exception of *Playhouse 90* and *Twentieth Century*. When Paley stopped me in midflight by saying quietly, "Fred, you are speaking beyond your competence," I turned in anger and departed. Unfortunately, Paley's office had two identical doors, and I charged melodramatically into his private bathroom. It took me five years to be able to laugh about that—and it was just about that long before I was in his office again.

Louis G. Cowan, who had become president of the CBS Television Network after the fabulous success of *The $64,000 Question*, did his best to try to retain the core of the *See It Now* unit, and by getting the *Small World* program on the schedule he made it possible for us to keep approximately half of our staff. But it was a sad time for all of us. Arthur Morse and Ed Scott, two of our veteran producers, had to find work elsewhere, as did cameraman Marty Barnett and others.

Small World had been our experimental attempt to secure a suitable vehicle for Eric Sevareid, whose skills had not yet found their proper framework in television. The program consisted of a four-way transcontinental conversation through overseas telephone lines, while cameras filmed simultaneously in four different locations. This was prior to the Telstar and Early Bird satellites, and the footage was then flown to New York where we spliced the dialogue into a half-hour broadcast.

Sevareid had made a pilot of *Small World* with Aneurin Bevan, Malcolm Muggeridge and Governor Theodore McKeldin of Maryland. Eventually a sponsor professed interest in the show, but only if Murrow was the interviewer. When Cowan said that the program could get on the schedule only if it had a sponsor, Eric graciously bowed out and Murrow agreed to conduct the program.

The press handled the death of *See It Now* with the stunned obituaries usually given to a real person who has died before his time. One newspaper ran a full-page drawing of a tombstone labeled *See It Now* in a graveyard beside *Studio One* and some of the other lamented casualties of television.

Perhaps John Crosby's epitaph in the New York *Herald Tribune* was closest to the mark:

> There were several historic occasions this last week. One was the end of Edward R. Murrow's *See It Now* after seven years of distinguished history. The other was the end of Elfrida von Nardroff after twenty-one weeks on *Twenty-One*. The events are more or less complementary.
>
> *See It Now* was born in the early days of television when it was thought that TV was a tremendous medium for the exchange of information and ideas. *Twenty-One* came along in the later phase when it was discovered that television was far better suited to play parlor games and give away money. *See It Now* enlightened us. *Twenty-One* stupefied us. One used television more or less as a public service on behalf of the viewers; the other uses it solely to sell as much of the sponsor's product as possible . . .
>
> There have been some dull *See It Now* shows, and some have been better than others, but it is by every criterion television's most brilliant, most decorated, most imaginative, most

courageous and most important program. The fact that CBS cannot afford it but can afford *Beat the Clock* is shocking.

Jack Gould, who knows as much about television and CBS as any person in or out of it, called me after he had written his last *See It Now* review, "Watch on the Ruhr," in July 1958, and said, "Sometime you and Murrow are going to have to tell me the real story of why *See It Now* was killed." I never have, because to this day I am not entirely certain, other than that it died of what the doctors sometimes call "massive complications." To say that "Statehood for Alaska and Hawaii" was the reason, which is what I believed at the time, is confusing a symptom for a cause. Production costs had something to do with it; the rising price of television time was also a major factor, for each time *See It Now* came on the screen there were too many empty seats in the largest and most expensive auditorium in the world. That Murrow and I were difficult to handle was another factor. It is true that we might have worked more diligently at getting along with the management, but it was our independence and Ed's sure-footed confidence in an era of groping and decision-making by consensus that made *See It Now* the force it was. Our autonomy did not exceed that of such independent souls as Ed Sullivan, Arthur Godfrey and Jackie Gleason, but impatience with them was tempered by their high ratings and sales value.

The fatal complication—all the other symptoms could have been treated—was the very strength that made Murrow unique. The man who could decide to do a program about McCarthy or Radulovich, or fly off to see Chou En-lai, or to report on smoking and lung cancer, could only do these broadcasts because of his fortitude and independence, and those same virtues which gave CBS distinction also brought it controversy, enemies and "stomach aches."

But even all of the above doesn't fully explain why *See It Now* died. For years afterward Ed would say, "There is still some missing part. I still don't know why the show was killed."

What Paley and Stanton did not realize at the time, and what we failed to articulate—if in fact we truly understood it—was that Murrow's independent spirit was the biggest asset the corporate body had. CBS couldn't afford a platoon of Murrows, but logistically and spiritually it could certainly support one responsible, universally respected, if not unanimously applauded, reporter who was able and willing to do and say precisely what a corporation could not.

It can be argued, perhaps with some justification, that a commercial business should not take a strong stand on, say, McCarthy, or have a point of view on segregation. What such a company can afford is a Murrow, a man of credentials and integrity who has his management's respect and confidence and who can go out on a limb. When the criticism came, the CBS management could always say, "We may not agree with everything that Murrow and *See It Now* do, but his job is to call his shots as he sees them." This is precisely what the publisher of the *Herald Tribune* said about Walter Lippmann and David Lawrence, what the *New York Times* says of James Reston, and what the Hearst papers said of Sokolsky.

At the time of the McCarthy broadcast, Paley and Stanton issued this answer to a *Newsweek* questionnaire:

> . . . In . . . feature or documentary program[s] . . . CBS . . . can and does at times delegate responsibility for the program content and for the expression of opinion . . . to one of its staff members . . . in whose integrity and devotion to democratic principles CBS reposes complete confidence . . .

Regardless of whether Paley and Stanton meant that as a statement of policy in 1954, or whether they had just improvised it to justify the McCarthy broadcast, no reporter or production team at CBS was ever again given such complete responsibility for "program content" or "expression of opinion," and the stomach aches and much of the luminescence created by Murrow ended when *See It Now* was extinguished.

I do not mean to suggest that all those who presided at the death of *See It Now* cheered at the funeral. The worst that can be said is that they sighed with relief even as they all called it a tragedy, something that "just shouldn't have happened."

A magnificent irony known to only three or four people is that if *See It Now* had survived for another six months, it could have served a purpose as important in its way as that of the McCarthy broadcast, and might have prevented part of the disgrace and humiliation of the television industry in the wake of the quiz scandals. In 1958 Bill Golden told Ed and me that there was some reason to believe that the big-money quiz shows were rigged, and that there was some damaging evidence. Bill wanted to know if we would be interested in doing a special documentary exposing the whole nasty mess; at least the company and the industry would then be exposing its own wrongdoings and this might considerably lessen the public's shock and revulsion.

We said that we would be interested in making such a report but that it would have to be done in our own way and on our terms, and that though we would welcome information from CBS, we would do our own investigating. Golden knew that we had no scheduled period of our own, and he volunteered to use his good offices to see if time could be arranged. Had *See It Now* still been on its own weekly or even monthly schedule, we would probably have gone ahead with the exposé.

But we never heard another word from Golden until long after the wreckage of the quiz shows had stunned everyone. "Too bad you never did that *See It Now* on the quiz shows," he said to me one day. When I asked him why he had never mentioned it again, Bill told me that the lawyers had stopped it: "They said it would have been in bad taste." He added, "Now what in hell do lawyers have to do with deciding what's good taste on the air and what isn't?"

This conversation took place at lunch one day in October 1959. Bill kept talking about the shame of the quiz scandals and the congressional investigations, and what had happened to the company whose good name he had helped to create through all its formative years. Like Murrow, he was one of broadcasting's last angry men, and like Ed, he loved CBS. He also loved Frank Stanton, whom he had known since both were young executives in the days of radio. As the lunch dishes were removed and the busboys set the tables for dinner, Bill's anger turned to sad despair about where the industry and CBS were headed. The last thing he said to me that afternoon was: "You guys should have done that show." Later his wife told me that he had talked about it all the way home that night. The next morning when I got to the cutting room, there was a message that Bill Golden had died in his sleep.

I felt I had to write Stanton and tell him that now we shared common scars. In a book about Bill Golden's vision Stanton wrote: "Those who tried (and most tried only once) by argument or by stratagem to get him to go along with less than what he thought was possible, or to discard what he knew was good, never got away with it. Bill could be inflexible, abrupt, impatient. But he was also gentle, kind, and warm. He could not be bargained with or cowed. There was fibre in his character . . ."

On occasion Stanton relies on ghost writers, but those words about Golden were all his own.

The Strange Birth of CBS Reports

"And if there are any historians . . . a hundred years from now and there should be preserved the kinescopes for one week of all three networks, they will find recorded, in black-and-white or color, evidence of decadence, escapism and insulation from the realities of the world in which we live . . . If we go on as we are, then history will take its revenge, and retribution will [catch] up with us."

Ed Murrow spoke those prophetic words in a historic speech to the Radio-Television News Directors Association in Chicago on October 15, 1958, just three months after the death of *See It Now.* But no one, including Murrow, knew how soon his prophecy would be verified. In the same talk Murrow said that he was "frightened by the imbalance, the constant striving to reach the largest possible audience for everything"—which of course was the drive that created the quiz shows in the first place, and which in the end made them dishonest.

In New Orleans one year later, almost to the day, Frank Stanton, who had been so upset by Murrow's speech, was being almost as critical: "And whoever may be to blame in this whole tawdry business . . . broadcasting has lost a degree of the public trust and confidence so essential to its effective performance . . . We should have been more thoughtful and critical of the whole idea of exposing to millions of families games in which contestants can win large purses. We really did not face up to the broader implications—whether such programs could ever be an appropriate form of widespread public entertainment—whether in their very nature they might contain the seeds of their own abuse and eventual destruction . . ."

In his Chicago speech Murrow also criticized the "money-making machine" for having "welched on [its] promises" and for having delayed a crucial address by President Eisenhower: "He [the President] was discoursing on the possibility . . . of war between this nation and the Soviet Union and Communist China—a reasonably compelling subject. Two networks, CBS and NBC, delayed that broadcast for an hour and fifteen minutes . . . about twice the time required for an ICBM to travel from the Soviet Union to major targets in the United States." If this decision was dictated by anything other than financial reasons, said Murrow, "the networks didn't deign to explain those reasons."

Earlier that year Stanton had said: "In the age of missiles—when time is reckoned not in months or weeks or even days, but in minutes—we do not have the luxury of time." In that same speech he also stated: "It is nothing short of providential that television has had a decade of constant growth to bring us to a position where we have a real chance of meeting [our] responsibility. It will be nothing short of tragic if through our own fault we muff it, or through the fault of others [a reference to the challenge of government control then being proposed by the FCC] we are kept from meeting it . . . If any industry developed at the right time and the right place to respond to the emergent demands of this ICBM age, it is the television industry . . ."

In spite of such pronouncements, 1959 was a disastrous year for CBS and the television industry; there were the fixed shows, too many speeches, Murrow's sabbatical, personal feuds that became public, executive sickness and fear of more government control.

It was the specter of the quiz scandals that overshadowed everything, however. A syndicated television columnist, Steve Scheuer, had first hinted that something was rotten with the big-money quiz shows, and *Time* and *Look* had alluded to the possibility of a hoax, but the libel laws made an exposé difficult. Then one contestant convinced a congressional subcommittee that he had been forced to lose to Charles Van Doren on NBC's quiz program *Twenty-One*, and the charade that had mesmerized a nation was over. All three networks had been warned; all three admitted that it was beyond their control; now all three hastened to clean up the mess.

CBS, where it all began with *The $64,000 Question* and its profitable offspring, *The $64,000 Challenge*, suddenly found many of its officers vulnerable, particularly Louis G. Cowan. Cowan, who never really knew whether he wanted to be a college president or a show-business impresario, and who wanted almost as much for television as he wanted for himself, was caught in the web of investigations. No one believed that he had played any part in the dishonesty, but his career and his elevation to the presidency of the CBS Television Network were so identified with the quiz shows that it was impossible for him to disengage himself from the wreckage.

In the midst of the uproar, Cowan was stricken with a serious circulatory ailment and was confined to a hospital in early November 1959, when he should have been in Washington testifying on his own behalf and the company's. In his place Stanton, in what was both his most humiliating and finest hour, sat before the outraged glare of Congress and the nation, taking full responsibility as far as CBS was concerned: "I want to say here and now that I was completely unaware, until August 8, 1958, of any irregularity in the quiz shows on our network. When gossip about quiz shows in general came to my attention,

I was assured by our television network people that these shows were completely above criticism of this kind . . . It is now clear that I should have gone further . . . This has been a bitter pill for us to swallow . . . We propose to be more certain . . . that it is we and we alone who decide not only what is to appear on the CBS Television Network but how it is to appear . . ."

Most of the spokesmen for the other networks were dazed, frightened, inarticulate towers of jello whose public statements only seemed to compound the faults that the quiz scandals had brought to light. In his austere, brutally frank willingness to assume responsibility rather than seek a scapegoat, Stanton may have saved the industry.

The congressional hearings were the climax of a year in which the industry's profits reached new highs and its public esteem plummeted to new lows. For Murrow it was his most frustrating period, and the correspondents who visited him in his office between the hours of six and seven forty-five while he waited to do his nightly radio broadcast, could not help observing the change that had taken place. He was weary—"beat from my youth," as he put it—not from too much work but from too much swimming upstream.

In addition to his radio news, Ed at this time was continuing with *Person to Person* and *Small World*, but the latter was no substitute for *See It Now*. Even the two documentaries we were allowed to do, "The Lost Class of '59," a report on the tragedy of Norfolk, Virginia's closed schools produced by Arthur Morse, and an interview with Field Marshal Sir Bernard Montgomery, were not permitted the title of our old series.

Unfortunately, Murrow had lent his name, voice and prestige to a program called "The Business of Sex," and the quakes resulting from its broadcast on January 19, 1959, further irritated the Murrow-CBS relationship and hastened his sabbatical plans. "The Business of Sex" was a radio documentary prepared by the public affairs department of CBS News; Murrow had agreed to narrate it in order to help a couple of people he liked and also to prove that he was a member of the CBS team and not just available for broadcasts he himself generated. The program, which revealed the alleged use of call girls by big business in their sales campaigns, was undoubtedly the most discussed radio broadcast of many years. There is every reason to believe in the authenticity of its producer's research, but such an exposé is judged by its documents, and George Vicas was undone by the promises he had been forced to make. The prostitutes whose recorded interviews provided the startling evidence for the documentary had been assured that their identities would not be revealed on or off the air, and therefore Vicas could not prove the truth of his contentions by releasing the evidence he had.

But when American industry, led by the National Association of Manufacturers, rose in righteous wrath to defend its honor, the target of their attack was not the producer of the program, nor the management of CBS News, which had asked Murrow to narrate it, but Murrow himself. All other business stopped as a steady procession of police inspectors, reporters and captains of industry came to question Ed, who waited vainly for the company to assume its responsibility. Murrow kept his silence, but he promised himself and me that he would never again narrate a program whose content he did not control. To this day there are some conservative Americans, including two who ran for President, who learned to forgive Murrow for the McCarthy program but will never forget "that fraud about those call girls and American business."

On February 16 Ed announced that, as of July, he was taking a one-year sabbatical from broadcasting "to spend a year traveling, listening, reading and trying to learn . . . with no need to look at . . . the clock . . ." The letters of request and permission were released to the press so that everyone would know that the leave of absence was amicable. I then proceeded to compromise Ed's position by asking him to continue to do *Small World* as he and Janet traveled around the world. He agreed, for he knew that it was probably the only way to retain what was left of the *See It Now* organization; the sponsor would accept no substitute for Murrow.

Next came Stanton's address to the Institute for Education by Radio-Television of Ohio State, on May 6, 1959, which later came to be known as "the *CBS Reports* speech." There was no reference to the quiz show or to Murrow's Chicago address, though cynics would say there was a cause-and-effect relationship. Murrow had referred to the Sunday afternoon intellectual ghetto and pleaded for what he called a "tiny tithe," by which some of the largest advertisers in television would give up one or two hours a year to sponsor hour-long reports on the great issues facing our society lest we discover too late that the "flickering" tube was used only "to distract, delude, amuse and insulate us" from realities.

Stanton's speech, perhaps the most eloquent of his career, also mentioned the critical need to inform the American people, and then went Murrow one better: "Next year the CBS Television Network is scheduling regular hour-long informational broadcasts once a month in prime evening time. We will report in depth on significant issues, events and personalities in the news. In the year following, we propose to make this a biweekly and after that a weekly program, if networks are permitted to retain their present structure. We are determined to press the medium to its fullest development as an informational force as effectively and as fast as we can . . ."

Stanton's address was, of course, in defense of the industry, but in his speeches during this period he was appealing to responsible self-interest lest "drastic cures" applied by government make television "a less effective advertising medium," in which news and public affairs would become the first victim.

Murrow had said in Chicago that responsibility rested "on

big business and on big television, and it rests at the top. Responsibility is not something that can be assigned or delegated. And it promises its own reward—good business and good television."

Rereading those Stanton-Murrow phrases today, one is saddened again that they could not have been said face to face, and that the two men were not more sympathetic. What Stanton's plan outlined was in many ways the resurrection of the *See It Now* concept; yet when Ed and I read the speech we were sure that Irving Gitlin's able public affairs unit, which was now responsible for the major share of documentary and discussion programs, would be given this assignment. Gitlin, an alumnus of the Murrow unit from *Hear It Now* days, had been the producer or executive in charge of *Twentieth Century*, "The Nation's Nightmare," "Out of Darkness" and *The Great Challenge*. Certainly no one in the trade press or at CBS mentioned Stanton's proposal as a project for the old *See It Now* unit.

The future was so bleak that when in June Sig Mickelson asked me to interrupt a brief vacation and come down to see him, I examined my contract to find out when my next option could be dropped. As I walked into Sig's office, a cigar in his mouth and the press release of Stanton's Ohio State speech on his desk indicated that he had appetite for the task before him. He read aloud the relevant passage of the speech, made clear that the kind of weekly informational program Stanton had in mind might not be a reality for several years, but that there would be eight in the next twelve months, that he wanted me to be the executive producer and that I would have a number of producers working under me.

I said, "Sig, are you sure you can get this cleared with the twentieth floor?"

Mickelson smiled and said that he was sure. Later I heard from several people that the decision had been Stanton's.

"I assume that this offer is made to the Friendly-Murrow unit . . ."

Mickelson had anticipated my question. "No, it isn't, but in any case, Ed leaves on his sabbatical in a month or so. What we are talking about is the executive producer's job, and the offer is to you." He added that he would like me to think about using Howard Smith as the reporter, but that I could employ any correspondents I wanted.

I told Sig that it was out of the question for me to undertake any such long-range series without Ed, who would be returning by the summer of 1960 at the latest, and that the program would then have to be a Murrow-Friendly proposition. Mickelson said that this would create "problems"; Ed could be the reporter on some of the programs, but it could not be "a Murrow series." I answered that I couldn't consider the project on such terms, but Sig suggested that I take some time to think about it.

When I talked to Ed he smiled wistfully and said, "You ought to do it if they'll give you authority and leave you alone." I thought too much of Ed to say anything so obvious as that I wouldn't take this assignment unless he told me to, but the meaning of my choice was not lost on either of us. I, who had become distinguished by virtue of my partnership with Murrow and his influence on my work, was being told that the heritage could continue under a new name; I could choose, but Murrow could not.

The first few months would be no problem. We had begun a documentary about the space program, "Biography of a Missile," and Ed could finish that broadcast and perhaps one or two others during his leave. The clash with the management would come in the summer of 1960; Murrow's return would coincide with the political campaigns, during which he should be particularly active, and unless his relationship to the series was clarified in advance, there would be more misunderstandings.

When I pointed this out to Mickelson he told me flatly that any chance of a Murrow-Friendly partnership was out.

The options were clear. I could decline the offer and go on co-producing *Small World,* in which case the new assignment would go to others. But as Ed pointed out, "If they fail, it might set the cause back many years." My other choice was to take the assignment and hope that by the time Ed returned, the corporate mood would have changed and he could assume his proper role. And if I took the job it meant the rejuvenation and even enlargement of the old *See It Now* organization.

Unthinkable though it was to do all this without Ed's full partnership, I *was* thinking about it; what made me feel particularly guilty was that if the situation had been reversed, Murrow would undoubtedly have rejected the proposal out of hand. I agonized for days over the decision and in the end compromised on the condition that Ed play a dominant role in the series after his sabbatical. By "dominant" I meant that I wanted him personally to report and co-produce at least twelve of the broadcasts in the second year, and play an editor's role in all of them. I told Mickelson that I had to hear this, in Murrow's presence, from the management of the company. This meant Stanton, for Paley was convalescing from an illness.

Also, Ed had urged me to insist that the executive producer have access to the management for consultation and appeal in matters regarding equal time and other conflicts emanating from the controversial subjects we might explore.

Mickelson agreed to both of these stipulations, but it was not until the night before Murrow left on his sabbatical that a meeting with Stanton was arranged. It began at eleven o'clock at night and ended shortly before one in the morning, and Mickelson was instructed by Stanton to formalize our agreement in a memorandum. This document stated that I would be the executive producer of the new series for a year and that at the time of Murrow's return a decision on the future would be made. In the meantime I could call on Murrow for advice as much as I wanted to; also I would have a reasonable opportunity to discuss with the editorial board matters of policy and the choice of subjects for the series. It was specified that I would not take advantage of this privilege unnecessarily, and that when the editorial board could not quickly be assembled I would deal directly with Mickelson or, in his absence, Stanton. The memo also stated that I would name the series, and that it was expected to be the most prestigious of public-affairs programs. As for its title, by a remarkable coincidence Stanton, Murrow and my wife each independently came up with the suggestion of *CBS Reports.*

Like most such *aides-mémoire,* this agreement was noteworthy for what it did not contain. However, it did end with a paragraph which stated that during the 1960–61 season Murrow would be employed in whatever capacity the company wished, but that his personal desire was to give up his daily radio program and *Person to Person;* he would prefer to have a regular once-a-week radio news broadcast, in addition to whatever duties he had on *CBS Reports,* when he returned in July 1960.

I must admit that I left that midnight meeting in the naïve belief that reason and conciliation had prevailed, and that if we had a successful first year with *CBS Reports* there would be so much momentum when Murrow returned that his full participation would be automatic.

Any such illusion, however, was shattered one week before the first broadcast. Again the quiz scandals were indirectly responsible, and when combined with the volatile Stanton-Murrow chemistry, an explosion erupted that could be heard from New Orleans to London.

The trouble began in New Orleans on October 16, when Stanton accepted an award from the Radio-Television News Directors Association, the same group which Murrow had addressed a year earlier. Then preparing for his congressional appearances and apprehensive about "this whole tawdry business," as he put it, Stanton decided to use the occasion to announce new program practices to eliminate what he called the "hanky-panky" of the quiz shows. In his speech he promised that CBS would be master of its own house: "We [assure] the American people that what they see and hear on CBS programs is exactly what it purports to be . . ."

Unfortunately the enterprising Jack Gould of the *New York Times* telephoned Stanton to get further and more specific details. In the interview Stanton said that in referring to programs being what they purport to be he meant dubbed applause and laughter, a trick that invites accusations of phoniness. There was nothing here that Murrow would not applaud, but then Stanton went on to cite Murrow's *Person to Person* as an example of shows that endeavored to give the illusion that they were spontaneous, when in fact they were rehearsed. The interview further quoted Stanton as saying that *Person to Person* guests should either be denied advance questions, or the audience should be told that the show was rehearsed. That Friday night Charles Collingwood, who had taken Murrow's place on *Person to Person,* was instructed to make a disclaimer that "advanced planning with our guests" is needed to determine "what we will show, what we will discuss and in what order," and also to pave the way for the equipment and personnel required to televise the program.

Quite apart from the awkwardness of the disclaimer, linking *Person to Person* to regulations designed to clean up the quiz hoax was a disaster. When Zousmer and Aaron, the producers of the program, called Ed in London to urge a strong statement to clear all their names, Ed responded with a blast that was as excessive as Stanton's: "Dr. Stanton has finally revealed his ignorance both of news and of requirements of television production . . . He suggests that *Person to Person,* a program with which I was associated for six years, was not what it purported to be. Surely Stanton must know that cameras, lights and microphones do not just wander around a home. Producers must know who is going where and when and for how long . . . The alternative . . . would be chaos." He concluded by saying: "I am sorry Dr. Stanton feels that I have participated in perpetrating a fraud upon the public. My conscience is clear. His seems to be bothering him."

Paley and Stanton instructed the CBS general counsel, Ralph Colin, a member of the board of directors, to fly to London to obtain either some kind of face-saving apology from Murrow or his resignation. Colin was back the next day without either. Ed never told him that it was the day of his twenty-fifth wedding anniversary.

Against this background, with the Murrow-Stanton headlines competing with the quiz scandals, and with Congress demanding the federal regulation of networks, *CBS Reports* made its debut on October 27 with "Biography of a Missile." Ed and I, who had virtually lived with what would have been Explorer VI and the Juno II rocket, which was to lift it into space, had announced that we were going to do the broadcast whether or not the rocket orbited successfully. Thus there was a good deal of suspense in the program, and Ed's involvement with the rocket and the German scientists who built it provided a dynamic beginning for *CBS Reports.*

One sequence will always stay with me, though we never got it on film. At the moment the rocket blew up, Murrow and I and the cameras were considerably closer to the blockhouse than we were supposed to be. When the range safety officer ordered the destruction of the missile, the flaming debris came dangerously close to us, scattering guards, cameramen and reporters under trucks, barricades and anything else at hand. As we squatted behind a jeep Ed, wearing one of my oversized shirts, drenched with sweat and covered with dust, looked up while the klaxon wailed and said laconically, "Well, you can't win 'em all."

In the post-mortem conducted by Dr. Kurt Debus at the scorched launching site, it was announced that two small diodes —part of the system to power the guidance of the rocket—had been improperly aligned in relationship to each other. So it was with those two complex, finely tuned instruments called Stanton and Murrow. But even if their "attitudes" could have been "corrected," as the engineers say—and only one person, William Paley, might have accomplished that—the rocket everyone was riding had a life of its own that no one could control. In his speech Murrow had said that he was "frightened by the imbalance . . . to reach the largest possible audience for everything"; this, more than the McCarthy broadcast or budget problems or the loss of a sponsor, had caused *See It Now* to lose its time period when *The $64,000 Question* achieved instant popularity. When the quiz shows fell to their death, engulfing everyone in their smoke, Stanton's desperate effort to extinguish the blaze cast doubt on the one unit whose integrity had never been in question.

The quiz scandals were slow to die and explosions continued for many months. The long year of 1959 came to a climax when, on December 8, Cowan and Stanton decided that they had had enough of each other; copies of Cowan's letter of resignation and Stanton's reply reached the wire services within an hour of each other, providing the newspapers with more headlines. Cowan's read in part: "You have expressed . . . your complete confidence in me and in the fact that I had nothing to do with the rigging of the quiz shows . . . in spite of my record and your confidence in my integrity you have suggested repeatedly, directly and indirectly, that I should resign . . . during these past two weeks you have asked me not to communicate with anyone at the office . . . You have insisted that any public statement place primary responsibility for my resignation upon my health. I have insisted on greater accuracy: My health is now excellent . . ." Cowan also charged that "you have made it impossible for me to continue . . ."

Stanton's letter contained equally blunt statements: "It shocks me that you should attribute to me motives that have no basis in fact whatever . . . Your talents and proven abilities are many indeed, but as you yourself have said many times, administration is not your forte . . . The next six months may well be the most critical in the history of the CBS Television Network . . ."

To no one's surprise it was announced simultaneously that James T. Aubrey, who only a year earlier had been hired by Stanton and Paley as Cowan's executive vice-president, was to replace the latter as president of the television network.

Aubrey's subsequent spectacular performance as a moneymaker for the company was in contradiction to the gloomy financial picture that Stanton had painted. A year earlier he had warned the affiliated stations that the high level of network profits was not automatic. "Softness in the national economy," plus the threats of FCC regulations and pay television, would require the television networks "to work and work hard" to maintain their current profits.

When Stanton gave that warning, on January 13, 1958, CBS's net profits were $22,193,000. When Aubrey took over, they were $25,267,000. Though profits slipped slightly for the next two years, they more than doubled between 1961 and 1964, reaching a high of $49,656,000 in Aubrey's last full year. No breakdown is available of figures from the television network division alone, but it is no secret that when combined with the five owned and operated stations, it represents by far the largest share of the profits.

In his 1958 Chicago speech Murrow had said: ". . . we

have in this country a free enterprise system of radio and television which is superior to any other . . . There is no suggestion here that networks or individual stations should operate as philanthropies. But I can find nothing in the Bill of Rights or the Communications Act which says that they must increase their net profits each year lest the republic collapse . . ."

Murrow may have known the Constitution, but Aubrey, to paraphrase a line from *The Music Man,* "knew the territory."

5 *As Murrow and Smith Go . . .*

For all its trauma, that 1959–60 season was not without its humor. Just a few weeks after Stanton's lecture on future broadcasting being "what it purports to be," we had an extravagant demonstration of "truth" in broadcasting. The occasion was a *Small World* program involving Murrow in London, Brendan Behan in Dublin, Jackie Gleason in Poughkeepsie and John Mason Brown in New York.

What started out as an entertaining dialogue on manners, morals and literature suddenly turned into what Gleason called a hundred-proof demonstration of the power to communicate. The gifted and uncontrollable Behan had eased his tensions with a fifth of "the crather," and realism was carried to new extremes. The Irishman took an instant dislike to John Mason Brown, and Brown, his nostrils visibly offended by the whiff of alcohol across three thousand miles, returned the feeling. But as much as Behan distrusted Brown, he enjoyed our *Small World* production assistant, Pat Bernie, a beautiful and resourceful English girl whose ingenuity was taxed to the ultimate as she removed from the Irish poet's grasp such fragile items as our mike boom, pitchers and glasses—and herself. When the program began and the boom man swung his microphone out of camera range, Behan rose in hot pursuit; every time it moved away from him he shouted, to the amusement of millions of viewers, "No, you don't . . . Come back here," chasing the mike as though it were a canary on the loose.

Behan also sang Irish ballads between reels and pursued Miss Bernie around the Dublin studio as Brown frowned in disbelief and Gleason and Murrow shook with laughter. At one point the poet shouted across the Atlantic: "How am I coming through?" Gleason answered: "Brendan, you're coming through one hundred proof."

In between his Falstaffian lunges, Behan provided commentary: "Americans—they're like a broken bicycle saddle. They give you a pain in the derrière." On the art of conversation: "It ended the hour the atomic bomb was dropped." Through missing teeth, he defined the speech of his three *Small World* partners: Gleason was speaking Irish-Gaelic, Murrow Scotch-Gaelic, and Brown was defending the Choctaw Indians.

At the end of one reel change—in those days we had to stop every eleven minutes as the film ran out—Brendan failed to return at the sound of the bell, and Murrow announced that the program would continue without the services of Mr. Behan, "due to circumstances beyond our control." John Mason Brown said wryly: "It's not an act of God, it's an act." Gleason disagreed: "It was an act of Guinness."

On November 8, 1959, we ran the program pretty much as it was filmed, to mixed notices. The New York *Post* called it "Murrow's revenge . . . If Dr. Stanton wanted realism Murrow certainly gave it to him . . ." The New York *Daily News* termed it "disgraceful . . . Murrow and CBS should be ashamed . . ." The New York *World-Telegram & Sun* criticized us, perhaps with some justice, for taking advantage of a man's illness. But if we had suppressed this program after all the advance publicity, we would probably have been accused of censorship—or at least that was part of our reasoning. In broadcasting circles the program was considered a mistake, but I prefer to think of Behan as a breath of fresh air.

. . .

1959 was also the year that I met Lippmann.

No one could have predicted one dividend of the quiz scandals—that because of them America's most civilized newspaperman, Walter Lippmann, permitted himself to be dragged kicking and screaming into television. Late in 1959 Lippmann wrote: "Television has been caught perpetrating a fraud which is so gigantic that it calls into question the foundations of the industry . . . The fraud was too big, too extensive, too well organized to be cured or atoned for by throwing a few conspicuous individuals to the wolves . . ."

Lippmann's thesis was that by constantly pandering to the largest possible audience in search of the most profitable advertising, television had become the opposite of free: ". . . in fact . . . the creature, the servant and indeed the prostitute of merchandising . . ." His solution was to give up on the networks and to "devise a way by which one network can be run as a public service with its criterion not what will be most popular but what is good." In the Lippmann plan, networks would pay part of their huge profits to help support the noncommercial network, which would be further endowed by the federal government.

The Lippmann plan disturbed me at the time because I was convinced that the networks had learned their lesson. If a fourth network was set up for public service, it seemed to me likely that the commercial networks would resort to doing their worst. I expected the idea of *CBS Reports* to flourish and spread to our competitors, and I did not want television's last best chance to be compromised by a nonprofit system which might give them the excuse to abandon any attempts to achieve the very excellence that Mr. Lippmann demanded.

One day when I was discussing this with Howard K. Smith, a close personal friend of Lippmann's, Howard suggested that I come to Washington to see the commentator, tell him what was wrong with his plan, and at the same time convince him to do a television interview.

The meeting was arranged. I wasn't very effective at convincing Walter about the weaknesses of his scheme, but when I realized that I wasn't going to change his mind I challenged him to use his wisdom to help television. If he wanted to improve broadcasting, the best way to do it was from within. He should sit down with Howard and be interviewed; he could do it well, and it was a way by which he could influence the medium right now.

Several months and two Metropolitan Club luncheons later, Lippmann finally agreed in May 1960 to submit to an interview in return for my offer to burn the film if it was no good. We didn't have to. Not since the Oppenheimer broadcast had one face so dominated the tube. Walter's frail voice, hardly audible in a living room, had, when amplified, an intensity that was hypnotic. I must admit that Howard and I did violate CBS policy by preparing an outline of the subjects to be covered. We didn't reveal specific questions, but Lippmann knew we were going to ask him about Berlin, Vietnam and Laos, De Gaulle, Khrushchev and the next President of the United States.

Lippmann wouldn't let us film the interview in his living room because he didn't want "any damn cameras and lights around," so we used Smith's new home in Maryland. Halfway through I knew that the program would be a model of lucidity and wisdom, but when I saw it in the cutting room the next day it exceeded my fondest hopes.

But this was in early May, and *CBS Reports,* nearing the end of its first season, was already having trouble with Aubrey in obtaining a night-time spot; for two months we had to sit on the film waiting for air time. The situation was made more complicated by Lippmann's objection to any kind of sponsor; however, with the other two networks and the BBC desperately trying to woo the columnist, it was out of the question that we wouldn't win our fight for an hour. When we finally did get a place on the schedule on July 7, 1960, some of the interview was out of date and Walter was at his summer retreat in Southwest Harbor, Maine. It was perhaps my greatest victory—and Helen Lippmann's bravest concession—that we were allowed to bring our cameras and microphones to Lippmann's porch, where we reshot portions of the program.

"Lippmann on Leadership," as we called that conversation, was a home run. Repeated both on television and radio, it was the first in a series of annual Lippmann programs which lasted until 1966. These broadcasts became events awaited by television audiences all over the world. I know of two Presidents who never missed one of them. Lippmann's publishers issued a collection of the interviews, which were conducted in turn by Smith, Cronkite, Schoenbrun, Collingwood and Sevareid. The book is dedicated to "Fred W. Friendly, the only begetter, who conceived and produced all this."

My fondest memory of the Lippmann conversations is something he said to me in affectionate arrogance one day. In the presence of my colleagues he was gently berating me for my heavy-handed tactics in dragging him into television. Half facetiously, half seriously, I lectured him on the power of the medium, and then, sparring out of my class, I said, "Walter, if it weren't for television and me you'd still be stuck in the classified pages of the Washington *Post* and the *Herald Tribune*." Lippmann looked up at me with his jaunty, jaundiced gaze and said, "And I made you respectable, young man."

Of all the Lippmann conversations, the close of the 1961 program is perhaps the most memorable. In answer to a question by Howard K. Smith about his "appeasement-like" approach to Laos, Vietnam and Cuba, Lippmann responded: "I don't agree with the people who think that we have to go out and shed a little blood to prove we're virile men . . . I don't think old men ought to promote wars for young men to fight.

I don't like warlike old men. I think it's their business to try as best they can, by whatever wisdom they can find, to avert what would be an absolute, irreparable calamity for the world."

Howard Smith was a perceptive and relentless reporter, whether questioning Lippmann, or Dr. Tom Dooley on "Biography of a Cancer," accompanying "Carl Sandburg at Gettysburg," or interviewing Prime Minister Nehru on India's birth-control problems. The latter was a segment of "The Population Explosion," the most successful broadcast of that first *CBS Reports* season. Smith also narrated "The Space Lag," an analysis of the squabble between the military and civilian administrations over responsibility for the space program.

For another broadcast Bill Leonard, then a producer, took his camera to the Dominican Republic and came back with a superb exposé of its tyrannical government, including a rare interview with dictator Rafael Trujillo, who was filmed partly on horseback. In the spring of 1960 Murrow did "Berlin—End of the Line," and returned from Europe in time to join producer Arthur Morse in Atlanta in May to report "Who Speaks for the South?"

The *CBS Reports* unit won every prize available to it that year, including three Peabody Awards; most encouraging of all, every broadcast except Lippmann's was sponsored. In the midst of the quiz affair Stanton had persuaded both Charles Percy, the young president of Bell & Howell, and John Collyer, chairman of the board of B. F. Goodrich, to sponsor *CBS Reports*. Both companies, particularly Bell & Howell, were very happy with the association, but at the end of that first season Aubrey and the sales department insisted on raising the cost of the series, and after some agonizing negotiations Bell & Howell bowed out. To this day, Percy talks of the bitter experience of being priced out of the program that he had helped to found; even a personal appeal by him to Stanton failed. Granted that the company had bought the series at special rates, they were exceptional sponsors in the Alcoa tradition and might have stayed for a generation. As it was, they transferred their sponsorship to a documentary series on ABC.

Murrow's return to full duty in the summer of 1960 was concurrent with another CBS fiasco: the Republican and Democratic national conventions. It was the year of Huntley and Brinkley, and CBS News "must have been doing something wrong."

Up until that Presidential campaign, CBS had dominated every convention. But David Brinkley and Chet Huntley had gotten their feet wet in 1956, and in 1960 they and NBC outmanaged, outgunned, outreported and outproduced CBS. When the Democratic Convention ended in Los Angeles, CBS was a poor second, perhaps more because of the wry, acerbic and astute comments of David Brinkley than for any other reason. In any case, CBS panicked. Under mounting pressure Sig Mickelson could not resist the clamor for a dramatic change, and he improvised a new anchor team of Cronkite and Murrow.

Both men were against the arrangement. Ed was not a facile ad-libber, and Walter liked to work alone. Besides, the professional respect which Cronkite and Murrow had for each other lacked personal rapport; on the air there was a heavy-handedness and lack of ease between the two correspondents. The viewer sensed this, and the NBC victory at the Republican Convention two weeks later was just as convincing.

In the fall of 1960 we broadcast "Harvest of Shame." Without other duties to divert him, Murrow was deeply involved in it. Even then his respiratory attacks were increasing, but he insisted on joining David Lowe, the producer, in the completion of his devastating study of the plight of the men, women and children who help to make us the best-fed people on earth.

It was Lowe's first assignment with *CBS Reports,* and he had lived with the migrants for almost a year as they worked their way up from Florida's orange and tomato crops, through Georgia's peaches, the Carolinas' beans and Virginia's corn, to the lettuce patches of New Jersey and the potato fields of Long Island. It was Murrow's kind of story, and as he stood in the rich Florida farmland describing the dawn shape-up, all the anger and eloquence of Steinbeck's *Grapes of Wrath* seemed to emerge. Together Murrow and Lowe fashioned a document of man's exploitation of man that was full of anguish and outrage. When it was broadcast on the day after Thanksgiving, it shocked millions of viewers.

Though "Harvest of Shame" attempted to reflect the growers' point of view as well, most of them were their own worst witnesses, and the president of the American Farm Bureau Federation lobby, interviewed on the report, compounded their lack of social consciousness by saying: "We take the position that it's far better to have thousands of these folks [the migrant workers] who are practically unemployable, earning some money, doing some productive work for at least a few days in the year."

Secretary of Labor James Mitchell, interviewed on the program, said that in all his years in business and government he knew of no greater pressure group than that leveled against anyone who attempted to improve the plight of these forgotten Americans. Murrow's ending was in the *See It Now* spirit and left no doubt where he stood: "The people you have seen have the strength to harvest your fruit and vegetables. They do not have the strength to influence legislation. Maybe we do. Good night, and good luck."

Not since McCarthy had we done a broadcast that created such impact, and never again would any of our programs create such clamor for change. Those migrants who were able to see it, as well as Secretary Mitchell and a few senators who cared, congratulated us. The big growers and their lobbyists yelled foul. They claimed that some of Lowe's Florida scenes had been photographed years before, and that the whole picture was distorted. They were wrong; it was a faithful, completely verified document. But the pressure from growers on the sponsor, a tobacco company, was so intense that they buckled and sent agents through the agricultural community apologizing for the program.

After he had seen "Harvest of Shame" Stanton called me and said, "I have never been so proud of CBS." Two weeks later I met Paley in the CBS elevator, and when I asked him what he thought of the program he said, "Excellent. I thought I told you I liked everything but the ending—" The elevator doors closed before I could ask him what he meant, but I guess I knew. The management was disturbed by complaints about such programs as "Harvest of Shame," even though they knew it was done fairly; what they always wanted was a "balanced" hour. But though objectivity is part of responsible reporting, all arguments, as Murrow had said, are not equal. The two sides to the migrant workers' plight could not counterbalance each other, and no reporter with a conscience could end such a report without letting the viewer know how he felt. As Murrow once asked, "Would you give equal time to Judas Iscariot or Simon Legree?"

(In light of this, it was particularly ironic that "Harvest of Shame" became a Roman candle that eventually exploded in Murrow's own face. Five months after it was broadcast the BBC scheduled it, and Ed, by then the newly installed director of the United States Information Agency, yielded to a Southern senator's appeal to ask the BBC to cancel it. Murrow's action was based on the premise that the broadcast was an analysis by and for Americans about one of our national blemishes, and not intended for export. The incident became a cause célèbre and was the only black eye Murrow suffered in his years in Washington. He himself called his lapse "both foolish and futile," but fortunately, when "Harvest" was broadcast overseas, foreign audiences were impressed by the freedom which allowed American television to expose such a national scandal.)

It was not only the protests about "Harvest of Shame" that made December hot. There was also the long-postponed climax to the Murrow-Stanton dispute; in addition, a schedule change necessitated by a new rating crisis increased the bitterness. Originally it had been decided that *CBS Reports* would be moved through the schedule in a wide variety of prime-time periods, and in the first year this procedure was followed. But during our second season another set of circumstances beyond our control caused a change. Aubrey, running far ahead in the ratings on most nights, was in trouble on Thursday night because of *The Untouchables* on ABC at 10 o'clock. For weeks it was rumored that he wanted to put *CBS Reports* into this time period on a regular basis, and finally the word came that the "accelerated schedule" of an informational program once a week was being advanced a year; we would be moved to Thursday night at 10 P.M. on January 5, 1961.

I did not resist the change. I quickly asked for one of those editorial meetings outlined in our midnight charter, and proposed to Paley, Stanton and the editorial board that *CBS Reports* continue every other week, but that in the alternate weeks there be a series of live debates. They would be modeled after the Nixon-Kennedy debates and would cover such issues as Medicare, recognition of Red China and nuclear disarmament. We were all in accord until I recommended that Murrow be named anchor man and co-editor of the entire Thursday night series. I reminded everyone that the midnight memo had left Murrow's participation open to future determination, and suggested that this was the time to decide it.

There were two complicating factors: the Stanton-Murrow acrimony over *Person to Person* had never been resolved, and Sig Mickelson, who had presided at the initiation of *CBS Reports,* had become a casualty of the news wars. The combination of Huntley and Brinkley's success and the emergence of Kintner's NBC team had impelled CBS to replace Mickelson with Richard Salant, first as chairman of the CBS News executive committee and two months later as president of the news division. Perhaps the most brilliant lawyer in broadcasting and a man of high principles, Salant believed that his respect for and devotion to news and public affairs would compensate for his lack of credentials and experience. His first task was to convince me that the Thursday night series should not be centered around Murrow—not a pleasant role for a man who revered Murrow.

After rejecting my recommendation of Murrow for *CBS Reports* and the debates, Paley said, "What do you have against Howard Smith?" I answered that I was a great fan of Smith's, a fact that Howard well knew, and that he would continue to be the reporter on many of the *CBS Reports* broadcasts and perhaps on some of the debates, but that I wanted Thursday night at 10 to be a Murrow-Friendly-produced-and-edited series. Employing Murrow would give the hour stature and continuity; the kind of debaters we wanted would be more inclined to accept an invitation from Murrow; people usually performed better in response to Ed's questions and presence; and last and most important, he was the best editor in the business.

The problem was not resolved at the meeting, and later Salant and I had the nasty job of battling it out. When he finally told me that my proposal had been turned down, I stalked out of his office saying that I would not do the series. Dorothy and I took the children skiing in the Berkshires, and Dick and I kept in daily contact by shouting at each other over the phone.

All of the *CBS Reports* producers joined me in my stand;

they said that they would resign with me if I chose to do so, rather than work on the project without Ed. A year before, I had yielded because Ed was leaving on a sabbatical; now my option was to resign or to compromise again so that the Thursday night series could perhaps break new ground for broadcast journalism.

When I finally told Ed what the choices were, he was hurt and disturbed but said that he had always known it would end this way. There was no point in attempting to place the blame on others or to brood about the past; the facts spoke louder than all the personality conflicts and errors of judgment that existed on both sides. Clearly CBS wanted the competence of the Murrow unit but not his prestige and outspokenness; they wanted the finest, most comprehensive information program in all television, but they would not allow the giant in his field to preside over it.

While I wavered, threatening to resign if Murrow was not accepted, trying to find some honorable settlement, John F. Kennedy resolved the situation and gained for his new government the most brilliant director the United States Information Agency ever had. (It was generally understood that another man considered for the post was Frank Stanton.) But the fact is that in January 1961, when Mr. Rusk and the President-elect summoned Ed for consultation concerning the appointment, I alone opposed it. I felt that Murrow was needed more as a reporter than as a propagandist. Paley said only that it had to be Ed's decision; he would be glad to have him stay at CBS, but he also understood the challenge of public service.

On January 31, 1961, Ed spoke his farewell to the CBS family in a closed-circuit program arranged just after President Kennedy announced the appointment. Even now it is a moving, emotionally charged experience to see the video tape of Ed's farewell as he spoke to the affiliated stations and to correspondents and producers who watched from crowded news rooms in New York, Washington and all over the country.

History will record that Murrow, in his thousand days, gave the United States a new voice. As Arthur Schlesinger wrote in *A Thousand Days:* "[Murrow] revitalized the USIA, imbued it with his own bravery and honesty and directed its efforts especially to the developing nations . . . USIA became one of the most effective instruments of Kennedy's third-world policy; and Murrow himself was a new man, cheerful, amused, committed, contented." Honesty and bravery were precisely what Murrow had to bring to television, but the symbol of that and so much more departed when he leaned into that camera in Studio 41 for the last time and said: "Good luck, and good night." And this time that strong, controlled voice broke.

Perhap it was inevitable that Ed would join government service sooner or later. He could have had the New York Democratic senatorial nomination in 1958, but Harry Truman, among others, told him that he was more valuable to the nation as a reporter. The day he walked out of that cluttered studio complex in Grand Central for the last time, he was walking into an eased exile from a profession he had helped to invent. It would be dishonest to say that he concealed his bitterness, or to forget the measured, if sad, relief that existed in some quarters of CBS at his departure.

Part of Murrow's role now fell to Howard Smith—as did part of the frustrations. When Ed had been summoned by Kennedy, he was in Birmingham, Alabama, beginning a *CBS Reports* broadcast originally intended to be a report on the *New York Times* libel case. Later, for legal reasons, the concept of the program was changed to an examination of the Alabama community called "Who Speaks for Birmingham?" Smith took over the reporter's role and was in Birmingham on May 18, 1961, when Sheriff "Bull" Connor's police stood by while civil rights workers were brutally beaten. Howard, a native of Louisiana, was appalled by the violence he witnessed at close range, and in recording the closing piece for the program, he quoted Edmund Burke at another time of crisis: " 'The only thing necessary for the triumph of evil is for good men to do nothing.' "

The management of CBS, deeply disturbed by the Birmingham program and its possible effect on the affiliated stations in the Deep South, ordered the Burke quote removed. It was an attack on the decent white citizens of Birmingham and it was an editorial remark, they said. At the end of a long afternoon in the cutting room there was a bitter row between the station relations vice-president and Smith, Lowe and myself about the content of the program. I never should have permitted the argument to take place, and I finally ordered the executive to leave. Unfortunately, the matter was referred to the management, and together with several other incidents about the forthrightness of Howard's commentary, it became the focal point of a bitter twentieth-floor luncheon.

Smith had been appointed bureau chief in Washington by Blair Clark, general manager of CBS News under Salant, and the Smith-Clark relationship had suffered from a series of other grievances, principally because Howard felt he was being held on too close an editorial tether. There were other problems, some of them personal, but the Birmingham situation brought matters to a head and ended, months later, with Paley's and Stanton's request for Smith's resignation.

I was outspokenly distressed at the loss of two great journalists in less than ten months, and with Salant's and Clark's knowledge, if not permission, I tried to see Paley and Stanton to prevent Howard's banishment. I was not able to see them together, but I did elicit high praise for Smith from each of them, and from Paley the opinion that he was perhaps the finest news analyst in the industry. I conceded that Howard was sometimes difficult to work with and perhaps better suited to be a correspondent than a bureau chief, but I argued that we could not afford to lose two broadcasters of Murrow's and Smith's caliber without seriously damaging our ability to do such programs as *CBS Reports.* Couldn't Smith be retained, with *CBS Reports* as his full-time job? Ironically, the reply this time was, in effect: What's your objection to working with Sevareid or Collingwood?

A brief, unsigned public notice was the only tribute to Howard's twenty years of devoted service: "CBS News and Howard K. Smith announced today that their relations are being terminated because of a difference in interpretation of CBS News policy."

Late that afternoon, as I walked down Fifty-second Street to meet Howard and tell him that there was to be no reprieve, I felt that I had been through this cycle too many times before. I wondered whether a pattern was developing, and if so why it was that I was always the survivor. Suddenly I remembered a bitter quotation Elmer Davis once applied to another man's moment of decision: "Yesterday afternoon [the] senator . . . wrestled with his conscience. He won." In both the Murrow dispute and the Smith dismissal, I too had wrestled long and hard with my conscience, and for the rest of my life I would wonder who had won.

Normandy, the Boston Bookies and the Awards Worth Keeping

The plane loaned to General Eisenhower by NATO lost its starboard engine just as we crossed the Channel coastline. It was August 1963, and we were on our way to Portsmouth from Normandy to film the beginning of "D-Day Plus 20 Years" from the war room, still intact, where the decision to proceed with the invasion was made on June 5, 1944. Among those on the Convair were former President Eisenhower, his brother Milton, his son John and William Paley. As the pilot began his final approach Walter Cronkite, with that droll sense of humor seldom projected on television, looked out at the feathered propeller and said, "Wouldn't you know it—Cronkite gets it in a plane crash, and all the dispatches will say is, '. . . Also on board was W. Cronkite.' "

We returned to Normandy to film the rest of the program, and the week we spent there meant something more than just another television program to all of us who were part of the small army of cameramen, producers, jeep drivers and distinguished camp followers, which the General referred to as "Friendly's Irregulars."

General Eisenhower had become a part-time correspondent for *CBS Reports* soon after he left the Presidency. Toward the end of his second term I had written Paley a note recommending that he approach his old wartime friend about making an electronic memoir of his years in office. The President expressed interest and asked Paley to mention the idea again in Gettysburg after January 20, 1961. As a result, we filmed three conversations on the General's Presidential years, several conversations on the state of the world, a *Town Meeting of the World* with Anthony Eden and Jean Monnet, and several other broadcasts. But by far the most rewarding experience was the sentimental journey to Normandy.

Each of us had his own favorite moments. Cronkite will never get over his ride on Omaha Beach with a seventy-three-year-old jeep driver from Abilene who didn't have an international drivers' license, or that final moment of the program when he and Ike walked along the rows of white markers in that green graveyard high above Omaha Beach.

What I remember best is the prelude to that sequence. The night before it was filmed Bill Paley, who had joined the Normandy expedition because he enjoyed the General's company and because he wanted to see how such a production could be completed in a week, gave a dinner party for General and Mrs. Eisenhower and the crew. At about eight-thirty the General said good night, pointing out that we all had a seven o'clock call in the morning, and as he left he asked me if he could talk to me for a few moments in his suite. When I knocked on his door ten minutes later, the General was sitting in a terrycloth bathrobe studying some notes. Looking troubled, he said, "Fred, this thing tomorrow at the cemetery is something I've got to do right. It's no time to talk about landing craft or air power or high strategy. This program is going to be seen by thousands of families who lost sons and husbands and fathers at Normandy."

Then, unashamed in his emotion, the old soldier talked of the inequality of sacrifice. "Tomorrow I'm going out there to talk to those families—I who came out of the war with enough glory to carry me on to other things. My own son was spared, and I've lived to see my grandchildren grow and prosper. What about those boys who died in that landing? What about their parents? What do they have to show that it was all worthwhile, that something decent and lasting came out of it besides military victory?"

"General," I said, "just say exactly what you've been saying to me. Say that tomorrow to Walter." I felt that I had caught a glimpse of him which only those few could have seen who were with him that rainy night before the invasion. The next day on the sea wall he was almost as moving; what the camera recorded was devotion to those thousands of dead:

> Walter, this D-Day has a very special meaning for me . . . these men came here, British and our other allies, and Americans, to storm these beaches for one purpose only, not to gain anything for ourselves, not to fulfill any ambitions that America had for conquest, but just to preserve freedom—systems of self-government in the world. Many thousands of men have died for ideals such as these, and here again, in the twentieth century for the second time, Americans, along with the rest of the free world . . . Now, my own son has been very fortunate. He has had a very full life since then. He is the father of four lovely children that are very precious to my wife and me. But these young boys, so many of them, over whose graves we have been treading . . . were cut off in their prime. They had families that grieved for them, but they never knew the great experiences of going through life that my son can enjoy. I devoutly hope that we will never again have to see such scenes as these. I think and hope, pray, that humanity will learn more than we . . . learned up to that time. But these people gave us a chance, and they bought time for us, so that we can do better than we have before. So every time I come back to these beaches, or any day when I think about that day twenty years ago now, I say once more we must find some way to work . . . to gain an eternal peace for this world.

I remember one other incident from that week in Normandy. While we were sitting one day in a small trailer on the beach near Arromanches with General Eisenhower, waiting for the rain to stop so that we could continue filming, Bill Paley was explaining the plans for the new CBS skyscraper on the Avenue of the Americas in New York. The General had visited the production center on Eleventh Avenue at Fifty-seventh Street, which had once been a milk barn, and he was confused about the functions of the two facilities. I facetiously explained that the difference was simple: "General, the decision-makers will be in the new building and the program-makers will be in the cow barn." Paley interrupted the laughter and aimed his finger at me: "Friendly, you make more decisions than anyone in that new building."

Paley had a point, for the truth is that during the five years that I was executive producer of *CBS Reports* I was more or less given carte blanche. Except for allowing the Murrow-Friendly partnerships to continue, every promise made at the midnight treaty was honored. There were times during those years when Stanton blinked and perhaps winced at what we were doing, but he never flinched. When we scheduled "The Case of the Boston Electra" after several unexplained plane crashes, and Captain Eddie Rickenbacker called to make certain that his old friends Paley and Stanton would do nothing to hurt "the growth of aviation," they merely referred him to me. Rickenbacker tried to talk me out of doing the broadcast, but it went on as planned. When we produced "The Teen-age Smoker," the tobacco industry, which is one of CBS's largest sources of revenue, protested, but the management stood firm—displaying courage made more conspicuous in retrospect by the fact that even today no other network has examined the relationship between cigarettes and lung cancer at such length.

The chemical industry applied pressure at the time of our broadcast about Rachel Carson's "Silent Spring," and Dick Salant's letters to some of the leaders in the field are souvenirs to be cherished. When Bill Leonard produced "Trujillo: Portrait of a Dictator," Senator Smathers attacked the program, its producer and CBS itself. The company not only backed us up but scheduled a repeat of the broadcast.

We had come a long way. No story better illustrates the maturity with which the management handled controversial subjects than the TFX plane incident. At the time of the vehement debate between Senator McClellan and Secretary of Defense Robert McNamara on whether favoritism had been involved in the awarding of the TFX aircraft contract, we filmed a one-hour program called "McNamara and the Pentagon." I had sought the Secretary's co-operation for such a telecast ever since he took over the Pentagon, and in 1963, with the aid of some lobbying from Ed Murrow, an ardent fan of McNamara's, and a gentle nudge from President Kennedy, the Secretary finally agreed.

The interview, with Harry Reasoner, took place in Mr. McNamara's office on two different mornings, and the hour we broadcast was a compression of about three hours of questioning. The Secretary spoke of Vietnam, about which he was then optimistic, of "wars of subversion," of the test-ban treaty, Russian poetry, lobby groups and why the multipurpose jet could be used by both the Air Force and the Navy.

Senator McClellan, who had been conducting Senate hearings on the TFX contract, said that if there was any additional information on the TFX in the McNamara interview, his committee wanted to see it. Though I told his staff that there was some unused footage but that little of it was important or newsworthy, the senator insisted that we send him either the film or the text. My position on this and all other interviews was that the material we published was public, but that the "out-takes" were the equivalent of a reporter's unused notes and therefore privileged. This had been Murrow's policy on *See It Now;* in the one instance when we subsequently used out-takes —the Oppenheimer interview—we had received the scientist's permission before doing so. At a time when McClellan and McNamara were locked in a bitter tussle, I felt that it would be unethical to furnish the senator what we considered privileged, if redundant and unimportant, information.

Senator McClellan and his staff made vigorous protests, and when the message from the powerful chairman of the Senate Permanent Subcommittee on Investigations came through to Stanton, the implications were loud and clear. Stanton not only said no, but went down to see the senator and explained our policy. At one point we were so concerned about a subpoena that I had the unused film removed to my home.

CBS also stood firm against the gun lobby when we produced "Murder and the Right to Bear Arms"; against the American Medical Association when they claimed that "The Business of Health" was a plea for socialized medicine; against the undertaking business and Forest Lawn's advocate, Congressman James Utt, when we produced "The Great American Funeral." Throughout, the company's backing was consistent except for occasional nervousness over broadcasts concerned with the race issue, when the sensitivity of the Southern affiliates was a complicating factor.

The Southern stations are a large and vocal part of any network's family. The morning after a *CBS Reports* on Birmingham, or on "Mississippi and the Fifteenth Amendment," a Southern station manager would be under considerable criticism in his community. This would affect New York in a variety of ways, the most immediate and destructive being that station acceptance of *CBS Reports* was always low in the Deep South.

To satisfy these stations and, for that matter, other affiliates about certain controversial programs (the Burlington, Vermont, station was sensitive about reapportionment reports; Charlotte, North Carolina, wanted to know about the filibuster program; Wichita was anxious about the farm program; Los

Angeles was worried about a broadcast on the demise of the Los Angeles *Mirror;* Arizona was concerned about the bomb-shelter report because part of it had been filmed in Tucson; and *everyone* inquired about our program on the radical right), and to give them an option, Stanton and Salant instituted a system of closed-circuit screenings several days in advance of each *CBS Reports.* This put the choice of programing a particular broadcast to each station, but it also applied certain conditioning restraints on our producers and reporters. It meant, in effect, that we had an editorial board of at least one hundred and ninety regional officials, and though many of them exercised remarkable restraint, some of the post-closed-circuit criticisms by telephone and telegram were livelier than the programs.

I must admit that this system tempered our broadcasts. The stations didn't try to influence our choice of subjects any more than the management did, but I found myself subconsiously applying a new kind of conformity to our documentaries. Looking back now, I suppose that I was subtly influenced to do controversial subjects in a noncontroversial manner. We did handle tough subjects and we often did them well, but there were no strong endings such as in the McCarthy, Radulovich or "Harvest of Shame" programs, or anything similar to Howard Smith's proposed ending for "Who Speaks for Birmingham?" Our techniques improved through the years, but in balancing arguments rather than objectively weighing them, we were sacrificing one ingredient of good journalism. As Elmer Davis once said, ". . . objectivity often leans over backward so far that it makes the news business merely a transmission belt for pretentious phonies."

The only times we really expressed a forceful point of view were when we turned to exposé-reporting. In such cases our investigatory reporting made a case so convincing that no "objectivity" was possible. But the trouble with exposé journalism, as every editor knows, is that most vital issues do not lend themselves to the technique. You can't do an exposé about disarmament, the water shortage, parochial schools, the Common Market or the Supreme Court.

Of course there were other times when *CBS Reports* continued to ring the bell, as when we addressed ourselves to problems so bitterly controversial—birth control, cigarettes, abortion—that merely broadcasting them had impact, or when we produced a report on a foreign subject like "The Trials of Charles De Gaulle," in which David Schoenbrun commented on Algeria; or on an inside look at East Germany, in which Dan Schorr's comments on the drab, sterile look of Communism did not require equal time balancing.

Early in 1960 I told Dick Salant that Jay McMullen was working on a special project in a New England city, that it might take more than a year, and that I thought it best for the company if I imparted no more details and took the responsibility myself. Security was most important, and in the event anything backfired, the less the company knew the better. I did tell Salant that the program had to do with gambling syndicates, crime and politics, and from time to time I reported to him that the project was going well.

When finally broadcast, on November 30, 1961, "Biography of a Bookie Joint" was not only one of the most sensational exposés we ever did, but also the most maligned. Half a city cried foul, screaming that we were dishonest, that we had staged and rigged the program, that we were irresponsible. Yet the broadcast withstood the hostile scrutiny, and proved again that electronic journalism can be as accurate and responsible as any of the older media of reporting.

I gave the program its title, but Jay McMullen gave it everything else, including two years of his life. McMullen is broadcast journalism's first and only investigatory reporter. Before he came to *CBS Reports* he had compiled a startling documentary on Jimmy Hoffa and the teamsters, and in 1960 he produced "A Real Case of Murder: The People vs. Peter Manceri," an analysis of the great game of justice in which the adversary system sometimes puts more emphasis on winning than on being right. This film was used in lectures at Harvard, Michigan and other law schools until the district attorney involved in the case asked that it be withdrawn. Out of a sense of what best can be described as a kind of statute-of-limitations mercy, we finally did so.

For another program, McMullen spent a year and a half pursuing opium from the poppy fields of Turkey, to the Middle East, to the Italian Mafia, and all the way into a junkie's arm on a Harlem street corner, in a program called "The Business of Heroin."

McMullen is a painfully slow worker who sometimes takes a year to pick his next story. He was a tremendous asset to *CBS Reports,* but we could afford only one of him. Stubborn and intractable, he could not be rushed, and I learned early that I could give him no deadline, not even the year in which a broadcast should be scheduled. When he first outlined the gambling program, we agreed that it could not be simply a general story on the subject, with a variety of arguments and positions, but that in demonstrating the relationship between the penny-ante bookie on the corner and the billion-dollar gambling syndicates, we had to produce evidence.

A few months later McMullen asked me, "What would you say if I told you that I thought I just might be able to get a camera inside a bookmaker's shop in Boston, and that with a little luck we might show policemen coming and going?" He had been working with the New England Citizens Crime Commission and had developed some good leads, but he needed a small camera that he could conceal and carry inside the bookie parlor. We authorized a small research-and-development fund, and Palmer Williams and McMullen set out to equip a lunch box with a tiny 8-mm. camera. For weeks the two men conducted experiments in and around New York before Jay was finally satisfied and returned to "location" in Boston.

McMullen rented a furnished room across the street from a small key shop at 364 Massachusetts Avenue in the Back Bay area. Day after day in June 1961, he and a cameraman equipped with long telescopic lenses photographed the store's customers. It was perhaps the busiest key shop in America, with as many as a thousand callers a day. Children on their way home from school watched the bookmaking traffic, the used gambling stubs were burned on the shop's sidewalk, and police officers dropped in continuously—often while leaving their patrol cars double-parked. This was all captured on film. In addition, McMullen was photographed entering the shop with his lunch box under his arm; then the action was picked up by the small hidden camera and microphone as he placed bets, watched the operations and proved the program's contentions.

McMullen is a better reporter than he is a cameraman, particularly when aiming with his elbow but the lunch box recorded some impressive data, and the long shots from across the street were almost too good—as CBS's legal department told us. The lawyers said that we could identify the visitors as policemen, but not in such a way that they might be individually recognized.

Late that summer McMullen arranged an appointment with Justice Department officials in Washington and ran the film for them. They thanked him for the information, as they would have any responsible citizen, but gave him no specific information as to what course, if any, they might pursue. We did have the impression that action would be taken, however, and McMullen's hunch was that we ought to have two camera crews in Boston during the last week in September.

In mid-September McMullen called me from Boston to warn me that soon there was going to be some publicity on our project. On Friday, September 29, Treasury agents swooped down in an unexpected raid on four establishments, including our key shop, and arrested eight persons. The spectacle of our cameraman photographing the action from the middle of Massachusetts Avenue outraged the Boston press, and the next day the newspapers had a field day. The Boston *Globe* ran an eight-column story headlined: "U.S. STAGES HUB RAIDS FOR T.V. 28 AGENTS HIT FOUR STORES . . . AS CAMERAS WHIR." The Boston *Herald* devoted only four columns on the front page to the story, allowing some space for the Syrian crisis: "T-MEN RAID . . . T.V. CAMERAS . . . RECORD ACTION"; and the *Daily Record* devoted most of its front page and two-inch headlines to "T-MEN RAID 4 FOR T.V." The *Evening American*'s analysis was: "They [CBS] tried for Ness [Elliot Ness of *The Untouchables*] and wound up with a mess." The fact that McMullen managed to have a camera present at the arraignment in federal court made us no additional friends.

In Washington, Edwin Guthman, then the director of public information for the Justice Department, confirmed the fact that CBS News had furnished the original information, but denied that any advance tip of the raid had been given to the network. The St. Louis *Post-Dispatch*, completely dependent on the wire-service stories, didn't bother to call us; in a blistering editorial they censured the Justice Department for co-operating in such a fiasco: "This performance is pretty much on a level with the Army's exhibition in Berlin for the Jack Paar show. Besides being a waste of the taxpayer's money, it tends to make law enforcement look ridiculous."

But *The Christian Science Monitor*, published in Boston, gave the story four columns on its front page and played it straight. When the coverage mushroomed and we were asked for an explanation, we issued a simple statement: "For some time, Mr. McMullen has been working on the business of gambling. In the most honorable and ancient tradition of newspaper journalism, we made certain information regarding crime available to the proper authorities." At the same time, I briefed Salant and he in turn prepared the management for the storm of protest that soon engulfed us—including denunciation by a cardinal of the Catholic Church and by CBS's own radio station in Boston.

Back in New York, McMullen kept insisting that the film wasn't very good and that he still didn't have a show, but I assured him that it was the most powerful exposé material to document a story that we'd ever had. My only problem was that Jay wanted to take the next six months to assemble the film and edit it. I told him that we couldn't wait that long, and we scheduled the program for November 30, 1961. Walter Cronkite narrated the broadcast, which was concerned not only with this bookie joint but thoroughly explored how the two-dollar bet corrupts the entire body politic, and how illicit gambling cannot operate without police protection.

When he saw the footage, Salant was as impressed as Cronkite and I, and he was helpful in keeping the CBS lawyers out of the editorial room, though we did need them in the cutting room. We knew that someday this film might have to stand the minute scrutiny of hostile counsel and we wanted every scene, every splice, to be beyond reproach in any libel action. The late Tom Fisher, and Joseph DeFranco, two corporate lawyers who were dedicated to getting tough subjects on the air, advised us to black out the program in Massachusetts and other areas of southern New England serving Boston because of the difficulty a court would have in selecting a jury from a panel of unprejudiced citizens. "Someday," Fisher said, "there'll be an item in the *Harvard Law Review* mentioning the fact that some CBS producers thought more of due process than showing a television show in Boston." We reluctantly agreed.

My chief regret is that "Biography of a Bookie Joint" did not appear opposite *The Untouchables,* as it normally would have been; true to form, the other networks had scheduled two pre-empting "prestige" specials opposite ours. But for all the competition, "Biography of a Bookie Joint" had a vast audience, and several New York hotel rooms were filled with Boston reporters, politicians and police officials taking notes and making pictures from the screen.

The next day, and for the next few months, the Boston papers in effect supplied promotion for our program. Sample headlines read: "T.V. SHOWS 10 BOSTON POLICE AS THEY ENTER BOOKIE SHOP" . . . "T.V. EXPOSE BLACKED OUT IN BOSTON" . . . "CHARGE BOOKIES HAVE LINKS WITH STATE REPRESENTATIVES" . . . "WHY DO WE NEED LAS VEGAS WHEN WE HAVE [the] HUB" After a special viewing John A. Volpe, a Republican governor in a Democratic city, promised a cleanup, and later demanded the police commissioner's resignation. Since Boston is probably the only city in the nation whose police commissioner is appointed by the governor, we were heroes in the State House and bums in City Hall.

The affair was further complicated when a small bookmaking ring was discovered in the State House. We were attacked on the floor of the Massachusetts House of Representatives by the Speaker (who was later indicted on charges of graft), and Representative Harrison Chadwick was actually censured by the House for having asserted on the broadcast that there was a link between gambling and certain members of the legislature.

Most of the Protestant and Jewish clergy praised the program, which some of them saw at a special showing, but the worst attack and certainly the most difficult to bear came from our old friend Cardinal Cushing. On the night of December 5, 1961, he stood on the stage of the Boston Garden in a confluence of spotlights as police bands played and the crowd roared, and defended the honor of the Boston police, whose chaplain he had been for years: "In my theology, gambling in itself is not a sin, it's the abuses that make gambling evil," he thundered. The Cardinal, who only a few months earlier had participated in the inauguration of a President, added: "Somebody betrayed us and I would like to know who . . . Whoever was behind it owes an apology to the city of Boston." The Boston police, dishonored and humiliated, may have had the *New York Times,* the Boston *Herald,* the Boston *Globe,* the Harvard *Crimson,* CBS and all the Brahmins in Boston arrayed against them, but they had the Cardinal in their corner. The Protestant leadership noted acidly that "gambling, Your Eminence, may not be a sin, but it happens to be a crime."

Before "Biography of a Bookie Joint" was off the front pages, defending the film became almost a full-time job. In an effort to prevent the discharge of the police commissioner, his lawyer accused "Biography of a Bookie Joint" of being a hoax. The Governor's Council, a committee of elected state politicians, some of whom were close friends of the police commissioner's, was convened to conduct the hearings on the police department, and the chief evidence at the investigation was the film itself. Because McMullen was to be a witness at the closed hearings of the grand jury, and because we did not think it proper for him to reveal his sources of information, we decided that I would take the film to the hearings of the Governor's Council at the State House and be the broadcast's defender.

The experience, which involved constant shuttling to and from Boston, was something that every producer who puts together a documentary ought to endure—once. My testimony required a detailed explanation of how a documentary is put together, and of McMullen's painstaking attention to detail. In addition, we sat for hours in that hot council room in the dark with the projectors running, dissecting the film foot by foot to authenticate each scene involving the police. When the police commissioner's lawyer claimed that one of the scenes had been photographed a year prior to the date we claimed and had not been made by CBS, I had to produce the coded symbols of each frame of film and evidence from the Eastman Kodak Company to prove the purchase date. When it was asserted that taxis in front of the key shop on Massachusetts Avenue carried advertisements that were not used after 1959, we enlarged the license plates of the cars in the film to show that they carried 1961 plates. At one point we enlarged, at the ratio of ten to one, a display card in the window of the key shop to prove that the movie advertised was indeed playing at the Uptown Theater in June of 1961.

Finally, at the end of one long, tedious day as I was still testifying, the hearings were interrupted by the police commissioner's lawyer, asking for a brief recess. A few minutes later the president of the Governor's Council announced that the commissioner had resigned.

It wasn't until after our "acquittal" in Boston that our television affiliate there would have much to do with us. At the time of the notorious federal raid, when all the heat was on, the CBS affiliate, WHDH-TV, owned by the Boston *Herald,* said that it couldn't take the chance of being associated with the program and wanted to know nothing about it. And our radio station, which was owned and operated by CBS, actually broadcast an editorial condemning "Biography of a Bookie Joint."

The thesis that "Biography of a Bookie Joint" attempted to make—that in most large cities there is a relationship between gambling and politics—was lost in the furor over the Boston police. We tried to make the point that the situation was not unique, that the same thing was going on in cities all over the country, but all the publicity obscured this. Boston's fascination over the show became so intense that the Massachusetts House of Representatives even passed a resolution requesting that the broadcast be run in their capital. Salant quite properly declined the invitation because of "the importance of individual rights involved in prompt judicial trials by a jury of peers, with no prior conclusions as to the guilt of the defendants."

Those "prompt" trials were finally held in February 1963, and there were some minor convictions. There were also some reforms in the police department, and power to appoint the police commissioner passed from the jurisdiction of the governor to the mayor of the city. But though McMullen testified before the grand jury for three days, and after every scrap of evidence was examined, indictments were handed down which led to convictions of the bookmakers, no police officer was ever convicted or dismissed.

"Biography of a Bookie Joint" wasn't shown in Boston until a year later, when we ran a nationwide repeat after the trials had been concluded. It had a tremendous impact even at that late date, and by then the Boston press corps had become our most loyal supporters, a far cry from those first stories at the time of the September raid. In my home today there is a silver bowl, given to the executive producer of *CBS Reports* by the Boston Press Club as their award for television journalism in 1961.

But the prize from the Boston wars that I most treasure is a gift sent to me in 1964 when I was appointed president of CBS News. It is a copy of the biography of Pope John XXIII, *Call Me John,* and under the inscription ("To Fred: Congratulations on your promotion and prayerful good wishes for the future") is the signature of the author, Richard Cardinal Cushing. There was no hint that His Eminence had forgotten, only that he had forgiven.

CBS Reports had its share of failures and near-misses. We never managed to do justice to the radical right or left; the one report we tried on economics was too diffuse; we never treated automation or the technological revolution; and we never found a way to investigate the business of sports. We made several attempts to give adequate treatment to the most unreported story of our time, Latin America, but during my tenure at *CBS Reports* we were never able to interest the American audience in the problems of those two hundred and thirty-seven million Americans. After my departure, however, Jack Beck and Charles Kuralt produced "Mexico: A Lesson in Latin," a startling report about one aspect of the dilemma.

Another failure that dogged me through four Presidential administrations was that I was never able to get two American Presidents together on the same broadcast. Exploring the power of the Presidency in such first-hand fashion has been a challenge to every television producer, and though no one ever had a better chance to pull it off than I, each time it eluded me. A confrontation between Truman and Eisenhower was unthinkable, because it took years of patience and diplomacy by their wives and friends before the other's name could be mentioned without a response too earthy for television. My best chance came in the early sixties when I had an opportunity to talk to President Kennedy and former President Eisenhower in the same week. Blair Clark, then general manager of CBS News, a Harvard classmate and close friend of Kennedy's, had taken me to see the President-elect on the day before the inauguration to discuss television and the Presidency. It was really a selling expedition to convince the President that in addition to the use of television for news conferences and so-called fireside chats, he ought to consider the interview technique employed in the annual Lippmann conversations he had seen and enjoyed as a senator. The President-elect told us that he would give the matter serious thought and asked us to bring the idea up again in six months.

Our first Eisenhower interview had just been completed when Clark and I went to the White House the next time. We were received in the Chief Executive's private quarters, where his valet was trimming the President's hair, and I can still remember the expression on his face when Blair suggested a dialogue with his predecessor. I won't try to quote the President, but in effect he said forcefully that he had no appetite for the proposal. The idea of a young President only a few months in office sitting down with an extraordinarily popular seventy-year-old ex-Chief Executive, with all the obvious comparisons of age, experience and wisdom, didn't appeal to him at all. He didn't think it would be good television, and he certainly didn't think it would be good for President Kennedy. However, he did agree to consider it, and he made a point of asking whether President Eisenhower was interested.

When I went to Gettysburg a few days later, I made a similar proposition to Mr. Eisenhower. His answer was just as quick and negative, and for the very opposite reasons: the General mentioned youth, the prestige of a President in office, and all the facts and figures at an active President's command. I never had the courage to tell either man the other's reaction, but I have often thought that their common instinct about what was right for their own image—though of course neither used that phrase—was one of the attributes that made each of them successful politicians.

I renewed my quest for such a dialogue years later, this time between President Johnson and General Eisenhower. Although there is considerable mutual respect between them, going back to the days when Eisenhower was in the White House and Johnson was Majority Leader in a Democratic Senate, I never had a word of encouragement from either of them.

In 1962, having given up on the idea of Presidential dialogues, we and the other two networks managed to convince President Kennedy that a television conversation was a worthwhile undertaking. Lippmann and others had been writing pieces about the President's lack of communication with the people, even suggesting that he had not yet learned the full use of television. Clark and I wrote the President and Salinger a series of letters on the subject, and finally, in December 1962, Pierre called to say that the Chief Executive had decided to do a one-hour conversation before Christmas. He quickly added that it was to be a three-network affair, but that the President had asked that CBS and I produce the program, and that the White House correspondents of the three networks ask the questions. Salinger cautioned me not to mention the idea to the other networks—there had to be a meeting at the management level—but that I could count on doing the program. A few days later the meeting was held, and the taping was set for December 16.

On that day, for almost two hours, a President of the United States used television better than it had ever been used before. But that afternoon also turned out to be the occasion of an embarrassing CBS domestic argument on how such interviews should be conducted.

The core of the problem was, I suppose, Stanton's 1959 statement that caused the flap with Murrow, and just how literal an interpretation should be placed on the phrase about programing being "exactly what it purports to be." I subscribed then, and I still do, to Stanton's ideal in theory, but having been involved in interviews with a series of such reluctant statesmen as Truman, Eisenhower, Chou En-lai and Macmillan, I know that a truer portrait of such men can best be captured by not imposing any time limitation, and then editing the footage to proper air length. A live interview with a man in office usually results in a *Face the Nation-Meet the Press* verbal fencing bout, in which a wary but nimble politician spends the half-hour trying to prevent his interrogators from getting him to put his foot in his mouth. Some important news breaks have come out of such panel shows, but the essence of the public official seldom emerges as it does in a distilled, carefully edited tape or film interview.

Before each "conversation" I would attempt to put the guest at ease by asking him to please relax and pretend that he was chatting with some old friends. I would also assure him that if he inadvertently revealed something that might endanger the national security, or made an incorrect statement, he had only to say so and we would make another take of his reply. Though I can't remember anyone ever exercising this option except to change a badly constructed sentence or an error of fact, it usually put the subject at ease. Particularly in the case of a President of the United States in office, it seems to me that this technique is essential, and I believe that most people in my position share this view.

On December 16, however, Salant and Clark told me that the management was reluctant to let us do the Kennedy interview in this fashion. I argued as persuasively as I could the case for a taped, edited interview—after all, these were the ground rules to which the President had agreed—and I finally won my case. I had also made it my business to confer with Jim Hagerty, then head of ABC News, and Bill McAndrew, chief of NBC News, and we were in complete agreement about how the interview should be conducted.

The timing of the program was nearly perfect. President Kennedy's second year in office was coming to a close, and the Cuban missile crisis had just ended. The three correspondents —George Herman, Sandy Vanocur and Bill Lawrence—had all done their homework, and so had the President. Don Hewitt turned Mr. Kennedy's office into a television set, with two of the five special cameras focused on the Chief Executive from an extremely close range, yet concealed in an alcove so that he was almost oblivious of them. The President wanted to sit in his big leather desk chair, but from past experience we knew that its swivel had a chronic squeak in it, and we prevailed on him to use his rocking chair.

A few hours before the interview began, I suggested to Mr. Kennedy that we divide the broadcast into two sections—"The President and the World" and "The President and the United

States"—and that we spend approximately forty minutes on each. When I thought the time had come to move from one to the other, I would suggest a ten-minute break. He had not been told any of the questions, but he was aware of the general areas we intended to cover.

"A Conversation with the President" began without fanfare or special announcement. After one false start in response to the first question, the conversation took off and didn't stop until fifty-five minutes later. We had made the transition on cue from foreign to domestic issues after approximately forty minutes, but no one had wanted to interrupt that flow and grace of language because we were all enthralled. The President was enjoying the three correspondents and was responding as though no cameras were present; when I finally called a temporary halt he was astounded that nearly an hour had passed.

Mr. Kennedy then invited everyone into the Cabinet Room for coffee, and I ducked out to our mobile truck on the White House lawn to look at the video tape. Just as Hewitt and I were congratulating each other on the quality of the tape, one of the technicians handed me a phone. It was Blair Clark in New York, and he began by telling me how well the interview was going—he had been watching it on a monitor in his office—but that he thought we had more than enough material and should stop shooting. When I protested that there was a three-network agreement to shoot ninety minutes and then edit, he said that in his and Salant's opinion, we had everything we needed. I pointed out that we still had some important ground to cover—integration and the University of Mississippi dispute, education, and a final summary of the past year—and that I had no intention of cutting the session short.

After I hung up on Blair I had a thirty-second walk across the White House lawn to cool off, but when I walked into his office, I faced an intuitive President. "What's the matter, Fred," he said, "you got problems with your brass?" At that moment I had no idea how much of the brass was watching and listening in New York, but I answered, "Mr. President, if I'm going to lose my job, this is as good a place as the next one. Let us proceed."

The next twenty minutes provided some of the high points of the program. The President talked about the Meredith case and civil rights laws, about education, and about the satisfactions and disappointments of his months in office. But the most poignant moments came at the very end when the young President, scarred by the Bay of Pigs fiasco, heartened by the outcome of the Cuban missile crisis, leaned back and said reflectively: "I must say that I have a good deal of hope for the United States just because . . . this country . . . criticizes itself and is criticized around the world. One hundred and eighty million people for . . . almost twenty years have been the great means of defending . . . the world against the Nazi threat, and since then against the Communist threat . . . If it weren't for us the Communists would be dominant in the world today, and because of us we're in a strong position. Now, I think that's a pretty good record for a country with six percent of the world's population . . . I think we ought to be rather pleased with ourselves this Christmas."

No one spoke for three or four seconds, and then it was over. The President stayed on for a few minutes afterward to look at the tape with us, and just as we were leaving hurriedly for the airport to catch the plane back to New York, he smiled at me and said, "Let me know if you need a job tomorrow."

By the time Hewitt and I got to New York, a three-network team had edited the audio tape. I had a few minor suggestions, and we all stayed through the night. Editors worked all day Monday to make the transitions smooth; by late that afternoon copies had been made for each of the three networks, and recordings for the many foreign broadcast companies who wanted to broadcast it the next day.

"A Conversation with the President" was carried on Monday evening, December 17, on all three networks. When Salant called to congratulate me on the broadcast that evening, I told him that I was going to see Stanton the next day to complain about the outrageous interference at the White House in the middle of the interview. In the endurance test of completing such a broadcast, there is no time to look backward, but now that it was over I wanted to protest the sudden change in midstream.

When I saw Stanton he was as calm as I was indignant, and listened attentively to my complaints about Clark and Salant. I couldn't work under such circumstances, I said, and I angrily threatened to resign. Stanton puffed away at his pipe, said he understood why I was upset, agreed that the last part of the interview had been well worth doing and gave me the impression that nothing like this would ever happen again.

Neither Salant nor Clark nor I ever discussed the subject at the time, but much later, when I was in Salant's job and carrying out orders which I didn't always approve of, I asked one of the two about that disagreement, "Was that your idea, or did it come from—?" Before I could finish, the answer was forthcoming: "I've been waiting three years for you to ask me that question."

Fifteen months after the first "Conversation with the President" there was another, but a new Chief Executive was in the chair, which now carried a small silver engraving on its leather back: "THE PRESIDENT, NOVEMBER 22, 1963." The opening camera shot slowly dollied back from that tight close-up to a room that had remained much the same. Bill Lawrence was there again, joined this time by David Brinkley and Eric Sevareid.

During the briefing before taping began, I brought up the Bobby Baker case to the President. I had been told that the only doubts he had about the interview were that it might turn into an inquisition over the Baker affair, and that the Presidential office would be embarrassed. Now Mr. Johnson told me that he hoped it would not be mentioned; the program should be concerned with more vital matters. As politely as I could, I said that I felt the subject had to be discussed, and that I had suggested that one of the correspondents specifically raise a question about it. I believed strongly that to ignore the scandal at a time when it was front-page news would have made the correspondents look silly, the President overly sensitive and the whole program stage-managed by the White House.

The interview was done in two long takes, interrupted by a ten-minute break, and when the second session ended with the President paying tribute to the public's steadiness during the difficult period of transition, he looked over to me as if to say, "Is it over?" This time it was my turn to be tense. I crossed the floor to where the four men were seated and said, "Mr. President, I guess I'm born to be the heavy, but no one has asked that question about Bobby Baker, and it just can't be ignored."

The President and everyone else grimaced, there was a long pause, and then in that wonderfully gravelly voice Bill Lawrence said, "All right, Fred, I'll ask it."

The tapes rolled again, and the President fielded the question skillfully. Without mentioning Baker by name, he indicated that any comment would be out of place until the Senate committee made its finding. The answer did not make news, but avoiding it would have.

The resulting broadcast was almost as effective as President Johnson's first appearance in the Congress two days after Kennedy's funeral. Gone was the stem-winding, back-slapping Vice-President; not yet present was the master of the teleprompter, peering through contact lenses at a moving speech board. On that Sunday afternoon in March 1964 his rapport with Sevareid,

Brinkley and Lawrence was something the audience could sense. They talked of President Kennedy, of protection for the Chief Executive, of Vietnam, De Gaulle, the new civil rights bill, and many of the other tasks confronting the new President after his first one hundred days in office.

President Johnson has since contemplated several other conversations, but so far none has materialized. Since such broadcasts are an effectual use of the Presidential office and of the instrument of television, it seems a pity to me that they can't become a semiannual or even monthly custom.

In all, *CBS Reports* as a regularly scheduled series had a life span of seven years—the same length of time that *See It Now* endured. Once, in 1964, when there were newspaper rumors that the series was through and that Aubrey was going to reclaim the time period for entertainment, I attempted to deflate this trial balloon by indicating that I would leave CBS if it happened. Another time I quoted Stanton as saying that he felt as strongly about the program as I did, and he supported me. Regardless of his motivation in 1959, Stanton willed *CBS Reports* into being, and by sheer strength of that will he kept it on the schedule when Aubrey would have killed or maimed it, when the sales managers wanted to cut it up into two half-hour segments in noncontiguous time periods, and when revenue studies were conducted to show that the six commercial minutes in that hour could be sold in an entertainment package for as much as $40,000 per minute.

During those years *CBS Reports* was often moved around; wherever the competition was toughest, we were assigned the time period opposite it. When *The Untouchables* finally began to fade and Aubrey could again compete on Thursday night at 10, we were moved to Wednesday night at 7:30, "to reach that important school audience" that couldn't watch at 10 o'clock.

But when the company had a Monday night rating crisis we were hastily shifted there in midseason, finally ending up on Tuesdays.

The series had some kind of sponsorship for most of those seven years, but individual programs were usually sold for less money than their production costs. When we were blessed with sponsors like The Travelers Insurance Company or IBM, a full-time rate was paid, but when there was no regular advertiser, the sales department would have to peddle the broadcast at the last minute for what are called "station payments." This was just enough money to be able to pay the affiliates their rent for an hour of precious night-time air; otherwise many of them would not agree to carry the program.

Advertising minutes on night-time television average $40,000 and can go as high as $60,000, depending on what the traffic will bear, and *CBS Reports* and an *NBC White Paper* don't bear what *The Beverly Hillbillies* and *Bonanza* do. Still, in 1965, my final year at CBS, our series was virtually sold out and produced sales in excess of $5,000,000. Though the name of the program has now been changed to the *CBS News Hour*, an omnibus title for a combination of cultural and in-depth news programing, it is still the only regularly scheduled informational hour in prime time, and I believe that it will remain there as long as Frank Stanton is president of CBS.

CBS Reports was a costly obligation by any standards, though it may have helped save the network at the time of the wasteland crusade, when Newton Minow and others called it one of the oases. The production cost for one of the old *See It Now* half-hours was somewhere between $20,000 and $25,000, or less than $1,000,000 for a forty-week season. The *CBS Reports* budget was seldom less than $80,000 or $100,000, and often well in excess of that. News projects, even long-range reports, can't always be budgeted or predicted, and often new developments would require us to scrap half a program already filmed—or even, if events overtook us, to kill a project entirely. A few broadcasts, perhaps one a year, were never shown, because they just weren't good enough. Newspapers and magazines can live with "overset"—that is, stories that are never printed—but in television an unused documentary can mean the loss of $100,000.

My feeling was that there is nothing more expensive than a bad show, and with television time as costly and scarce as it was, we could not justify scheduling an inferior program just to reduce the inventory, any more than we could stop reporting on Mississippi or the Sino-Indian war when these stories were front-page news. The accountants didn't always understand this, and even Paley himself grew weary of the economic strain. But *CBS Reports* remained Stanton's child, even if it occasionally embarrassed him.

Of such disturbing programs, David Lowe produced some of the most effective: "Harvest of Shame," "Who Speaks for Birmingham?," "Sabotage in South Africa," "Murder and the Right to Bear Arms," "Abortion and the Law" and "Ku Klux Klan: The Invisible Empire." Two nights after a marathon in the cutting room to finish the latter, David died of a heart attack.

Lowe was troublesome to handle, seldom brought a show in on schedule, was always over budget and never did a report that didn't annoy some special-interest group. I wrote more letters inside and outside the company defending him than I did for any other five producers. David had tremendous heart, and his problem was one to be cherished: he just couldn't learn how to be neutral about some issues, and when he died he was mourned by people in the slums of Birmingham and Johannesburg, and in the migrant shacks of Florida.

In that 1958 Chicago speech Murrow quoted Heywood Broun's "No body politic is healthy until it begins to itch . . ." and then he added: "I would like television to produce some itching pills rather than this endless outpouring of tranquilizers." In those seven years we broadcast one hundred and forty-six *CBS Reports.* All of them were respectable, and perhaps 10 percent of them were itching pills. In retrospect this may not seem like much of a ratio to brag about, and far too many of the best programs occurred in the early years of *CBS Reports.* Those broadcasts that attained professional excellence and an impact far beyond their air time had an honest point of view and the empathy of the correspondent.

Reporters are generally better writers than producers and directors, especially when they see and feel the tragedy and controversy firsthand and then write from their own conviction. The correspondent unwilling to get mud on his shoes or pick up an amoeba bug in Asia, or get hit by a beer can in Mississippi, is not a journalist but a narrator. It is the man on the spot who can lift a report out of its anticipated mold and make it soar. I think I have produced more television documentaries than anyone else, so I feel qualified to attest that no broadcast without the full dedication of the reporter on the scene ever yielded a sense of accomplishment, or the brickbats which made us realize that the viewer had become as involved as we had been. Most producers would agree that these are the only awards worth keeping.

7

What Every President Should Know

If anybody in television today remotely resembles Elmer Davis, it is Harry Reasoner. Like the sage from Aurora, Indiana, Reasoner seeks out and destroys the pretentious and the obvious with dry wit and economy of language. On March 2, 1964, when I replaced Salant as president of the CBS News Division, Reasoner's first words to me were: "Well, I see that the lunatics have taken over the asylum." The irony that I, who was not renowned for budget control or strict adherence to bureaucratic dicta, had suddenly been made chief administrator of a news organization with an annual budget in excess of $30,000,000, was lost on few within the company.

By 1964 CBS News, which had pioneered in broadcast journalism, was, in spite of its distinguished corps of correspondents and producers, resting uncomfortably in second place. NBC News, whose assets included the competence and appeal of David Brinkley and Chet Huntley and the relentless drive of Robert Kintner, had finally established itself as the news leader, in spite of the fact that CBS's staff was superior. Kintner, who seldom slept and who lived with monitors tuned to each of the networks, had, with the backing of Sarnoff, tripled the NBC News budget, and had given the organization zip and momentum.

Both within news circles and out, my appointment was generally well received, and several editorials made the obvious point that someone identified with Murrow had been selected to restore CBS's damaged prestige. As Jack Gould of the *Times* put it: "Mr. Friendly's rise to one of the key posts in journalism is expected to begin a new era of reportorial vigor on the home screen," and then, in a statement more prophetic than accurate, he wrote a few days later: "The factor of time really goes to the core of . . . the issue. William R. McAndrew, head of NBC News, does not hesitate to break into the schedule and stay with a story. He has a boss, Robert E. Kintner . . . who is an incurable news hound . . . What really cooked between Mr. Friendly and Dr. Stanton, and what, in turn, are they cooking up for NBC? If 'The Big Moose' or the 'brilliant monster,' as Mr. Friendly is variously nicknamed in sundry CBS quarters, can pull the big switch at will, the contest for news supremacy is surely on." Ironically, less than two years later both the "incurable news hound" and the "brilliant monster" were unemployed.

Friends have asked me why I ever accepted the offer of a job which at best had a life expectancy of three years, when I had a long-term contract with a higher salary as executive producer of *CBS Reports.* (In the strange economics of broadcasting, news executives are always less rewarded than producers and correspondents; many producers are better paid than company vice-presidents, and many of the Washington reporters make more money than their bureau chief, who has far more responsibility.)

I took the job partly for the reason it was offered: because Stanton was desperate. There had been five news chiefs since 1946, and each of them, from Murrow to Salant, had left disillusioned. Although Salant and I had earlier proposed a plan in which I would serve as his executive officer in charge of all news programing, it became obvious that Dick was not going to be able to retain his post.

More pragmatically, I took the job because I worried about the rumor that an administrator, rather than a man experienced in the news field, might be brought in from the outside, and that in the dismantling which might follow, *CBS Reports* would be jeopardized.

If a more idealistic reason is required, Thomas Carlyle supplied it: "[Edmund] Burke said there were Three Estates in Parliament, but in the Reporters' Gallery yonder, there sat a Fourth Estate, more important [by] far than they all." This is not a figure of speech; in these momentous times it is a truism, for when America's survival depends on self-appraisal and global understanding, news, particularly television journalism, may well be the first estate. To think in such terms as "The stupendous Fourth Estate whose wide world-embracing influences what eye can take in?" to quote Carlyle again, may seem pretentious, but I believed that the news division could focus that influential eye on the moon and Vietnam, on parliaments and senates, on the slums of Harlem and Johannesburg, and provide our society with knowledge and insight. I was also just enough of a competitive animal to believe that the staff could handle our competitors, and that I could handle the executives of the company.

Of course I discussed the offer of the job with Murrow, then recuperating from lung surgery in La Jolla, California. He advised me to take it if I thought I could handle it, but not to agree "to report to any ten-man committee." A few days later I told Stanton that I would accept if I was responsible only to himself as president of CBS, and to Paley as chairman. He not only agreed but went so far as to say that if he ever left the company to take a job in government, or that if he or I ever thought my return to production was advisable, my old contract would again be in effect. Stanton was also gracious enough to send hand-initialed announcements of the appointment to a wide circle of the broadcasting and Washington communities, including several CBS expatriates now working at other networks.

At the time of my appointment Paley was vacationing in Nassau, but I was assured that he was delighted with the decision. When I did see him at our next Tuesday news luncheon, which became a fixed ritual, he told me that he believed CBS had become slightly complacent over news and that perhaps it was his fault as much as anyone's. "Maybe I'm getting old and have been too willing to believe that we are still on top," he said. He regretted that we had let NBC seize the initiative in live coverage of vital events, which they had exploited to their advantage. He also felt that we had been too firm in curtailing news analysis, and that this had taken some of the spice out of our broadcasts. We discussed the comparatively low ratings of our news programs and agreed that something had to be done to bring them up to the Huntley-Brinkley level. The statement that Kintner had ordered run at the end of each Huntley-Brinkley broadcast—"This program has the largest daily news circulation in the world"—hurt Paley the most.

The chairman was also concerned about the discrepancy in advertising sales between the two news divisions. Many of our documentaries and specials were now sustaining or were sold for station payments, while NBC was sold out at their regular rates. An arrangement that NBC had concluded with an oil company, which provided sponsorship of unscheduled programs covering special news events and "gavel to gavel" coverage of conventions and other live broadcasts, gave our competitors a decided advantage.

Salant, who was asked to return to the twentieth floor as special assistant to Stanton, was understandably wounded by the abrupt decision. What he had accomplished under near-impossible circumstances cannot be minimized. The 7 P.M. half-hour news program was the product of his dogged determination to broadcast more news despite the opposition of the affiliates, and especially the CBS owned and operated stations, and the election unit he and Blair Clark had set up under Bill Leonard was the beginning of the Vote Profile Analysis system, an analytical tool which has revolutionized election reporting more than anything since the advent of the telegraph.

The company I now found myself in as one of seven division presidents and one hundred and twenty vice-presidents, was far bigger than the one I had joined in 1950. But even for a man who considered himself an expert on CBS's organization structure, it was much more complex than it appeared from the news floor, and I spent my first hundred days being reoriented.

Two monuments to the dreams and style of Frank Stanton are symbolic of CBS: its July 16, 1951 table of organization, and the imposing skyscraper on the Avenue of the Americas, completed in January 1966. Of the two, the table of organization is far more important because it set in motion the divisional plan which caused a proliferation of presidents and vice-presidents, each competing with the others in what Aubrey and others have described as "the adversary system."

CBS was founded in 1927 and purchased in 1928 by William S. Paley, the imaginative heir to a Philadelphia cigar fortune. In 1935 Frank Stanton, a young psychology major with a doctorate from Ohio State University, came to CBS to establish audience research methods; eleven years later, at the age of thirty-seven, he became president of the corporation.

Until 1951 the company had all the advantages and disadvantages of a small family business; thereafter it had all the advantages and disadvantages of a corporate enterprise. Although the change came at a time when television sales were expanding in almost geometrical progression, some observers trace the company's phenomenal financial success since then to that 1951 plan.

However, the table of organization did not take full effect

until 1959, at which time CBS News became the final separate division. Some have claimed that CBS News has never been quite the same since becoming a separate but equal entity. It is unequal because it is a dangling division; not a profit center, it is instead a supplier as well as a customer of the television and radio divisions.

Though CBS is a confederation of one hundred and eighty-seven independently owned stations, it owns, as do its two network rivals, five (the limit permitted by the Federal Communications Commission) very-high-frequency television stations in five extremely rich markets, as well as seven radio stations. These affiliated stations are serviced by the network and share their revenue from the sale of time. For example, if CBS sells six commercial minutes on *The Ed Sullivan Show* for $62,000 each, and the pro-rata share for KHOU-TV, Houston, is $237.50, the network and the station divide this money on a formula of approximately 70 percent for the network and 30 percent for the station. This is an approximate figure; some stations get slightly less, and if the broadcast is, say, a news program that they are not eager to carry, they may get more. The day-time formula favors the station less, sometimes paying them as little as 7 percent of their card rate. Obviously the station makes its money on the adjacent time periods, sold locally. In the case of NFL football, none of the $70,000-a-minute revenues is paid to the station; instead, they are permitted to sell a certain number of minutes to local advertisers. The sustaining service that the affiliated stations receive from the networks on important public events, such as elections, Presidential news conferences, news programs and documentaries, is one of the principal reasons that they maintain a network affiliation, in spite of their reluctance to carry many of these broadcasts.

At CBS, when television and radio were split into separate entities in 1951, each with its own president, the relationship and balance between them were shifting. As television expanded, radio shrank, but because the profit-and-loss statements were kept separately, radio was required to show a profit of its own, thus creating an unhealthy rivalry between two crucial media which were never allowed to complement each other's services. (Until late 1965 CBS television could not be used to tell its audience that a certain special event was to be broadcast on radio, and vice versa.)

In 1958 further fragmentation of responsibility occurred when the television division itself was split in two—the CBS Television Network being established as one profit center under Louis G. Cowan, who had become broadcasting's "man of the year" by virtue of *The $64,000 Question,* while Merle Jones, who had been head of all television of the company, gave up one of his hats to become president of the CBS owned and operated television stations. These two profit centers—each of which soon became as large as the division from which they had been separated—then competed against each other for profits in the same marketplace. As a result, a decision that served a station's financial interests might be made at the expense of the network. For example, WCBS-TV, New York, or KNXT, Los Angeles, might not broadcast a certain special news event because it would mean pre-empting a popular local program which brought in a great deal of advertising revenue. Paradoxically, what was good for CBS was not necessarily good for CBS, one might say.

When CBS News became a separate division, the arrangement seemed to give more responsibilities to its president, Sig Mickelson, but it was only an illusion of responsibility without sufficient authority or power. Each time CBS's corporate cells split, another contraceptive layer was placed between Chairman Paley, President Stanton and the working echelons of decision-makers below them. Moreover, when the news division was given its new status, the layers were compounded. CBS News became the supplier of news programs to the radio and television networks, and to the television stations. But our largest customer, the television network, also became our largest supplier, because it sold the news division a variety of facilities such as studio space, cameras, mobile units, long lines for remote broadcasts and—of all things—radio studios.

The apportionment battles over how much the radio, television and station divisions should be charged by CBS News and how much, in turn, the television network should bill us, required a special assessment committee which satisfied nobody. When the television network complained that coverage of a four-day space flight cost more than $1,000,000, the news division retorted that almost half of that money was traceable to the excessively high prices the television network charged us (for example, $2,400 per day for a single video-tape machine and editor; $5,000 per hour for a crew and studio with full facilities). We might have rented such facilities on the open market for less money, but we were captive customers. At one point all the division presidents submitted a plan by which the parent corporation, Columbia Broadcasting System, Inc., would be charged for all news and public events as an institutional service and responsibility, but this was rejected as an organizational step backward.

The greatest effect of so dividing the table of organization was that it split authority over decisions that had to be made almost instantly on special events. Of course if it was an earth-shattering news story such as the Kennedy assassination or the Tonkin Gulf incident, higher judgment did not have to be consulted; but in those grayer areas where no editor could be certain of the accuracy of his news judgment until the event had taken place, one had to weigh the public need against the divisional one. The head of the news division, who was in charge of covering the event, also had a secondary interest in the profits of the affected division; on the other hand, the head of the television network was responsible for producing larger profits each year, and had only a secondary interest in the success of the news division.

Sometimes this stalemate of command could be settled only from above, and often there was no one answering on the bridge. At times Paley and Stanton were willing to impose their will; at other times their judgment was as uncertain as the shaky structure that was set up to make decisions, and the result was division and diffusion of responsibility. The 1951 table of organization may have been good for CBS's profits, but it was bad for news coverage.

It was always my understanding that Paley only reluctantly agreed to the division setup, and to everyone's certain knowledge, Murrow was critical of it. In a speech he once said: "Responsibility . . . rests at the top . . . [and] is not something that can be assigned or delegated." When that responsibility was exercised by Paley and Stanton, it was usually in the public interest, but when it was left to lower authority, the pursuit of profit often won. For example, during the critical moments of the United Nations debate over Vietnam in 1966, CBS News provided a special half-hour summary on important developments in the Security Council, but the CBS television station in New York did not carry the program because this would have meant delaying the start of its afternoon movie. When I finally reached Stanton to tell him that we were "blacked out" in New York, he was shocked. He did not have to tell me, however, that he was not going to order an "autonomous" division to broadcast any specific program, but the television viewer had no way of knowing why he had been denied the right to see and hear what was happening at the U.N.

However, the system of autonomous divisions was not without its virtues for the news division. It kept the executives of the television and radio networks out of the news room and out of the business of deciding the contents of our programs. Aubrey never understood why we should be permitted to do a

CBS Reports broadcast on cigarettes and lung cancer, but he would never have presumed to interfere; nor could Aubrey or Arthur Hull Hayes, head of CBS Radio, tell us what correspondents to assign to certain broadcasts, or order a correspondent to plug a sponsor's product. The rule was that policy decisions which could not be settled at the division level were to be brought before the CBS News executive committee; however, in the two years that I was president of CBS News, few meetings were scheduled. Most of the decisions concerning such crucial matters as scheduling were painfully ground out by bitter argument, and sometimes these contests of will required more energy than that required to beat the competition.

Our main competitor, NBC, was organized differently; President Robert Kintner, who came to NBC in 1957, was personally in charge of all operations, and when news and entertainment collided, he automatically gave news the right of way. One day in 1964 Bill McAndrew, head of NBC News, and I were returning to New York from Washington by plane. Over Philadelphia, word was flashed to us that Nikita Khrushchev had fallen from power. As soon as we landed we each called our offices, I to plead with Aubrey, and then Stanton, to get a half-hour for a special report that night, and McAndrew to hear that Kintner had already ordered a one-hour program. The fact that I did not get approval until five o'clock was one reason why NBC did a better job that evening.

Another organizational factor influencing news budgets—and therefore decisions—is that NBC is owned by the Radio Corporation of America; though the network is a highly profitable part of this giant complex, it represents less than 25 percent of RCA's net earnings. The CBS television operations are estimated to represent as much as 71 percent of the parent company's profits; therefore, $1,000,000 spent in news coverage by CBS may affect profits proportionately more than the same expenditure by NBC affects RCA. Furthermore, RCA, which makes a great deal of money from color television sets and television tubes, prospers from "loss leader" activities—that is, money-losing programs which increase the sales of television sets. NBC also carries prestige programs which the RCA corporate family can afford, whereas at CBS the television divisions of the company provide its main profits.

The CBS headquarters building in New York is about five hundred feet high, and all Stanton. He once described to an interviewer the way he felt about his creation: "You dream about it at night, you think about it in the morning on the way to the office. You spend time on weekends, you spend time with the architect. I can't quantify it . . . you give everything you've got to making sure you get what you want."

Not everyone feels that this handsome, austere building is an aesthetic success. Ada Louise Huxtable, the architecture critic of the *New York Times,* liked the skyscraper's exterior, but called its interior "a solid gold, corporate cliché . . . [an] anonymous vacuum-packed commercial shell that it was never meant to be . . . And CBS," Mrs. Huxtable added, "does not become, as Saarinen had hoped, a whole and 'soaring thing.' It is a great building, grounded."

There are those—I among them—who believe Mrs. Huxtable's comments may fit television more than they do 51 West 52 Street. Stanton has reason to be proud of the creative role he played in the design and detail of this building, which enriches the New York skyline and which has won many architectural awards. He would not and could not claim that influence on the television schedule.

The difference between the headquarters building and the garish structure which is today's broadcast schedule is that the latter was not built under Stanton's or Paley's close supervision and control. In contrast, during Columbia's early years Paley laid the original foundations with solid blocks of talent. It was due to his efforts that the New York Philharmonic was broadcast regularly on CBS. He discovered such entertainers as Bing Crosby, Morton Downey, the Mills Brothers, Kate Smith and Myrt and Marge; to these he added *The Columbia Workshop* and the *American School of the Air*, as well as a news department with the help of the editorial skills of Edward Klauber, a brilliant newspaper editor who was the real founder of all broadcast journalism.

In the late forties Paley added strength to his growing company by hiring away from NBC Jack Benny, Edgar Bergen, Red Skelton and Amos 'n' Andy. In those days, while Paley made CBS glow, Stanton transformed the business into a well-oiled machine, drew the blueprints for the television network, and did more than anyone else at CBS to establish it.

With the sudden expansion of television, CBS grew beyond everyone's expectations, but the company soon marched to the beat of a distant drummer called the ratings. In 1936 Paley had warned, "Too often the machine runs away with itself . . . instead of keeping pace with the social needs it was created to serve." On that same occasion he said, "I believe that we are forming, in a sense, the present fulcrum of a future lever long enough to move the world. We must move wisely. . . ." Thirty years later the house that radio built was a tower of film reels expected to double its growth every four or five years, and it had a life all its own; "the social needs it was created to serve" had been subverted for the needs of profit.

By 1965 the schedule was so far out of control that one of the company's top executives publicly stated that most of what was broadcast no longer reflected what he himself would watch or could enjoy, but what would win the rating game. Paley and Stanton looked on while programs proliferated which assaulted their sense of taste, and even decency; they seemed incapable of stopping the inexorable flight from quality.

Because the broadcast structure, unlike the headquarters on

Fifty-second Street, cannot afford not to continue to grow, and because there are no more hours in the days to sell, the company, in its search for expansion and more profits, has had to diversify to other areas of investment. Hence the acquisition of a television-set manufacturer, a tube division and an amusement park, each of which was a failure; an electric-guitar factory and *My Fair Lady,* which were gold mines; and the New York Yankees. The quest for new properties continues lest the future not provide anything to grow on, as the profit centers continue to produce excess cash that must be invested.

On March 2, when I addressed the news-room staff after assuming the presidency of the division, I said that I was giving up the best job in television for the toughest. It turned out to be the toughest *and* the best. But if I was telling the story of my years in this job through the medium of a television documentary rather than in a chapter of a book, the opening sequence would be that one in the news room just described, and then the scene would switch to the annual stockholders' meeting one year later. The chairman of the board was presiding; at his sides the various presidents of the CBS divisions were seated, ranging from Dan Topping, president of the New York Yankees, to Goddard Lieberson of Columbia Records, to Jack Schneider, Jim Aubrey's replacement as head of the television network division.

We had all been briefed on how to handle the itinerant hecklers who roam from one stockholders' meeting to another, and there were prepared answers for questions on Aubrey's departure, why Yogi Berra had been fired as manager of the Yankees and why Huntley and Brinkley were ahead of us in the ratings. Still, I went to the meeting expecting to hear some minor words of praise for the news division, for we'd had a constructive year. What I was not prepared for was a startling revelation by Paley. After announcing that preliminary figures for the first quarter of 1965 indicated that net sales had increased about $8,000,000 over the previous year, the chairman said that net income for the same period was down $900,000 from 1964. One of the reasons behind this decline, he stated, was "that the three television networks were more evenly matched in ratings in prime evening hours." But then Paley added a sentence that brought me up straight in my seat. Unscheduled news coverage of events such as Sir Winston Churchill's death, the space program and the civil rights issue, the chairman declared, affected "first-quarter programing costs [so as to reduce earnings] by six cents a share."

My immediate reaction was one of relief that Murrow was not present to hear Sir Winston's funeral mentioned in terms of corporate earnings. (It is relevant to point out that at the time of President Kennedy's assassination, Stanton made a magnificent decision, involving minutes and millions, to cancel all commercial programs for the next four days, and that he never publicly related the financial sacrifice involved.)

Paley's statistics also reminded me of a phone conversation with Aubrey and Stanton, who were at Television City, Los Angeles, at the time of Churchill's death. I had been urging all-day coverage for this state funeral; jet flights carrying BBC video tape would be arriving by midmorning, and I knew that three Telstar satellite passes would make it possible for us to be on the air most of the day. Over the telephone I told Stanton that if we were showing cartoons while NBC was broadcasting the funeral cortege, we would regret it for the rest of our lives. I won that argument, and even our competitors were willing to admit that the Churchill funeral had been a broadcast of which CBS could be proud, thanks to Charles Collingwood's commentary and the inspired coverage available to us through the BBC and the Independent Television Authority.

My last reaction to the linking of Sir Winston's name

with a per-share loss was that I didn't think anyone at that stockholders' meeting or anyone reading about it in the newspapers the next day would quite believe it. Wall Street and Madison Avenue both knew that Aubrey's phenomenal rating streak had been broken, and that it was the NBC-ABC parity that made the difference in earnings.

It was this tug of war between profits and "unscheduled news"—a rather curious term—which made the presidency of the news division the toughest job I ever had, and it demonstrates the never-ending conflicts of interest within a network. Two decisions I had to make in 1965 may help to establish perspective. Though neither of these was run-of-the-mill, the dilemmas they posed and the implications they raised were symbolic. One crisis was the hastily called Presidential television appearance involving minutes; the other was the Pope's visit involving millions.

The freedom march arriving in Montgomery on March 25 was live television coverage at its best and station relations at its worst. That afternoon on the platform in front of the Alabama State Capitol, with its Confederate flag flying, a white folk singer leaned over and kissed Harry Belafonte. Within minutes all the phones on my desk were ringing and there was a roll call of Southern stations that resembled the beginning of the Civil War all over again. Earlier we had decided to stay on the air from Montgomery only until 2:30, and to return again at 4 P.M. for Martin Luther King's oration. The Southern stations resented our extensive coverage; the manager of our Charlotte affiliate, for instance, threatened to call a protest meeting of the station advisory group, and demanded prior warning of any future "propaganda events." Some of our Northern stations, on the other hand, reported that they were swamped with calls protesting our return to normal programing for almost ninety minutes.

That night, on U.S. Highway 80 between Montgomery and Selma, a white civil rights worker from Detroit, Mrs. Viola Liuzzo, was killed while driving freedom marchers home.

The next day, March 26, our "unscheduled news" programing called for live coverage from the White House while President Johnson pinned medals on Gemini III astronauts Virgil Grissom and John Young. The ceremony began shortly after 11 A.M., with the President among the speakers, and ended up predictably with NASA officials using the air time for a long public relations speech. Harry Reasoner stayed with the action until noon, describing the handshaking, child-hugging and other festivities. NBC had elected in advance to stay on the air after the White House ceremonies in order to cover the parade to Capitol Hill, where the astronauts were to attend a congressional luncheon. Watching this on the bank of monitors in my office, my colleagues and I rejoiced that we had decided against televising the motorcade, for it was a rainy, windy day and there were no crowds. For once we had guessed right, and NBC was trapped.

Suddenly there was a call on my direct line to the Washington office. It was Bill Small, our bureau chief, who said that word had come from the White House suggesting that we keep our cameras ready; the President might come on the air again in a few minutes. In the instant it took me to ask Small the question I knew he probably couldn't answer—"What's the President going to talk about?"—I was aware of our plight. We were back with our soap operas, while NBC, now stuck with that damp procession, would welcome a chance to switch to the East Room even if it were only to televise Mrs. Johnson welcoming a garden club.

Fully aware of the passion with which millions of women follow the slow-motion plots of midday serials, I called the television network people to ask what problems it would cause if we interrupted scheduled programing at 12:30. The answer was: "It would cost thirty thousand bucks, and you've interrupted *Search for Tomorrow* half a dozen times lately." Besides, they asked, what was the President going to say that was so important that it couldn't be delayed until regular news? I said that I would try to find out. I called Stanton to ask his advice, but he was in a meeting.

At 12:25 Small called again to ask whether we were going to cover the President's appearance or not. "Bill," I asked, "can't you find out what he's going to talk about?"

"George Reedy [the Presidential News Secretary] says it's important, but he won't tell us anything. Why don't you call him?"

In thirty seconds I had Reedy on the tie line. "George, just for my ears, is the President going to talk about the Liuzzo killing?"

Reedy answered, "I won't say yes and I won't say no." He was trying to avoid a leak.

I was on the spot. If we went to the East Room and the President then chose to talk about plans for postal reform or to discuss the appointment of a new ambassador, I would be the goat with the television network and with all those soap-opera fans. If I decided against coverage—on my monitor NBC was already announcing the momentary appearance of the President—and his subject turned out to be newsworthy, we would read about the absence of CBS in the newspapers from coast to coast the next day—and would deserve the scolding.

At moments such as this my office became the equivalent of the "slot" of a city news room. At 12:35 the bank of monitors on my wall reflects the various options before me. NBC is still televising its rained-out parade, but is continually switching back to the East Room. ABC has entertainment; on the CBS screen is *Search for Tomorrow*. On one of the closed-circuit monitors I watch the White House correspondents filing back into the

East Room and the cameras being uncapped. Small calls to say that the President is due in two minutes. My office is filled with editors and correspondents urging me to switch to the President. The phone on my desk rings. It is the sales department: "Can we assume you are not going to interrupt? Remember, it's thirty thousand bucks."

"No, you can't assume anything," I say. Suddenly the Presidential seal fills the screen of the monitor, the signal to the networks that the President will appear in thirty seconds. The phones on my desk continue to ring. On the tie line Small calmly says, "Well?" I take a deep breath, look up at the monitors blinking back at me and breathe "Go!"

In less than five seconds Reasoner's calm voice is interrupting the network, and millions of television sets respond to our signal. The phones from CBS headquarters are jangling but there is no time to pick them up. Suddenly the seal is gone, but the President has not yet entered the room. In the interval Reasoner discusses the earlier events of the day, and speculates about the Liuzzo killing. Then one can sense from the hush spreading across the room and the turning of heads toward the door that Mr. Johnson is approaching. At last he enters with two familiar figures: FBI Director J. Edgar Hoover and Attorney General Nicholas Katzenbach. We've guessed right. It must be the Liuzzo case and there must be news of an arrest, or Mr. Hoover would not be there.

It's March and my office is air-conditioned, but the back of my shirt is a wet dishrag. Gordon Manning, a vice-president and my deputy in charge of hard news, sighs with the relief that means we are safe until next time. The President announces the arrest of the alleged assassins and departs, Reasoner wraps up the telecast smoothly, and by 12:50 P.M. we are back to normal programing. Small tells me that he is going to lunch. There are a few messages from the other building, including one from Stanton congratulating us on our decision. If I had guessed wrong there would have been a few phone calls too; it goes with the territory.

Stanton did not participate on that occasion, but he often did play a part in such split-minute decisions. At the time of the Dominican crisis on May 2, 1965, the White House had all three networks on tiptoe from 6:30 P.M. until 10. Without any advance information about the content of his speech, we stood by to interrupt *Lassie* at 7 P.M., *My Favorite Martian* at 7:30, *The Ed Sullivan Show* at 8 and *For the People* at 9, and finally *Candid Camera* at 10 P.M. At about 9:15 I talked to Stanton, who had been in Washington to attend a meeting. Did he have any way of discovering the importance of Mr. Johnson's remarks, and would it involve the deteriorating situation in Santo Domingo? In less than ten minutes Stanton called back to say that he had reason to believe that the President was planning to deliver a major speech. At 9:58 P.M., when I gave the signal and the Presidential seal appeared, I felt distinctly queasy on discovering that we were the only network which had elected to cover the speech, especially when I remembered that the loss of advertising in pre-empting *Candid Camera* was well over $100,000. Moreover, the President's first paragraph had no real news meaning, and for several minutes I thought we had guessed wrong; soon, however, the prompter began to function and he got down to his text.

The next day CBS was praised for being the only network to carry live the announcement that we were sending thousands of additional troops to Santo Domingo. That night we had made an educated guess that proved correct, but there were times when we guessed wrong, and Bob Kintner, who was addicted to live coverage regardless of prebroadcast intelligence, had a better attendance record than we did.

Then there was the tortuous decision over the Pope's visit. In early September 1965 our veteran Rome correspondent,

Winston Burdett, sent us word that the long-expected visit of Pope Paul VI was now definitely set for October 4. As the plans were subsequently announced, the first pontiff in history to visit North America would depart Rome shortly after midnight, New York time, arrive at Kennedy International Airport at nine-thirty in the morning, and after a full day of processions, meetings, an address to the United Nations General Assembly, a mass at Yankee Stadium and a visit to the Vatican Pavilion at the World's Fair, would depart again for Rome that night. We immediately joined the other networks in a three-way pool of all technical facilities so that our combined resources, augmented by the New York independent stations, could furnish coverage at various key points around the city stretching over many square miles. CBS's share of the pool budget and our own unilateral coverage would cost nearly $300,000. We also announced, as did NBC, that we would provide coverage of the Pope's arrival and all the important events on his itinerary.

The Pope's visit was obviously going to be one of those momentous news events of our time when the three networks would be competing head-to-head with one another, and each news division was determined to distinguish itself. In mid-September Gordon Manning proposed an intriguing idea: instead of having one of our regular correspondents interpret the mass at Yankee Stadium, why didn't we invite Bishop Sheen to be our "house expert"? I told Manning that it was a brilliant idea but that we should not limit the Bishop's commentary to the mass; we should use his expertise all day. Manning agreed to try to arrange it, but ten minutes later he was back with a long face to tell me what we both should have remembered—that Bishop Sheen was in Rome attending the Ecumenical Council. "Go see him," I said. "I'll go over the weekend," Manning replied. "Tonight, Gordon," I said, and the next morning Manning and the Bishop's lawyer and adviser were in Rome.

Within forty-eight hours Manning cabled that the Bishop had agreed to work with us.

While Manning was in Rome we had our usual Tuesday news luncheon meeting. Stanton was out of town, but Bill Leonard and I briefed Paley on our plans for the Pope's visit. However, when I mentioned that we were thinking about all-day coverage, the conversation died with my sentence still dangling. The chairman said he was not at all convinced that the Pope's visit warranted such extensive programing. Paley, who is known for his generous support of all religious denominations both on and off the air, simply believed that we were overemphasizing the importance of the story and that we could not afford it. Would we do this for a Nehru, a Ben-Gurion or the head of any other state? Leonard and I argued that this was a rare event in history, but that in addition to the pomp and ceremony, the Pontiff's address to the United Nations made it a political as well as a religious mission. Paley agreed with this, and suggested that we telecast live the arrival at the airport and the speech at the United Nations, but that the other events be covered on the evening news broadcasts and perhaps in a special program late at night.

Our inconclusive discussion lasted for the remainder of the luncheon, and it was decided to continue it the next week, when Stanton would be present. I did not have the fortitude to tell the chairman that we had already committed ourselves to the technical pool and that we had arranged for Bishop Sheen to be our consultant and interpreter.

For the next few weeks the debate continued. Stanton participated in the discussions but, as often when the chairman and the news division were in conflict, reserved his judgment. Still, I did sense a growing concern on his part that CBS might be underplaying the event. In one private conversation I told him that we were still hoping for full coverage, and I predicted that we would all end up with "Pope fever" a week before the Pontiff's arrival. I had finally told Paley about Bishop Sheen and he thought this was an imaginative stroke, but it in no way altered his concept of the value of the story. At one meeting, projections were submitted showing that the cost of coverage excluding air time would be approximately $300,000 regardless of the extent of our programing, but the really disturbing figures were the dollars that would be lost by pre-empting the entertainment schedule for the entire day. Schneider had submitted a rough estimate which showed that the company would lose between $900,000 and $1,100,000 in advertising revenue.

Meanwhile NBC had announced full coverage, with no commercial messages scheduled for the entire day. At our final Tuesday meeting prior to October 4 the matter was still not resolved. My colleagues and I were sick.

Then, late on September 29, I was asked to attend another meeting with Stanton and Schneider, but since Paley was absent, no definite conclusions were reached. The next afternoon, four days before the Pope's arrival, we went at it again, this time with the chairman, Stanton, Schneider, Arthur Hull Hayes, the president of CBS Radio, and Craig Lawrence, who represented the CBS owned and operated stations. The debate went back and forth with little progress, and all the obvious arguments for and against all-day coverage were rehashed *ad nauseam*. At one point Paley excused himself to seek "a valued friend's advice." When he returned he told us that his consultant felt that full coverage was not required—indeed that many parts of the country might resent it. Since the chairman had also made the point that saturation coverage of a religious leader's visit might not be in the national interest, I was somewhat concerned by this added opinion, but I doggedly kept pushing for all-day coverage. Finally a decisive comment came from someone not directly involved in the television operation. Arthur Hull Hayes, who had been quiet all afternoon, said simply, "For what it's worth, there are over forty million Catholics in this country, and if we don't broadcast this story properly we may offend them all." Schneider was for as much coverage as possible, but he was new to the job and his position was understandably restrained. Stanton was still silent, and we decided to postpone a final decision until the next day. Later I was told that the chairman's "valued friend" was a CBS public relations consultant.

On Friday, October 1, we finally committed ourselves to full coverage—with qualifications. We would revert to regular programing at 4 P.M. and return to the Pope at 9 P.M. in Yankee Stadium. Later I managed to have this moved up to 8:30 P.M. The major compromise we made was that we would televise the mass live in New York but would use a normal delay pattern elsewhere across the nation. This meant that the Midwestern stations would see the event an hour later and the Far West three hours later.

The Pope's day began at nineteen minutes after midnight, October 4, when all three networks switched to Rome via satellite for his departure from Fiumicino Airport. Early in the morning crowds poured into New York and took up positions all along the planned route of the cavalcade to St. Patrick's Cathedral. Walter Cronkite had flown over to Rome in order to ride back on the Pope's plane, and after the official party had disembarked, he told the television audience about the trip and narrated a film shot on board the plane. As Cronkite rode into town with the Pope's procession, Reasoner and Winston Burdett reported what was happening, assisted by our guest, the Most Reverend—and lucid—Fulton Sheen. They were a superb combination, and for grace, wit and interpretation CBS had no equal that day.

Schneider watched the telecast throughout the day, and after the Pope had ended his address and was ready to leave for a tour of the United Nations, later to attend a private reception with the delegates, he suggested that we go off the air at 4:30 P.M. I pointed out that the Pope was at that moment talking with Secretary of State Rusk, United Nations Ambassador Goldberg, Soviet Foreign Minister Gromyko and French Foreign Minister Couve de Murville, and that I thought we had to stay with the story until he arrived at the Holy Family Church. At 4:30 I begged for a further delay until 5. When Schneider insisted at 4:45 that we call it quits at 5, I told him that the Pope was running behind schedule and that if we could not televise to the network any longer, I at least wanted to continue programing so that our New York station could keep broadcasting. Both Schneider and the New York station agreed to this.

In about an hour the telegrams began coming in from cities which had suddenly lost coverage at 5 P.M. The most caustic one came from the president of the Boston *Herald,* which owns CBS's affiliate in that city. His description of their embarrassment in this large Catholic city, where the Pope's itinerary was unexpectedly interrupted, at having to return to normal programing on one network while the coverage continued on another, was one of those telegrams you save in an asbestos envelope.

The mass that night at a special altar over second base at Yankee Stadium was an inspirational television spectacle, and I was proud of television's part in such an epic. Watching all three networks, I felt that Bishop Sheen added an insight and style which some might consider too rich and too dramatic, but which I found electric. The music echoing back and forth across the cavernous stadium, the small ceremonial bell tinkling its ancient summons, and the batteries of lights and tiny candles formed a dazzling pattern against the colorful red robes and aura of serenity surrounding that indefatigable man of peace.

When the Pope had finally departed on his eleven-thirty plane and we said good night to Bishop Sheen at midnight, I told him that he had helped provide broadcasting with one of its finest, if longest, days. I did not tell him that I had a sheaf of telegrams from the Midwest protesting that CBS had run one hour behind NBC all night long because of the decision to use a delay pattern.

The next day at lunch with Paley and Stanton, both of whom were enthusiastic about our coverage, I decided that a brief post-mortem might be helpful. I described the harrowing case history of our telecast and suggested to the chairman that we ought to try to find a better way to make such decisions in advance. If the news division had guessed wrong or if it had rained that day, I would have been in trouble for committing all those funds and facilities, and for employing the services of Bishop Sheen. (We had offered to pay a suitable honorarium to the Society for the Propagation of the Faith in return for his help, and if we had not been able to use his commentary extensively, I would have had difficulty in justifying it.)

Paley was most critical; he was disturbed that I had committed our facilities and money without his or Stanton's approval. I answered that it was my job to go out on a limb, even at the risk of being wrong occasionally, and that if we had waited until the Thursday before the Pope's arrival to join the network pool and arrange for Bishop Sheen's help, it would have been too late. What I was trying to establish was that the news division, which was involved only in news and public affairs decisions and was not distracted by the myriad problems of the entertainment schedule, the FCC, diversification and so forth, ought to be able to count on its recommendations for unscheduled news events being accepted—especially when the company usually ended up adopting the course we had suggested in the first place.

"You mean," said the chairman, "that you committed us to all that coverage at the time I was against it?"

"Yes, sir. I had to take that chance or we would have been left out in the cold."

"You had no right to proceed. Your job was to convince top management, or not to do it."

Paley needs no sermon from me on news judgment. He was making decisions that built CBS News and prepared America for its role in World War II when I was still a radio novitiate in Providence. One of my favorite Paley anecdotes concerns a news decision he made in 1929 when Prime Minister Ramsay MacDonald of Britain visited the United States and made a special address to the American people under an exclusive arrangement with NBC. When Paley heard about this he protested vehemently, to no avail. Not only was he willing to give up the entertainment schedule for that time period, but to dramatize his protest, he ordered the CBS network to go silent and remain off the air for the period of MacDonald's speech.

During the Munich crisis and all through the war, Paley and CBS never hesitated to interrupt the radio network schedule for special programs from Berlin, London and Paris. In those days nobody bothered to figure out how much advertising revenue was lost. Even in the early days of television all one required was a high batting average in news judgment, but in 1965 the formula dictated that news judgment be weighed against displaced revenue.

As I sat there with Paley and Stanton, going over this ground for the nth time, the chairman pointed out that our budget for unscheduled news was already in the red, and that the displacement of advertising because of the "news explosion" could get out of hand. He was as disturbed with our haphazard manner of decision-making as I was—but for different reasons. Prosperous as CBS was, he declared, we had limited funds, and we simply could not do everything we might wish without affecting our earnings. "We're still running a business," he said, "and we aren't going to be able to support the kind of news organization you want if we can't stay economically healthy."

The conversation that followed did more to make me understand the agony of being the head of a vast broadcasting empire than had all the other experiences of sixteen years. "Mr. Paley, let me ask you what may be a naïve question. Why do we have to make more money every year? There's an old Wall Street expression: 'The tree doesn't grow to the sky.' "

"That's a pretty good question," said the chairman, "but we have many small shareholders across the country and within the company. Some of our employees have worked for us for a long time. Their entire security is tied up in their equity; many of them have stock options. Management's obligation is to protect the interests of those stockholders."

I resisted the urge to talk about what I have always thought of as the *other* stockholders, the one hundred ninety-five million citizens who grant CBS and the other broadcasters the franchise to use their air; I had once engaged in such a debate with Stanton in the presence of the full advisory board, and it had left scars on both of us.

Paley went on to expound the theory that if the management didn't maintain its growth and profits, it ran the risk of losing control of the company.

Then the chairman of the board, who owns over a million and a half shares of CBS stock, was silent for a moment; looking at Stanton, he said, "I suppose the mistake we made was in ever going public." This was a reference to the stock capitalization of the company, which had previously been fully controlled by Paley and other top officers of CBS. (CBS stock was not listed on the New York Stock Exchange until 1937, although there was some public ownership as early as 1932.) At other times there had been comments about the freedom of the Sulzberger family, which owns so much of the *New York Times,* and the

Bingham family, which owns the Louisville *Courier-Journal* and its broadcast operations; without the demands of outsiders in search of profits and stock growth, such companies need not be so responsive to shareholders.

That conversation provides a clue to the agony that plagues honorable men who must constantly try to balance the public good and private need. Nobody in that room doubted in his heart that broadcasting the Pope's visit or Sir Winston's funeral was in the public interest, nor that it might adversely affect earnings to a degree—though it might be argued that the long-range stability of the company was best served by assuming such public-service obligations. The question is, What is enough profit? And conversely, What is enough public service? If profits had stayed at $1.27 a share, where they were in 1958 when Stanton said that CBS would have to work hard to stay at that level, all the public service we could have conceived in our wildest dreams would have been within our means. But 1958's profits had to be increased through the years, and by the end of 1965 the "proper" balance between revenues and public service had permitted the net income, like the company's growth, nearly to double, to $2.47 a share. Too many unscheduled news programs could drive those figures down, could make Wall Street change its optimistic evaluation of CBS as a high-growth stock, could impel those mutual funds, foundations and universities to invest in something else.

In an effort to reduce those costs of which Paley spoke—and of which we were all too well aware—we occasionally tried "selective" coverage of unscheduled news events, and I publicly defended this system. But the flaw in this is that though full-day coverage of an event does not always maintain a high level of interest, the caliber and content of the regularly scheduled daytime programs one returns to can only induce schizophrenia. It makes little sense to interrupt, say, a space mission to return to ancient cartoons, situation comedies that have been broadcast half a dozen times before, or the soap operas whose plots move imperceptibly in the time it takes a space capsule to orbit half the earth.

Moreover, selective coverage is particularly painful when one has a competitor like NBC. Besides its policy of going live for almost every big news event, NBC had one additional advantage, mentioned earlier: because of its lower day-time audiences and sales, the cost of interrupting the schedule for news was far less than that of CBS. (CBS, which prides itself on the fact that it has thirteen of the top fifteen day-time programs, may now be realizing even larger profits from its day-time operations than it does from its evening prime time.) As a result an unfortunate pattern developed: because NBC could more easily afford to cover all of an unscheduled news event, the news-oriented viewer would choose that network on such occasions, while the "escapist" housewife stayed with CBS. Thus, our share of the audience grew larger except when something vital was taking place; then NBC, with maximum coverage, usually had the maximum audience.

My worst blunder as president of CBS News was not due to an error of judgment but to a lack of will power and stamina. The Republican Convention in San Francisco in July 1964 was held during my first few months as president of the news division, and although the newly formed election unit had done well in the 1962 off-year elections and in most of the primaries, this was its first national convention, and NBC did a superior job. It has been argued by many observers that no network adequately covered the Goldwater takeover of the G.O.P. apparatus; in any case, we lagged far behind in content and audience.

Paley, who was in San Francisco throughout the convention, agreed that the final two days showed definite improvement. I remember saying to him as we left the Cow Palace for the last time that this was a new team and that if we didn't panic but allowed the election unit to gain experience, we would eventually have a seasoned organization, a luxury that the news division had not had for some time. Back in New York I found that Stanton agreed with me, and Bill Leonard and the election unit immediately set about correcting the mistakes made in San Francisco.

I believe that what aggravated the situation was a full-page story in *Variety* which heralded NBC's overwhelming victory and predicted that nothing could stop Kintner until after 1968. I was summoned to a meeting with Paley and Stanton, and after an exhaustive post-mortem the suggestion was made by the chairman that perhaps the problem was Cronkite. It was true that Walter had not been at his best in San Francisco; he had been uncomfortable about sharing the anchor booth with Sevareid, who did his analysis from there, and occasionally he had been unresponsive to the producers' instruction to switch to other correspondents on the floor. But the decisive difference had been the sprightly staying power of Huntley and Brinkley, and some aggressive reporting from the floor of the convention hall by NBC's Chancellor, Vanocur and McGee.

When my superiors suggested that we replace Cronkite with a new team, Roger Mudd and Bob Trout, it struck me as a debatable solution, but I agreed to think about it. At subsequent meetings I realized that it was not so much a suggestion as a command. Two of the other executives in the news division with whom I discussed the proposal were violently opposed to it. My own reaction, which I expressed to Paley and Stanton, was that the proposed change resembled CBS's panic in 1960, which had resulted in the unsuccessful Cronkite-Murrow partnership. Furthermore, the shift would upset the morale of the election unit and the news division, where Walter was much respected, and might humiliate him so that he would feel impelled to resign. Lastly and most important, change merely for the sake of change was not likely to work. Mudd and Trout were two correspondents in whom I had unlimited faith, but nothing was going to stop Huntley and Brinkley at the Democratic Convention in August, and it would be better to stay with the combination we had, gain experience and rely on the lessons learned in San Francisco.

After it became obvious to me that I was expected to replace Walter, I spent the entire afternoon walking around New York. It seemed to me then that I had little choice; I was convinced that if I resisted this drastic step, the future of the news division and my own authority to make long-range changes in the news division would be jeopardized. I now believe that if I had stood firm and refused to substitute anyone for Cronkite I could have prevailed. At the time, Cronkite was in California with his family; because it was unthinkable not to let him hear the news face to face, Bill Leonard and I flew out to meet him at the Los Angeles airport. By the time we got there I had his demotion all couched in euphemisms, and had conceived a plan by which Walter would play a dominant role from the convention floor. But he knew exactly what was happening, and in the way he took the demotion, he turned my worst moment into his finest.

There were so many stories in the press about the change that Walter was finally forced to hold a news conference in New York in which he said that the decision was strictly a matter of ratings and that he understood the company's position. Our announcement of the shift employed some fancy language about the uniqueness of the Democratic Convention requiring a new kind of coverage because its Presidential candidate had in effect already been selected, but we did not fool anybody and it hurt our credibility as a news organization; as many people pointed out, if CBS had won the ratings in San Francisco, Cronkite would still have been there. The cruelest blow came from Hal Humphrey of the Los Angeles *Times*. Under the caption "There's No Business Like TV News Business," he wrote:

"Last week's scuttling of Walter Cronkite . . . put him on the same level as a comic whose jokes weren't registering high enough on the laugh meter."

In point of fact, Mudd and Trout did a remarkable job at Atlantic City in August. The entire unit had spirit, and the notoriety of the sudden midcourse maneuver almost brought us even with NBC in the ratings some of the time.

Cronkite came out of the affair a bigger man than before, and I learned how to apply the courage of my convictions at least enough to insist that he be the national editor at the November elections. Mudd, Trout, Reasoner, Mike Wallace, Sevareid and Louis Harris, the political pollster who was one of the developers of the Vote Profile Analysis system, all played pivotal roles on that occasion, and the whole unit achieved a comprehension and clarity unmatched in any election night. This single broadcast may have been the turning point for us. We lost the rating battle, but not by much, and nobody cared, not even Aubrey, who called me at four o'clock in the morning to congratulate us.

New Hand on the Big Switch

For all the endless meetings and struggles for allocations, I relished the presidency of the news division. Though it was not as creatively satisfying as producing *CBS Reports,* it was rewarding because I was able to help lead a comeback of considerable proportions. In those two years we did not reach all the goals we had set, but we stopped losing. Walter Cronkite's news program, a better journalistic job than its NBC competition, passed Huntley and Brinkley both in size of its audience and in its serious interpretation of the news, particularly Vietnam. Our Washington bureau, previously flabby and incohesive after a series of four bureau chiefs in four years, became, under Bill Small, one of the most respected news organizations in Washington.

In the crucial area of special reports and documentaries, we not only maintained the leadership of the past, but we were sold out and finally stumbled into the black. *CBS Reports* and its alternating broadcasts on Tuesday nights were fully sponsored, and we had letters from one advertiser offering to buy more time if we could find a place in the schedule for more programs.

One of our most publicized successes happened because of a speeding ticket I received. I used to travel on the West Side Highway between Riverdale and Manhattan as often as four times a day to be on hand for a major newsbreak or family birthday party or school play, and on one such midnight ride I was given my third summons in an eighteen-month period. There is an excellent New York State regulation that all such chronic offenders must report to the Motor Vehicle Bureau to hear a patrolman's lecture and take a brief written examination. I passed, and went back to the office determined to give the test, or rather a more graphic television equivalent of it, to the television audience.

After the program *Time* wrote that "when Fred Friendly has a headache, he thinks the whole world is in pain." Still, almost thirty million people saw "The National Drivers' Test," which may mean that more people took an examination simultaneously than ever before. The broadcast has become an annual event, and for the first time that I can remember, we had advertisers bidding against one another for sponsorship.

After "The National Drivers' Test" we gave other exams on health, taxes, citizenship and current events, and NBC paid us the compliment of trying—unsuccessfully—to launch a series of its own. Such programs, testing the responses and awareness of millions of viewers and increasing their knowledge of a subject like public health, are a useful tool to the broadcast journalist, but they can never take the place of the hard-hitting, point-of-view documentary. However, as two-way automated-feedback testing techniques are developed, such mass examinations could play an important role in educational television.

Because of the remarkable sales record of Tuesday night and the success of the Cronkite evening news broadcast, the CBS News balance sheet improved to such an extent that though our annual budget was at an all-time high in my last year at CBS, we came within $500,000 of breaking even. It was rather ironic that the news division president, who was known as "the last of the great spenders," and who had once chartered a special jet to fly the tapes of Churchill's funeral from Shannon Airport to

Nova Scotia, helped CBS News to achieve its most economically successful year in an age of inflated television costs. In part this was due to David Klinger, vice-president for administration, who had made my life miserable as a producer, taught me how to read corporate millions without the last three zeros and brought order to our budgets. Thanks largely to him, one of the last and nicest things Paley ever said to me was to compliment us on our "remarkable record in numbers," both financial and in the ratings.

I worked a long day, from seven o'clock, when I received the first calls from the news room about, say, special footage from Vietnam for the early-morning news shows, until one or two the next morning. As one of my children said, "You don't do anything now but dictate memos and talk on the telephone." I was a maximum viewer and listener and a constant heckler. I encouraged, cajoled and raised hell about scratched film, slow cues, sloppy reporting and correspondents who had not done their homework. I fought a few battles, winning some and losing others, to make it possible for correspondents to do the kind of yeasty news analysis that might make a difference. I strayed too often into producers' control rooms, second-guessed too many colleagues, prompted a few false starts, insisted on last-minute changes that probably made no difference, made Charles Collingwood the Atlantic Ocean's first commuter, needled Sevareid into doing a news analysis five nights a week, and ordered Ernie Leiser, the executive producer of the Cronkite program, to use it every night. Once Sevareid, on the eve of a reluctant trip to Santo Domingo, where he did a fine job, said, "The trouble with you, Friendly, is that you don't realize that hypochondriacs get sick too." And another colleague complained, "Friendly, you'll never have a nervous breakdown, but you sure are a carrier."

Most of all I looked and cared and made decisions, for in broadcast journalism, decisions have to be made at the rate of ten an hour and a bad decision is better than none at all. You live by your batting average, and you are as good as your confidence in your people—and therefore their confidence in themselves. On the day I left CBS the same man who had called me "a carrier" said, "You made it here because you believed in us so much that we believed in ourselves."

One area where I failed everybody was in not being able to do something about the nightly 11 o'clock news program, whose inadequacy, particularly during the newspaper strikes, the blackout and the subway strike, caused us so much embarrassment in New York. The constant criticism all of us in the news division heard almost every place we went, and one constantly reiterated in the newspapers, was: "When are you going to do something about the eleven o'clock news?" I would tell critics that the news division's responsibility stopped at 11 P.M., and that the New York local news at that hour was produced by our autonomous New York operation, Channel 2. But after a while I realized that no one other than scholars of the curious CBS table of organization would know the difference between CBS News and WCBS-TV.

Over the years Channel 2, New York, has been the most profitable individual station operation in the world. It is no secret that some stations make well in excess of $10,000,000 a year, and Channel 2's advertising rates are among the highest. At one time the profit from this one station, I am told, was almost as large as that of another entire network. In spite of this, the Channel 2 news operation has been a cause of unhappiness to almost everyone in the CBS hierarchy, Paley and Stanton included. In 1963 the management had separated the Channel 2 news operation from CBS News because it was decided that both should be autonomous. This meant that there were two CBS news units in New York, often competing with each other. It also meant that the head of CBS News and his staff of editors had no authority over the flagship station in our largest city.

When the secession took place, Channel 2 set up its own independent operation and hired news editors and correspondents from local stations all over the country. Many of the new men were only qualified to be a desk assistant in our news room, though some had considerable potential to develop if given the proper training and experience. Suddenly New Yorkers were watching a new generation of scrubbed young men who did not know Mosholu Parkway from Gowanus Canal. More important, it was inexcusable of Channel 2 to turn its 11 P.M. news into a local edition, when millions of New Yorkers who couldn't get home in time for Cronkite at 7 P.M. were watching their first news of the day.

Like "selective coverage," "local autonomy" is one of those phrases which does not mean what it is purported to mean, but I must confess that to this day I am not certain why the division between CBS News and Channel 2 continues. The theory is that it involves money, but this does not make sense because the duplication of these news units costs well over $300,000 annually, and an integrated operation would end the ridiculous custom of sending two competing units from one company to cover the same event.

It is possible that CBS News' known opposition to the excessive insertion of commercials in regularly scheduled news programs was a factor. Curiously, standard network practices permit only three minutes of commercials in, say, *The Beverly Hillbillies* because it is scheduled between 7:30 and 11 P.M. The Cronkite and Huntley-Brinkley news programs are included in the day-time pattern. Since "prime" time ends at 11 P.M., in 1966 Channel 2 news at that hour has seven minutes of commercials and as many as five additional sponsor identifications. Perhaps it was because it was known that CBS News would not agree to any such debasement of news and personnel that we were not permitted to operate Channel 2's New York news program.

I never discussed this problem publicly, and for eighteen months avoided talking about it with my immediate staff or with Paley and Stanton; I was convinced that if we continued to improve and the local station continued to flounder, we would be asked to step in. But after the newspaper strike of 1965, the blackout and the subway strike, I made reintegration a matter of priority in my meetings with the chairman and the president. Unfortunately, I never received much encouragement; when I asked Stanton why Kintner and McAndrew, who unified all NBC news operations in 1962, didn't have the same problem about autonomy, he replied, "I don't know, but someday they are liable to lose their license over that." Once, at the end of a long, unrewarding conversation on the subject, Paley did say, "Nothing is forever, you know, Fred." I replied, "Well, when it happens, I hope somebody will remember to say, 'Too bad Fred couldn't have lived to see it.' "

Another point of irritation between the television network and the news division was the reporting of sports.

Schneider belonged to the school of thought that sports broadcasters were announcers, a sort of human score board or house voice on the public-address system at the ball park. When an automobile sponsor agreed to buy minutes in the Cronkite evening news in 1965, Schneider and his sales manager told me it was with the proviso that there be a five-minute sports package at the end of the broadcast. Schneider wanted a sports announcer of Jack Whitaker's caliber, whom he had known in Philadelphia, or Frank Gifford. I happen to be a Gifford fan and friend, and if he is ever permitted to be a newsman instead of an announcer hired and selected by football management and doing commercials for beer and gasoline, his expertise and grace might make him a fine sports analyst; but the idea of imposing five minutes of sports on an already crowded evening news program, which had only twenty-three minutes of actual news time, was out of the question. Even if I had ordered it, Cronkite and Leiser would have resisted it. I did agree to try to program the last five minutes of Cronkite with so-called "back of the book" news, which would include sports when the story warranted it, but I refused to hire a sports announcer to do it. Paley and Stanton witnessed some heated debates between Schneider and me on the subject, and Jack wrote me some rough memos about my risking $5,000,000 worth of billing.

The essence of the conflict is that broadcast news cannot be a mature form of journalism when it operates on a double standard for sports news and other news. Of course sports is news, but if sportscasters overlook, say, the mistakes of a referee when the isolated playback clearly indicates that he erred, or if the sports announcer is not permitted to say that a game is dull or is urged to build up tension in a one-sided contest in order to build ratings, he is affecting the credibility of all broadcast reporting.

Twice in my tenure as president I observed Paley's anger at close range, and though in one episode I was the target, I admired him greatly on both occasions.

The first involved James Aubrey when I was attending my first television-network budget meeting. These annual rituals, complete with printed presentations and color slides, are rehearsed and programed not only to secure budget approval but to defend profit schedules. At the meeting Aubrey, explaining the bonanza year of 1963 and his projections for 1964, spent more than an hour showing that entertainment sales ratings and the gross were higher than ever. All these figures were in black, but the news costs, which reduced profits, were always in fire-engine red and underlined. At least five times—and each time he spoke the words, red figures flashed in the darkened board room—Aubrey said, "You can see, Mr. Chairman, how much higher our profits could have been this year if it had not been for the drain of news." Each time I gritted my teeth and silently reread the reminder I had scribbled to myself before entering the meeting: "Don't interrupt and don't lose your temper."

I intended to make a strong, restrained statement when Aubrey had finished his presentation, but it wasn't necessary. Paley complimented Aubrey on his overall figures, and then told him and everyone in the room how offended he had been at the constant use of the news division as a whipping boy. "It should not be forgotten," he said, "that news and public affairs helped build CBS and everything we are today . . . Without it we might not be able to continue." At the close of the meeting Aubrey left the room without speaking to anyone, and I later wrote Paley a note of thanks.

The only serious reprimand that I ever received from Paley was delivered with such verve and for so good a reason that at the time I did not know whether to resent it or thank him. A one-hour documentary called "The Berkeley Rebels" employed what Stanton and Paley believed was an excessive amount of background jazz and dramatic effects, which made the program stimulating but not necessarily a news-oriented presentation. Looking back on it now, it seems to me that Stanton and Paley were too responsive to the prebroadcast protestations of President Clark Kerr of the University of California, who was understandably nervous about any further publicity about the Berkeley campus. It was for this reason that they had made one of their very rare requests for an advance screening of the broadcast.

Nevertheless, I also believe now that Paley and Stanton were more right than wrong. Bill Leonard and I ordered many changes in the final editing of "The Berkeley Rebels" and removed some of the cinema techniques to which the management objected. Arthur Barron, one of our most creative and responsible young producers, had accurately portrayed the circumstances and issues of student revolt, but in so doing had allowed himself certain license which threatened the program's integrity. After considerable struggle we made enough changes to nearly satisfy Paley and Stanton—and to infuriate producer Barron. At one point, after I had reiterated to Paley my faith and trust in the producer, the chairman interrupted me forcefully: "You have in your hands the most sacred trust that CBS has. Your job is to keep CBS News holy—and I expect you to do it." I will always remember that the most inspiring sentence the chairman of the board ever said to me was spoken in anger.

One concept that has never quite been formulated at CBS or in broadcast journalism in general concerns news analysis, and many a luncheon with Paley and Stanton lasted until mid-afternoon when we discussed the fine line between interpretation and editorializing. Paley wanted more interpretation, but he asked me to consider retaining a stable of carefully selected outside commentators from newspapers and magazines who would provide a spectrum of balanced commentary. I opposed this on the grounds that it would put our own correspondents in an untenable position; why should newspaper columnists be allowed to express opinions on our air when they were not?

Stanton, who has the most literal, exacting mind I have ever been exposed to, wanted our policy spelled out in black and white, but his ideas of radio and television news reporting are much like those governing the newspaper wire services. Just as he disliked the word "show" in connection with news, he frowned on the use of the word "editorial" as applied to such traditional journalistic terms as "judgment" or "decision." Paley, I believe, sincerely wanted analysis because he knew that responsible news interpretation was as much a part of journalism as raw facts. But he still wore the scars of the Murrow and Smith altercations, and once when I used Elmer Davis as an example of the kind of low-key, highly disciplined breed of news analysts we needed, he answered, "You don't know the kind of fights I used to have with Davis over those five-minute commentaries of his." Some people close to the commentator believe that he did not return to CBS after his service with the Office of War Information because of this friction, and there are others who wonder whether the company really wanted Davis to return.

Sevareid and Collingwood had developed a kind of terse cryptanalysis that was well suited to the Cronkite news program, but their best work occurred during extended special reports that required reflective interpretation on Vietnam, the Dominican situation or civil rights. Nevertheless, news analyses of the Watts riots or a Mississippi freedom march continually aggravated the situation between the management and the news division.

The guideline on news analysis which I laid down for editors in the news room was that a full understanding of certain stories required interpretation, and that where an assignment called for a seasoned correspondent to provide interpretation, his responsibility was to stop short of making up the viewers' minds on a recommended course of action.

This bothered Stanton, who believed that the audience had a right to make up its own mind about, say, McCarthy without being told about the man's distortions of the truth, and that in a documentary (which is a form of interpretation) on the U.N., the foes of that organization had every right to have their views equally represented. Over the last two decades there have been several examples of interpretative broadcasting—among them Murrow on Korea, Sevareid on John Foster Dulles' foreign policy, Howard K. Smith on Alabama and Morley Safer on Vietnam—which had embarrassed and upset Stanton, but which have won these men awards and recognition.

Broadcast journalism needs more, not less analysis. To take only one example: Vietnam today is not only the first war that television has been able to cover fully; it is also the news analysts' greatest challenge. No conflict in modern history has been obscured by so many subtleties and implications; in Southeast Asia, black-and-white words like "victory," "defeat," "majority," "democracy" and "appeasement" have relatively little meaning, and the complexities and nuances of the situation demand interpretation. As James Reston has said, today's reporter is forced to become an educator more concerned with explaining the news than with being the first on the scene.

Stanton, with his well-developed sense of order, who had never produced a news program or edited a newspaper—just as I had never met a payroll—believed that a new fact was in itself news, and that any serious attempt to grade and assess such facts was close to editorializing. I maintained that a raw fact, unexplained, is not really news and that turning broadcast circuits into conduits for unanalyzed information is not only bad journalism but even slightly dishonest. Occasionally Stanton would talk about using news readers like those of the BBC, where the writer and the speaker are often separate personalities. He wanted no help in making up his mind about Santo Domingo or Medicare. I argued that I did not want our correspondents to make up our viewers' and listeners' minds on a course of action, but that for Sevareid not to add perspective on the Santo Domingo situation, or for Collingwood not to accent the contradictions in Vietnam, or for Marvin Kalb to ignore what he knew to be the facts in favor of a State Department handout would be more of a news slant than the hard facts alone.

I do agree that the science of news analysis is not something to be entrusted to every reporter regardless of his enterprise. Newspapers have always differentiated between those skilled correspondents from whom they invite analysis and those who are expected simply to report the basic news story. I believe that Paley understood this distinction and would have liked to see it drawn on our broadcasts; Stanton, however, always wanted the differences spelled out in a policy paper. Several patient attempts to do this by Herb Mitgang, executive editor of CBS News, failed to elicit a reaction of any kind from the president. When I asked him about a new draft, his only comment would be: "It didn't go far enough."

The fact is that journalists have always despaired of defining the difference between reporting and interpretation too precisely, though Ed Klauber came close in a paragraph he wrote in 1939 that established the standards for CBS reporting in World War II:

> What news analysts are entitled to do and should do is to elucidate and illuminate the news out of common knowledge, or special knowledge possessed by them or made available to them by this organization through its sources. They should point out the facts on both sides, show contradictions with the known record, and so on. They should bear in mind that in a democracy it is important that people not only should know but should understand, and it is the analyst's function to help the listener to understand, to weigh, and to judge, but not to do the judging for him.

In public policy statements Stanton has delineated the difference in similar terms: "Analysis is concerned with things as they are, or as they were, or, judging from present facts, what they probably will be. An editorial is concerned with things as they ought to be." The problem lies in the semantics. For example, Howard Smith's Birmingham analysis—" 'The only thing necessary for the triumph of evil is for good men to do nothing' "—was not an editorial by Stanton's characterization; yet, admonitions such as "Drive Carefully Over the Labor Day Weekend" or "Get Out and Vote" literally do fit his definition. Terms of reference in a critical analysis of Mao Tse-tung, De Gaulle, George Wallace or Robert McNamara are inevitably predicated on the commentator's distance from his subject. It is far easier to be critical of De Gaulle or Johnson from a distance of three thousand miles than it is in Paris and Washington, respectively. Whether we like it or not, geography and the temper of the times lend license to news analysts in all media.

News analysis is a matter of good judgment and reliance on serious journalists whose restraint you trust. Reducing it to paper any further than the above is much like defining a partnership in marriage. Once you determine that you require news analysts, and that, say, Elmer Davis, Ed Morgan, Howard Smith, Eric Sevareid or Charles Collingwood is the man you want for the job, then you learn to live with his interpretations —and occasionally to be embarrassed by them. The analyst is not going to be on target every time, and occasionally he may step over the line. Even then, responsible editors will usually be able to convince the correspondent to moderate his copy enough to live within the spirit of the policy. In my one hundred weeks as president of CBS News, no correspondent had one of those chronic face-to-face encounters with the management that had plagued CBS through the years, and I believe that the news division's reporters felt that the opportunity to do more meaningful interpretation had been partially restored.

In discussions with my colleagues, in public speeches and in my frequent defense of such analysis to my superiors, I stressed the fact that news without interpretation only provided, as Murrow once put it, "the illusion of power without responsibility." As a graphic example, I would often use three different treatments of the same story—a 1964 campaign stop of President Johnson—to define the differences between reporting, analyzing and editorializing.

A straight news broadcast might read as follows:

Providence, September 28

The largest crowd in Rhode Island history thundered its welcome to President Lyndon Johnson today on narrow Fountain

Street as his motorcade was engulfed by a solid mass of humanity estimated by police to be in excess of 150,000. Repeatedly the candidate, obviously stimulated by the enthusiasm of the crowd, stepped out of his open convertible to shake hundreds of outstretched hands. Several times the President became separated from his Secret Service guards, who were obviously concerned about his safe return to the motorcade. By evening the Chief Executive's right hand was blistered and had to be bandaged.

A news analysis of the same story might say:

Twenty-four hours after the publication of the Warren Commission Report, which stressed the difficulty of protecting the President and asked for new safeguards for Presidential motorcades, Lyndon Johnson gave a practical example of the dilemma of protecting a chief of state when he is a candidate in motion. In the narrow streets of Providence today, the President of the United States, emotionally stirred by the roar of 150,000 people, left the comparative safety of his motorcade at least six times to shake the hands of Rhode Island voters. Mr. Johnson's right hand was visibly sore, and later Band-Aids were required to cover his blisters. Several times the Secret Service guards despaired of retrieving him from the crowd, and one officer was heard to remark, "One more day like this and we can't be held responsible for his safety."

The United States government, which has lost four Presidents by assassination in the last one hundred years, has just been given suggestions by the Warren Commission on the restructuring of federal lines of responsibility for protecting the Chief Executive. Today's events indicated some difficulties not anticipated in the Commission's report: Candidate Johnson, no more than any other politician running for election, is not going to keep a safe distance from 150,000 voters.

When Johnson was asked last winter if he always followed the instructions of the Secret Service he replied, "I want to be a people's President, and in order to do so, you have to see the

> people and talk to them and know something about them and not be too secluded. I think they'd feel safer if the President kept 100 yards distance from every human being, but that is not practical."
>
> Candidate Johnson's conviction that elections are not won by staying in the White House has much truth to it. But it is also a fact that a dead candidate never got elected to anything either.

This last passage has purposely been written on the borderline between news analysis and editorial, and because of the human factor in broadcasting it is an example of how unenforceable an ironclad written directive can be. If delivered over a dramatic film sequence of a Presidential assassination, or depending on the sequence preceding or following it, or if spoken in an hortative style, these words could be editorial; if spoken quietly and with an understanding of the pressures and excitement of a campaign, they could be interpretative.

An editorial on this subject might be something like the following:

> The spectacle of the President of the United States courting the roar of the crowds in a Providence street and flirting with the threat of violence or even understandable hysteria, is enough to chill Americans who have seen four Presidents shot down in the past century and witnessed attempts on three other Presidents or nominees in the last fifty-two years. The disturbing element about Mr. Johnson's car-hopping this afternoon was that it occurred the day after the warning of the Warren Commission Report, which clearly defined the difficulty of protecting Presidents during motorcades.
>
> This nation spends millions of dollars on special jet planes, trains and other facilities to protect its President; hundreds of dedicated Secret Service agents stand ready to risk their lives to defend the life of the man whose continuous service to the country and the world cannot be measured as less than the safety of

the Republic. Lyndon Johnson must remember that the ultimate protector of the President of the United States is the President himself. The fact that it is his own life he risks makes it no less an obligation than if it were any other national asset he might be jeopardizing, and if he himself won't protect the life of the Chief Executive, legislation will be required to lay down some guidelines. We would support such a law.

Individual stations have a mandate to editorialize, and Stanton has been a forceful advocate of this. But most stations claim that they have limited or no credentials to editorialize on international and national issues, and the networks, which have no "license" to do so, do not editorialize. Therefore, at a time when many Americans get most of their news from broadcast sources, it is essential to fill the void between a "just stick to the facts, boys" attitude and recommending a definite course of action. Abdication of this opportunity because of technicalities or fear of overstepping the line is to "throw the reader into a sea of facts and leave him on his own whether he can swim or not," as Lester Markel, associate editor of the *New York Times,* once put it.

Part of the job of running CBS News involved the radio network; specifically, 65 percent of the network radio schedule was news. Apart from Arthur Godfrey, who is still a one-man broadcasting system, news was the radio network's raison d'être. The tragedy was that news was blatantly secondary to the commercials, merely a filler to separate the layers of advertising. When Ed Murrow once asked a radio executive the reason for the rash of five-minute weekend news programs, the response was: "It seems to be the only thing we can sell."

CBS has ten-minute news reports every hour on weekdays, but the radio network and its affiliates have created such a complex schedule for their news, sandwiched in between commercials, that the correspondents have to be timing experts who literally do two or three shows at a time. One day in the Berkshires I tried to listen to Mike Wallace on two radios—one from Albany, one from Pittsfield. On one station Wallace ran two and a half minutes longer than on the other, and I heard three news stories from Pittsfield which weren't in the Albany broadcast. In all, the two live reports were identical only about two-thirds of the time, and if I had been monitoring a station in Illinois or California, I might have found the discrepancy even larger.

The explanation for this lies in the fact that many radio news shows are constructed with "soft news" openings and intervals, so that national or local commercials can be inserted. Individual stations also terminate the programs at will for local news and advertisements. Wallace and the other radio correspondents have no way of knowing how much of a given report their listeners in Washington, New Orleans and Denver have heard.

The most painful part of this adulteration is that there are many kinds of stories radio can do faster and with more time for interpretation than television. But the criteria for getting most regularly scheduled shows on the air is: "Can you sell it?" Network radio, which in the late forties was the rich older brother of television, is now a starved relative by comparison. Instead of being allowed to complement television by attempting to cover subjects that the visual medium cannot do as well, or doesn't have the time for, CBS Radio as a separate division must show a profit or perish. Lee Hanna, who made a valiant effort at CBS to rebuild the radio news schedule, was continually fighting an uphill battle, and even his pleas to do documentaries on budgets of $500 were turned down as extravagant.

The finest radio news report now on the air, aside from Ed Morgan's nightly analysis on ABC, is the CBS *World News Roundup*, and I constantly tried to extend it to thirty minutes. But recently the vice-president in charge of the CBS owned and operated radio stations was quoted by *Variety* as proclaiming that the *Roundup* is a relic of another era, and he implied that it should not be on the schedule. Nevertheless, some radio stations, such as WCCO, Minneapolis, continue to fight the good fight, and James Seward, who was at CBS almost from the beginning, has striven for many years to retain the medium's dignity and vitality.

Network radio is, I have always believed, about as secure as Arthur Godfrey's health; CBS, the nearest proximation to a bona-fide radio network system may well vanish with his retirement. But at this writing I am convinced that the death rattle of network radio is more than a murmur; its untimely demise could well predate Godfrey's retirement. The tragedy is that in a moment of national emergency this medium, which has limited power requirements, would be far more crucial than television. One thinks of the night of the power blackout in 1965, when for six dark hours radio was the difference between panic and order. Permitting network radio to die because it is less profitable than other uses of the franchise is like permitting a coast-to-coast railroad system to be dismantled. But this medium deserves a book of its own, and if I ever write another, it will be about radio's days of glory and of how it was permitted to become a shrill, strident barker, beating out, in Marshall McLuhan's phrase, its "tribal magic."

Although it has become difficult to uphold a high standard of broadcast practices in radio and television, the news division's insistence on maintaining the separation between sponsor and program has been sacred, and in my tenure as president the support from Paley and Stanton was usually unflinching, even when it cost the company money. With Paley's and Stanton's solid backing, CBS has never permitted a sponsor's advertising logo to appear on the anchor desk during a space shoot or a national election. Other networks do so, but we stuck to our guns even when very desirable advertisers said that without the trademark they wouldn't advertise.

We also turned down many an advertiser because they wanted the right of approval on subject matter. Moreover, no sponsor ever saw a broadcast until it was on the air. Several computer companies wanted to sponsor documentaries about automation; our firm response was that if and when CBS News decided to broadcast such a program, no manufacturer involved in the marketing of such a product could sponsor it. Several firms manufacturing rockets for the space agency were constantly offering to sponsor broadcasts on space exploration, and a large automobile company could not understand why we would not let them advertise on "The National Drivers' Test" program. Once we rejected the commercials on a broadcast about the Polaris submarine because the advertiser, a cigarette company, had slyly placed a model of the Polaris missile on their pitchman's desk in an effort to identify their product with the program's content. The announcer had to fly in from Hollywood to retape the commercials the night before the show, and CBS agreed to reimburse the sponsor the $10,000 for the substitute advertisements.

Our reasons for this attitude were twofold. A sponsor's commercial appearing in a documentary about his field, whether space, medicine or automobiles, gives him a decided advantage over his competitors and makes the entire hour appear to be one long commercial for his product. But perhaps even more important in the long run, if certain subjects are scheduled because they are sponsored, it follows, conversely, that certain other programs might not be broadcast because they are unsponsorable. That is why I always opposed buying serious news documentaries made outside the company. An independent producer, no matter how lofty his motivations, is going to choose subjects which he knows he can sell. By extension, the advertisers could then determine what should be broadcast. The one exception to this rule, which I reluctantly recommended, was *The Making of the President 1964;* in that case, the subject matter itself, Theodore White's integrity and his willingness to supervise every phase of the production assured us that our rule would not be abused.

I am against sponsors deciding that there should be a series of television programs on behalf of the United Nations because someday there may be a sponsor who wants to buy an anti-United Nations broadcast, and I have always been proud that Frank Stanton refused to consider the Xerox series on the United Nations. I was disappointed to see that in June 1966, CBS News did accept a program about Wall Street produced outside its division, and that the Hughes Aircraft Company should have been permitted to suggest and sponsor a one-hour report on the Surveyor moon project. However, I believe that CBS has lived to regret these two decisions and is not likely to repeat them. It is no secret that many people in the news division warned against both departures from policy.

Stanton's finest attempt at statesmanship to date, I believe, concerns the connection between cigarettes and lung cancer. He lost the battle, but with perseverance he may win the war, and if he does, this victory will deserve a place in broadcast history. Like Paley, Stanton does not smoke cigarettes, and there is no doubt in his mind about their effect on the public's health. For years the cigarette industry, one of broadcasting's largest sources of revenue, claimed that there was no such relationship, but in the months preceding the release of the Surgeon General's report, Stanton insisted that CBS had to begin formulating a policy. His plan was that well in advance we should announce that on a specified future date we would eliminate all cigarette advertising, for which, I was once told, CBS received approximately $70,000,000 annually. Stanton believed that this amount

—almost half of a total of over 150,000,000 cigarette dollars spent in broadcasting each year—could be replaced by other advertising revenue.

Stanton lost his first round partly because of pressure from the radio division and partly because the birth of CBS was associated with tobacco interests. However, he is a relentless adversary when he has decided on a course of action, and if the government doesn't order it first, I predict that eventually Stanton's name will be associated with the limitation or rejection of cigarette advertising on television. He is too much of a realist to believe that an industry licensed in the public interest can indefinitely accept $150,000,000 a year—a sum apt to increase—to promote a habit that is, beyond a shadow of reasonable medical doubt, against public health. Using the public air to spread a disease that may kill three hundred thousand Americans in 1967 is a palpable disgrace that should make the quiz scandals look like a harmless parlor prank. In many other civilized nations, cigarette advertising in broadcasting has been banned and in England replaced by antismoking campaigns, and Stanton is too intelligent a man not to understand the inevitability of that step in this country. In 1959 he said that CBS would be responsible for what goes on the air. Congress believed him then, and I do now.

On April 27, 1965, I was flying over the Atlantic on my way back from a two-day meeting with Hugh Greene, director general of the BBC, and his news chiefs, in which agreements had been worked out for the restoration of the old BBC-CBS relationship. We were over the Irish Sea when the stewardess came back with a message for me relayed from Shannon. "Your friend Mr. Murrow died today," she said.

The plane was two-thirds empty and it was as good a place as any to be silent for five hours. When we got near enough to the United States for communication, I asked the pilot to give CBS in New York a brief message to be sent to all bureaus and correspondents. In it I quoted something Ed said in his last radio broadcast to the English people when he left London after the war: "You lived a life instead of an apology." My message said that this quotation fit Murrow as much as it did the British people, and that it was something for the profession he left behind to aim for.

In *Remembrance Rock* "The Old Abider," the term of affection Ed and I had for Carl Sandburg, wrote: ". . . The shroud has no pockets . . . the dead hold in their clenched hands only that which they have given away." Ed Murrow, who slept too little and worked and smoked too much, had always said that he wanted "to wear out, not rust out." He did. He went to his grave with nothing—not even his voice was left at the end—but for a man with no pockets in life, he died the richest man I've ever known.

During the period of Murrow's service in Washington and his long illness, there was no more attentive a friend than Paley, and this meant much to Murrow. The chairman traveled to La Jolla, California, to visit him, called him often for advice on news matters and made it clear to Ed, as did everyone in the news division, that his return to CBS as an active broadcaster or as a consultant was both needed and desired. I think that Ed would have been pleased both by the fellowship set up in his name jointly by CBS and the Council on Foreign Relations, and by Paley's eulogy: "He was a resolute and uncompromising man of truth. His death ends the first golden age of broadcast journalism. I shall miss him greatly, as will all of us at CBS. But one thing we know, his imprint will be felt by broadcasting for all time to come."

Murrow disliked long obituaries. Other than at President Roosevelt's death, the only eulogy he ever felt a need to deliver, that of Sir Winston Churchill, he couldn't do because in the final months of his own life he was too ill.

I don't know which of all the farewells would have pleased him most, but two brief paragraphs from Eric Sevareid's broadcast of April 27 come closest to what I felt:

> There are some of us here, and I am one, who owe their professional life to this man. There are many, working here and in other networks and stations, who owe to Ed Murrow their love of their work, their standards and sense of responsibility. He was a shooting star; we will live in his afterglow a very long time.
>
> I never knew any person among those who worked in his realm to feel jealousy toward him. Not only because he made himself a refuge for those in trouble, a source of strength for those who were weak, but because there was no basis for comparison. He was an original, and we shall not see his like again.

9 *Air Time for Vietnam*

Explained a network spokesman, "The decision was reached by management not to cover the hearings because we felt that what went on for six hours could be digested and carried on the regular news broadcast. We were not motivated by commercial considerations. The loss of advertising revenue did not enter into the decision. We just didn't feel it was the kind of thing to carry. Nobody's looking at it, not even housewives."

Newsday, February 11, 1966

The specific cost incurred by the CBS Television Network in covering the . . . Vietnam hearings, for example, amounted to just over one million . . . Obviously, since CBS News cannot be self-supporting, we must pay some attention to the economics of broadcasting in making decisions involving such costs.

FRANK STANTON, February 25, 1966

Schneider said he felt "the essence" of yesterday's testimony could be "distilled" by CBS newsmen for more effective presentation in capsule form on the Walter Cronkite evening newscast. He said he thought the volume of testimony carried in the coverage of last Friday's and Tuesday's Vietnam hearings could have resulted in "obfuscating" and "confusing" the issues.

New York *Post,* February 11, 1966

. . . [television's] uniqueness is in its power to let people have that intimate sense of meeting the great figures of the world and actually seeing many major events as they happen . . . Great events of all kinds do not have to be filtered through the appraising accounts of reporters and editors. They can be witnessed by the people themselves, who can make their own judgments.

FRANK STANTON, May 6, 1959

The machine which Chairman Paley once warned must not be allowed to run away with itself "instead of keeping pace with the social needs it was created to serve," had a life of its own on February 10, 1966. No one person at CBS said, even to himself, much less to anyone else, "I would prefer to have our network broadcast a fifth rerun of *Lucy* today at ten o'clock instead of the Kennan testimony on Vietnam." It was not a matter of deciding between two broadcasts, but a choice between interrupting the morning run of the profit machine—whose only admitted function was to purvey six one-minute commercials every half-hour, all of which had been viewed hundreds of times before—or electing to make the audience privy to an event of overriding national importance taking place in a Senate hearing room at that very moment. (In the February 20 issue of the New York *Herald Tribune,* the paper's Washington Bureau chief called those hearings "much more than sheer entertainment. For they grappled with great national questions and brought them out into the open, into the light and air for the public to see and judge.")

When the dispute over the choice of *Lucy* instead of Kennan had ended, someone who had watched CBS cover three wars and wage a few public ones of its own, later wrote to me: "Nothing has really changed in the last thirty years except for some of the participants."

The following is an account, in chronological detail, of what happened at CBS in February 1966. If broadcast journalism is to be held accountable for what it puts on the air, then the decisions which influence it are important and subject to public review.

During the six months prior to February 9, I had been in constant disagreement with Stanton over CBS News' reporting of the Vietnam war. Though on January 28 Stanton had made an eloquent speech to a trade association about our coverage, and had shown a brief, edited film of some of our combat reporting at its convention, the irony was that he had been critical of much of the footage at the time it was originally broadcast. He had never concealed his uneasiness about Morley Safer, whose reporting from the combat area was, in my opinion, superb, and who has since won almost every possible honor. In all fairness, Stanton's public support of our reporting never wavered, and on one occasion he wrote an inspiring defense of Safer's dispatches of the burning of Cam Ne to a senator who had been critical.

But Stanton was also disturbed that several of the correspondents' pieces on Vietnam and the Santo Domingo crisis had crossed the line into editorializing, and he was particularly irked by a report from Murray Fromson in Bangkok on January 6 which said that American pilots based in Thailand were bombing Communist supply lines moving along the Ho Chi Minh Trail in Laos. Stanton claimed that all correspondents had agreed to embargo this information, but both Fromson and Sam Zelman, our bureau chief in Saigon, denied this. I pointed out to Stanton that two prominent United States publications, the *New York Times* and *Time*, had run detailed stories, complete with maps, of our Thai bases ten days earlier; to this he replied, "Since when are those publications examples of our journalistic responsibility?" He was disturbed, he said, lest Fromson's report cause the Thai government, which was nervous about the bombing, to kick us out. When I asked Stanton if he thought for one moment that the fact that the bases were being used to bomb the Ho Chi Minh Trail was a secret to the enemy or to the people of Thailand, he admitted that it was not, but he believed that mention of their existence had embarrassed our government. I insisted that the news editor who had cleared the material had acted well within the bounds of our guidelines, and that killing the story would have amounted to censorship.

Later, Assistant Secretary of Defense Arthur Sylvester called me at home to protest this same story, as well as another in which Fromson had reported that the United States was so short of ammunition that we were buying back supplies from some of our European allies. (This was eventually confirmed by Defense officials.) When I told Stanton that the Pentagon was quite upset about this particular broadcast, he answered, "I know, indeed . . ."

In the summer of 1965 I had reached the conclusion, shared by my CBS colleagues and others in the profession, that journalism generally was failing to explain the complexities of the Vietnam war. In the fifteen-year history of reporting on that foreign-aid mission which began with eight transport planes in 1950 and grew into the deadly undeclared war in which we are now engaged, the correspondent in the field is entitled to far better marks than his editor and the interpretative journalist on the home front. When I proposed that the news division depart from its usual August schedule of documentary repeats and instead originate four extremely low-budgeted "Vietnam Perspective" broadcasts with a cast consisting of the Secretaries of State and Defense, the United States Ambassador to the U.N. and the Presidential assistants, all to be interviewed by our Washington staff, Stanton first resisted these programs on the grounds that our policy in Vietnam had already been made and that such analysis would be redundant, but we finally got them on the air.

However, whenever Stanton's prebroadcast reservations changed to favorable postprogram reactions, he was always the first to compliment the producers, and if a program which had been put on the air over his objections did not come off, I never once heard him say, "I told you so." Thus, in July 1966 CBS distributed a picture booklet, *The Face of War,* containing scenes from the Vietnam specials which he had once opposed, and accompanying the pictures was the text of an address he had made to the Canadian Broadcast Executives Society.

On another occasion a projected half-hour interview with Senator William Fulbright conducted by Eric Sevareid and Martin Agronsky so upset Stanton that he said, "What a dirty trick that was to play on the President of the United States . . . I didn't know about it until I saw the news release." However, "Fulbright: Advice and Dissent" was the portrait of a tortured and concerned man who confessed to hard questioning that he felt he had erred in voting approval of the 1964 Tonkin Gulf resolution; this had in effect given the President considerable latitude in enlarging the war.

Now in late January and early February 1966, as the bombing moratorium was ending in Vietnam, the news division pushed for a series of debates with Senate and House leaders on the forthcoming resumption of bombing and escalation of the war. Although we had commitments for appearances by an excellent representation of congressional hawks and doves, Stanton resisted the continuation of the "Vietnam Perspective" broadcasts. The January 30 debate, "Congress and the War"—with Senators John Stennis and Karl Mundt and Congressman Hale Boggs representing the hawks, and Senators Wayne Morse and Joseph Clark for the doves—was literally forced onto the air by a series of nagging phone calls and a slightly offensive memo of mine that finally caused Stanton to rescind his objection three days before the broadcast, "if you really feel that strongly about it."

The resulting broadcast was a spontaneous, constructive debate; Sevareid kept the senators and congressmen to a strict agenda and concluded with a brilliant summation. Senator Morse urged the President to accept the Pope's advice and take the matter to the United Nations, which the President did the next morning. Morse and Stennis were evenly matched, and for ninety minutes the two of them turned our Washington studio into the floor of the United States Senate. Toward the end of the program Stennis interrupted an attack on Morse and the doves to say: "This has been a real congressional debate, [with] nationwide television coverage," and afterward Stanton called to say that it had been one of the best produced, most useful programs of its kind we had ever done.

The Washington and press reaction to that broadcast was most rewarding; the other networks were challenged to keep up with CBS's pace in interpretation of the war. The next day Stanton flirted with the idea of letting us do a weekly series on Vietnam, but when I pursued the matter I ran into opposition.

Stanton, something of an expert on military affairs, chairman of the board of trustees of The RAND Corporation, and a top adviser to the United States Information Agency, had journeyed to Vietnam the previous summer and was well informed about the struggle. His objections to such broadcasts were, he told me, partly financial (though each of the Vietnam debates cost no more than $10,000), but were mainly based on his concern that too much "dove-hawk" talk unsteadied the hand of the Commander-in-Chief. I believed, for my part, that healthy debates by responsible leaders could build national understanding of the President's position, and that the spectacle of congressional leaders debating the war was far better than the epidemic of one-sided teach-ins and hostile demonstrations that had filled the void in the absence of a national debate. In my opinion, responsible debates and the subsequent Senate hearings actually de-escalated the demonstrations and draft-card burnings that so embarrassed the Administration.

Two days after our January 30 "Congress and the War" debate, Ambassador Arthur Goldberg took the Vietnam matter to the Security Council. We recommended doing the debate live from the United Nations, but when faced with the cost of all-day coverage we settled for brief two-minute reports and a thirty-minute summary at 4:30 P.M. Leaving instructions with the crew that if the debate justified it they should interrupt regular programing for Goldberg and the Soviet delegate, Fedorenko, I left for the regular Tuesday news meeting with Paley, Stanton and Schneider. I should have stayed at the Broadcast Center (as the production center on West Fifty-seventh Street was now called) and monitored the debate myself; my colleagues were so conditioned not to spend the $80,000 per half-day it cost to throw the switch that the courage of their news convictions failed them. We did not broadcast Goldberg's speech, and neither did the other two networks; the next day the newspapers criticized all of us severely.

Two days later Ambassador Goldberg gave me his own reaction over the telephone. He said that the debate was extremely important and that we should have been there. To compound the injury, a half-hour summary of that important day at the U.N., skillfully edited and narrated by Dick Hottelet, did appear across the nation at 4:30 P.M., but was not broadcast in New York. When Gordon Manning, who supervised such special reports, heard that Channel 2, the CBS owned and operated station in New York, was not going to carry the program, he pleaded with the vice-president in charge to change his mind, but the executive refused to sacrifice part of *The Early Show*. Thus, the television critic of the *Times* saw the summary via Hartford at his home in Connecticut, but it was blacked out of the largest city in the world and the home of the U.N.

At that Tuesday news meeting Stanton was still enthusiastic about our Vietnam debate two days earlier. He then surprised everyone by suggesting that perhaps we should consider doing a weekly television report on Vietnam. I enthusiastically seconded the motion and suggested Sunday as the obvious day for the program; with no more football for the season, we could broadcast from 4:30 to 5:30 P.M. at very little cost to the company. But Stanton said that he wanted to think over the proposal before committing himself. I suggested that in the meantime we do a program the next Sunday called "The U.N. and the War." I finally got permission for this late on Thursday afternoon. It was not a very lively broadcast but it was productive and I think everyone was glad that we did it. However, the idea for a regular weekly Vietnam broadcast never went any further, despite my urging.

On January 28, Secretary of State Rusk had testified before the Senate Foreign Relations Committee on Johnson's request for supplementary foreign aid. Had we been on our toes we would have had it on the air live, but the Secretary's testimony was a sleeper and all the networks were caught off guard. On the afternoon of the testimony, the editors of the Cronkite news broadcast told me that they had more material than they could use for the program that night; the footage of Rusk under interrogation was excellent. I remember someone saying with a guilty look, "I don't suppose they would have let us televise that with live cameras, do you?"

When I saw the Cronkite evening news I knew that we had blundered. We had three minutes of absorbing testimony about Vietnam; Huntley and Brinkley had used five. When I yelled at Ernie Leiser, the executive producer of the program, and asked why he did not use more footage, he answered, quite correctly, "Because there was just too much other news."

By the time I got the Washington bureau on the phone, Small was ready for me: "We had twice as much good stuff; New York couldn't use it."

"Bill, I'm afraid to ask this because I think I know what the answer will be, but would they have allowed live coverage?"

"Certainly they would have," he snapped, "but you never could have gotten the air time and you know it."

I said lamely, "I wish you'd let me make these decisions next time." Then and there I promised myself that if we ever had another whack at those hearings I'd prove Small wrong.

The opportunity came on February 3 when Small called to ask whether we wanted live coverage of David Bell, then administrator of the Agency for International Development, who would also be testifying before the Fulbright committee. I asked whether the other networks were planning to have cameras there, and Small said he would find out. Half an hour later he called back to say that NBC had not decided whether to do live coverage, but that they would have cameras there and that we could work out a "pool" with them. This is an arrangement by which cameras cover an event for several networks; then each news division can determine whether it wants to broadcast it live, extract it for summaries or digest it for its news shows. I agreed to go into the pool and told Small I'd let him know about live coverage as soon as possible.

Schneider was away, so I called John Reynolds, who had just taken up duties in New York after being in charge of West Coast operations for the network. When I told him about the hearings and their importance, he was extremely co-operative and told me to follow my own news judgment. "Will you need a half-hour, or more?" he asked. I told him that the testimony was scheduled to commence at 8:30 A.M., which relieved him because it meant interrupting only *Captain Kangaroo:* "We'll get some squawks from the mothers, but there isn't a lot of money involved. Try to keep it to a half-hour if you can."

I explained that I did not know whether our telecast would run for thirty minutes or several hours, but that the proceedings might be quite slow. I added that Bell was reported to be surprised that anyone would want to carry his appearance live because he had only "a dull prepared statement." However, I had the feeling that Fulbright and Morse might be in hot pursuit of Bell, as they had in the case of Rusk, and that we ought to be prepared to stay with the hearing more than a half-hour. After further conversation we agreed to advise the stations that we were going on the air at 8:30, that we would stay a minimum of a half-hour and that we would make the necessary news judgment as the hearing progressed. That night we announced our coverage on the Cronkite news show.

At 8:30 the next morning, February 4, both CBS and NBC were covering the testimony live. Roger Mudd explained the hearings and the background of Rusk's testimony the week before, and then Bell began reading his prepared statement. I was still watching at home in Riverdale and preparing to leave for the office when Gordon Manning called from the control room to ask me to stay where I was. "This looks as if it will be pretty good stuff, and I don't want you on the parkway when we have to decide whether to carry it longer or cut it off," he said. I agreed.

At 9:20 Gordon called again. The hearing was beginning to heat up; it was obvious that the senators, unable to debate the issue of Vietnam with the President himself, were using Bell, his foreign-aid deputy, as a substitute target. We decided to stay with the testimony until 10 A.M. Again Manning asked me to stay within reach at home. "That damn phone in your car never works right and I may have to call you. The television network people will be calling soon and I'll need some moral support."

I stayed put. It was snowing that morning and I did not want to get stuck, en route, out of range. Both Gordon and I were well aware that the dollar price on each half-hour increased as the morning progressed. Not running *I Love Lucy* at 10 A.M. would mean the loss of about $5,000, and *The McCoys* at 10:30 about the same, but cancellation of *The Dick Van Dyke Daytime Show,* another rerun scheduled for 11:30 A.M., would cost the network about $25,000 or $30,000. In effect, we were really playing double or nothing.

As Fulbright, Morse, Mundt, Clark and the other senators took their turn questioning Bell, the hearing turned into the first bona-fide unstaged Vietnam senatorial debate on television. NBC was staying with the testimony too, but with their weaker day-time schedule, the programing they gave up during the morning cost them less than half of what it cost CBS. Every twenty minutes or so Manning would telephone to say that he was getting calls from network sales and from John Reynolds, asking how much longer we were going to stay with the story and at the same time mentioning the cost. But the testimony seemed too important and we decided to continue. I stayed at home by the phone until noon, and though Reynolds called me twice, he did not try to influence my decision other than to keep us up to the minute on the cost.

We had just finished broadcasting from Washington when I finally reached my desk at 12:30. When I called Stanton to tell him what had been going on and to find out what he thought, his secretary told me that he was unavailable. The hearing resumed, and once again CBS was there live at 2:34 P.M. It is worth noting that NBC did not continue their broadcast. Had we not returned to the air when we did, the Senate hearings might have been covered differently from then on, because it was our lead that later caused NBC to go back to continuous coverage.

That afternoon I was in Ambassador Goldberg's office when Manning called: our White House correspondent had reported that President Johnson and his top advisers were flying to Honolulu to meet South Vietnam's Premier Nguyen Cao Ky on Saturday, and we had interrupted the hearings to announce this. After I had hung up I told Ambassador Goldberg about the President's trip, which was a surprise to him. The purpose of my call on Goldberg had been to try to convince him to participate in our Sunday "Vietnam Perspective" broadcast, but once I had mentioned the President's plans, his interest in our project drained away and he seemed anxious to get rid of me so that he could be brought up to date by the State Department.

Earlier during this meeting, Goldberg had again chided me for neglecting to televise live the February 1 United Nations debate. I winced then, but cherish his wrath now; he was right, and his criticism helped to condition me for the struggle over Vietnam air time that lay just ahead. Later, when I told Stanton about the dressing-down Goldberg had given me, he seemed disturbed. "What right does a U.N. ambassador have to concern himself about what we broadcast?" he said. I answered that Goldberg had been critical, not managerial, and that it was certainly not the first time we had heard a complaint from members of the Administration, nor would it be the last.

Administrator Bell testified the whole afternoon of the fourth, pre-empting all the soap operas and game shows, with their many valuable commercial minutes per half-hour. At the end of the day I was told that we had cost the television network some $175,000 in lost revenue (though I believe much of this money was recaptured in "make-goods" at later dates).

I called the Washington bureau to tell them what a splendid job of coverage they had done. Small said that the feeling in the trade was that we had been more comprehensive than NBC, that the organization Kintner left behind when he departed had lost some of its momentum and that now our competitors were, in effect, following our initiative.

When I called Stanton to see what he thought of the day's coverage, he said he did not know that we had been on the air all day. When I told him that we would have some tough decisions to make the next week about the Gavin, Taylor and Rusk testimonies, he sighed in such a way as to let me know that there were big hurdles ahead.

Later that night I received a telegram from our affiliate in Tampa complaining bitterly about the day's hearings and the interruption of the entertainment schedule on such short notice.

I was also told that the New York switchboard had received one hundred and fifty calls, but that a remarkably large number of them were enthusiastic about the hearings. Usually almost all such calls were critical of any interruption of the soap operas or Art Linkletter.

On Saturday, February 5, our new half-hour Saturday evening news made its debut. It was a good beginning because earlier that day the President and the Secretaries of State, Defense, Agriculture and Health, Education and Welfare and their combined staffs had departed for the meeting in Honolulu. We had sent along a large cadre of correspondents and editors, including Reasoner, Kalb and Pierpont. In addition, Peter Kalischer flew in from Saigon with Premier Ky, and his broadcast account of his playing poker all the way across the Pacific with the young chief of state, on his way to a crucial meeting with the President of the United States, is an indication of the lack of preparation by at least one of the participants for that hastily arranged meeting.

The war was escalating, and the hearings also escalated in importance with the appearance of Lieutenant General James Gavin, who, in a letter to *Harper's Magazine,* had criticized the conduct of the war and called for its stabilization by the establishment of enclaves along the coast. Walter Lippmann and others praised this approach, and when Secretary of Defense McNamara and General Maxwell Taylor condemned it, Gavin called a news conference to amplify his proposals.

I knew that there was going to be a battle with the management to get the Gavin testimony on the air, and so I called the general in Boston to determine the exact day he was scheduled to testify. Gavin told me that he had been called for ten o'clock Tuesday morning, February 8, and that he welcomed the opportunity to answer McNamara and to clarify his position, which he felt the press had distorted. There was no doubt in my mind that he would be a provocative and important witness.

Normally this was the kind of decision to be taken up at our Tuesday news meeting, but obviously we could not wait, and my colleagues urged me to push for a decision immediately so that we could announce our coverage early. I took my case to Stanton, who knew Gavin and the kind of witness he was likely to be, but he warned me against getting "boxed in," as we had with Bell's testimony. When I told him about my call to the general and argued for an immediate decision, his reply was to ask me to consider the financial damage that another all-day session would cause. I said that we would monitor the hearing closely and use no more air time than necessary, but he kept bringing up the cost. In desperation I reminded him that for the first five months of the fiscal year the news division had been under budget by more than $500,000 for the first time in many years. Stanton admitted how pleased he and Paley were about this, but urged me not to cover the Gavin testimony live; we would only be using some of our precious budget surplus, which we would certainly need for other special events later in the year. Finally, he asked me to talk with Schneider; I did, but received no clear-cut answer from him either.

Meanwhile, in Honolulu the President managed to take away some of the headlines about the hearings. Then, shortly after Fulbright had stated that Gavin would definitely testify on Tuesday, the President announced that he would be flying back on Tuesday afternoon and that the Vice-President would meet him in Los Angeles before flying on to Honolulu and a tour of the Far East, including a visit to South Vietnam. This meant that Tuesday was going to be a heavy day for news and that we ought to be thinking about doing a special program that night. I always carried in my pocket a weekly summary of the network's schedule which pinpointed its "soft" rating spots; in an emergency these could be pre-empted for news extras or specials. For Tuesday night the soft spot was CBS News' own hour, in which *CBS Reports* or its alternate broadcasts appeared. That week the program was to be a one-hour color presentation called "Sixteen in Webster Groves," an examination of teen-age America filmed in an upper-middle-class suburb of St. Louis. I always believed that if we were willing to pre-empt *Candid Camera* or *Perry Mason* for news, we had to agree about shifting our own broadcasts when they were not too topical. Certainly "Sixteen in Webster Groves" was postponable, and I hastened to suggest to Schneider that we pre-empt it for a special, "The Councils of War," based on the President's mission and Gavin's testimony. Furthermore, I proposed calling the sponsor to offer them this special program and promising to run "Sixteen in Webster Groves" as soon as possible in the future. I asked for a price for the hour, and was told that we could offer our special program for $100,000. In short order the sponsor agreed to the arrangement if the special broadcast became necessary.

On Monday afternoon, when I again urged Stanton that we do the Gavin hearings live, he suggested that we simply edit it and run it on the 10 o'clock special program. Our argument continued until 6:30, at which point I received what I considered reluctant permission to go ahead, and Cronkite announced the next day's coverage on his news program.

The Gavin testimony was brilliant television. An intellectual military man and a quietly effective speaker, he did alter what appeared to be the main thesis of his *Harper's* piece. Various senators made speeches directed at him, and in their questioning Symington and Hickenlooper seemed to be critical, but they all praised the general for appearing. And once again our competitors, who usually gave as good as they got, had to admit that this was our day; at one point they were so rattled that they had our taped replay on their air.

I called Stanton to say that we were going ahead with the special because the testimony was so vital and because the President's plane was due to arrive in Los Angeles between 10 and 11 P.M. When I mentioned the good job our Washington staff had been doing, Stanton said that he had not been watching. Still, I considered the day's time and money—another $175,000, I was told—well spent.

That afternoon word came from Hawaii that the President would not be arriving in Los Angeles until 10:30, New York time, because of headwinds; also that he was aware cameras would be at the airport and that he would have a statement to make when he met the Vice-President. After their special on the President's trip, NBC would be in the middle of a two-hour movie, and ABC had an hour show from 10 to 11. CBS might have the entire event, plus the Gavin summary, to itself.

I decided to go home for dinner that night and return to the office for the special. When I got back to the news room at 9:15, Manning and Bill Leonard, who'd had dinner at The Ground Floor, told me of a curious little episode. At the restaurant they had bumped into Chairman Paley, who had asked Leonard what was going on. When Leonard told him enthusiastically about our great day on the air with Gavin and the one-hour special for that night, Paley said that he had not known anything about it. The chairman repeated this to me the next day.

The 10 o'clock special that night opened with Cronkite in New York, Sevareid and Mudd in Washington and Kalb and Kalischer in Los Angeles, where they had flown from Honolulu just in time to participate in the broadcast. After a brief opening summary of the council of war between Premier Ky and President Johnson, as well as the testimony that day before the Fulbright committee, Roger Mudd introduced a twenty-five-minute edited version of Gavin's remarks; this was followed by a series of brief but pertinent filmed interviews with Rusk,

McNamara, General Taylor and Premier Ky. Those interviews, done by Reasoner, Kalischer and Kalb while they were in Hawaii, were particularly effective following the "enclave" theories of General Gavin. There was one dramatic moment when Kalischer asked Ky if he would be willing to negotiate with the National Liberation Front. The Vietnamese leader glared at Kalischer and said, "National Liberation Front—our enslaving front?" then added, ". . . never talk with me . . . on the Front of Liberation . . . if you want to go back to Saigon."

Throughout the broadcast Cronkite kept the audience posted on the progress of the President's plane as it approached the West Coast, and when it became obvious that Mr. Johnson would arrive after 11 o'clock, Walter reported that we would keep our cameras ready at the airport. The last section of the broadcast was a five-way electronic round table between the correspondents, in which Sevareid, Kalb and Kalischer were skeptical about the purposes and conclusions of a meeting that "was thrown together with rather short notice," and speculated that the public embrace of Premier Ky might lead to complications. In addition, Kalb reported that definite differences had been aired, and that there was reason to believe the meeting had not gone well.

The President's plane touched down at 11:24 P.M., New York time, and we immediately switched to the airport and stayed with the story until he disembarked over an hour later. NBC was there the entire time, ABC part of the time. It was one of those dreadful watches; we could not afford to leave the President, for he and Mr. Humphrey were expected to make an appearance momentarily, and yet the pressure to return to the regular schedule was enormous because the Eastern stations were agonizing over the loss of *The Late Show*. Each network was trapped, and it was well past 12:30 before the President and the Vice-President made their statements in the hangar.

As I drove up the West Side Highway at one-thirty that

morning, it seemed to me that the total silence from the management of the company was the loudest sound I had heard all night. Next to being told how much money one has spent in such coverage, the worst notice is to hear nothing, and my only communication had been a phone call from Reynolds asking how long we were going to stay with the President.

A few hours later I was back on the West Side Highway, bound for an early-morning meeting with Stanton and the CBS advisory committee. I was particularly anxious to attend because I had an encouraging report to make about the news division's improved budget situation. As I rushed into the new building the elevator starter asked me to pick up two messages. One was the news that the advisory committee meeting had been canceled at the last minute. This must have been a sudden decision because several of the participants had already arrived from out of town; moreover, Stanton was always most precise about notifying everyone of such changes well in advance.

The second message was to call Mr. Paley. When I reached him he complimented the news division on the 10 o'clock special the night before and said he wished that I had alerted him to the Presidential coverage at midnight; he had missed it because he had not known about it, he said, and he asked me to feel free to notify him personally of any future special news programs. This conversation made me slightly uneasy because I knew how many times he and Stanton talked every day.

When I reached my desk I immediately called Stanton and said I was sorry that the advisory committee meeting had been canceled because I had hoped to talk to him and Jack Schneider for a few minutes afterward to settle two unresolved and urgent matters: Kennan's testimony before the Fulbright committee the day after, and next Sunday's "Congress after Honolulu" debate. Stanton said that he was much too busy with another matter involving Paley, and that I would have to work out these matters with Schneider. Unfortunately, I was either too tired or not listening closely enough to realize at that moment what I was being told. When I called Schneider shortly thereafter to say that Stanton had left the decision on Kennan and the Sunday Vietnam special to the two of us, he seemed slightly surprised but asked me for my recommendations. Of course I urged that we schedule both.

At about noon Stanton asked me if I could see him at twelve-thirty. His manner was grave when we met and he showed me a news release to the effect that the board of directors had asked William S. Paley to continue as chairman of the board past his sixty-fifth birthday. Stanton said that this had been a last-minute decision and that what it really meant was that he would have different duties and be removed from any active participation in the broadcast activities of the company. Then Stanton discussed his own future in considerable detail. He also explained that Jack Schneider had just been appointed to the newly created position of group vice-president, supervising the activities of all broadcast operations—the news division, the television and radio networks and the owned and operated stations. He added emphatically that he did not like this turn of events, but that it had been the recommendation of the management-consultant firm which had been studying the company.

I told Stanton that I had no personal objection to working with Jack Schneider, but I did want reassurance that the news division's decisions would continue to be made at the news committee meetings consisting of Paley, Stanton, Schneider and myself. (Manning, Leonard and sometimes Mitgang also attended.) To my shocked dismay, Stanton explained that in the future neither he nor Paley would have such duties, and that Schneider would be the decision-maker.

"But, Frank," I said, "you know that when I took this job two years ago you told me that I would be responsible only to you and the chairman." Stanton said that he was all too well aware of this promise and that this was why he had wanted me to know about the decision before it was announced. I answered that this changed all the ground rules and that I would have to think about it. "What would happen," I asked, "if I decided I could not continue as president of the news division because I thought my responsibility to you and the chairman was altered?" I remember Stanton's exact reply. He grimaced, held up his hands and said, "It would be the worst thing that could happen, dreadful for the news division, dreadful for the company. I think if you put it that way to the chairman he would take it all back himself."

When I arrived back in the office at two-thirty, Manning was pressing me for a decision on the Kennan hearings, Leonard wanted to know about "Congress after Honolulu" for Sunday, and Small in Washington wanted to know about both. When I told them and the rest of my immediate staff about the Schneider appointment, there was unanimity that the scheduling of the Kennan hearings was no longer in doubt. Someone said, "Jack isn't going to throw his weight around on his first day in office."

I then dictated two memos, one to Schneider about the Kennan hearings and one to Paley. In the first I congratulated Schneider on his new job and then made my recommendation:

> At tomorrow's hearings of the Senate Foreign Relations Committee, George Kennan is going to testify. Senator Fulbright considers that he will be the most important witness of the entire hearings. He is one of the world's greatest authorities on Russian-Chinese relations. It may also be a climactic day in the hearings because Kennan is bound to polarize the conflicting points of view of the doves and the hawks of the committee. It should develop a national debate.
>
> General Maxwell Taylor has been postponed from next Monday until Wednesday, February 16. Secretary Rusk is

due to testify on Thursday. The committee tells us it's possible these two dates will be reversed, but both will testify and there will be hearings on Wednesday and Thursday.

It is my strong recommendation that we broadcast the hearings of all three days, continuing the pattern that existed when Mr. Bell and General Gavin testified.

We at CBS, at the highest level, have constantly spoken out for access to congressional debates and hearings. The fact that this opportunity to broadcast these hearings, which reflect one of the great challenges facing this democracy, makes the responsibility to do these hearings—and to do them well—most important.

Broadcast journalism has, once or twice every decade, an opportunity to prove itself. Such an opportunity were the events leading up to World War II; such was the McCarthy period. The Vietnam war—its coverage in Asia and in Congress—is another such challenge.

I am aware of the financial burden that such coverage places upon the Television Network, and the electronic editing and self-discipline of the past year have reflected the concern of the News Division in this regard. But I consider these hearings as a matter of conscience for this company and this executive. This is public service in the most basic sense. I am sure you agree.

Fred Friendly

At four o'clock Schneider called me to say that he had my memo and that he thought my oral presentation earlier that day had been more convincing. Although my most extended argument over the hearings and general coverage of Vietnam had been with Frank Stanton, it was the newly appointed group vice-president who told me that his decision was final: "We are not going to carry the Kennan hearings."

Schneider discussed money and his feeling that opinion leaders would not be watching, and said that housewives weren't much interested in Vietnam. After a long argument—

and I remember speaking these words quietly, though I expect that Schneider probably remembers me as shouting them in anger—I said, "Jack, I find this situation untenable. You are making a news judgment but basing it on business criteria, and I can't do this job under these circumstances. I want you to know just how strongly I feel about this, and I'm going to ask the management for clarification."

"I don't want to pin you down," Schneider said, "but what exactly are you going to do?"

I read him the note that I had composed and was about to dispatch to Paley:

> Mr. Paley:
>
> Two years ago when I was asked to head the News Division, I was told that my responsibility would be directly to the Chairman and the President. I gather from today's announcement that this is no longer so.
>
> Because of the seriousness with which I regard this matter, I would like to see you at your first convenience.
>
> *Fred Friendly*

Later that afternoon Paley's secretary called me to confirm a noon meeting the next day—the same day that Kennan was to testify.

Despite my own gloom, there was optimism back in the news room on the evening of the ninth that we would win our argument to televise the Kennan testimony. Those concerned with the evening news even insisted upon writing an announcement for the Cronkite program so he could report what time our coverage of the next day's hearings before the Senate Foreign Relations Committee would begin. It was our turn to provide pool facilities, and Small was told to have Mudd and Sevareid ready at 10 A.M. the next morning. The Huntley-Brinkley news program announced that they would be broadcasting the next day's hearings, but though we had calls from some of the stations and the New York *Daily News,* the *Tribune* and the *Times,* all asking about CBS's coverage, we had no statement to make.

At nine-thirty that night Manning and I talked again and decided that one of us had to call Schneider to expedite a decision about the Sunday congressional broadcast. Manning volunteered, and half an hour later told me that after due deliberation Schneider had agreed to the Sunday broadcast. They had also discussed the Kennan hearings again, but with the same negative result. Manning, a low-key but highly effective advocate, had made the point that the decision could be left open until air time the next morning. He would be in the control room, I would be in my office, and the hearings could be on the network at the push of a button, he told Schneider.

But at 10 o'clock the next morning, February 10, CBS was running *I Love Lucy* while NBC had Senator Fulbright interrogating George Kennan. The scene in my office was one of such tragicomic polarity that if it had been part of a stage play no one would have believed it. Aside from the juxtaposition on the monitors in my office of *Lucy* on CBS, the Kennan hearings on NBC and a movie on ABC, there was present, by prior appointment, an earnest young man from still another management-consultant firm, part of a second wave of efficiency experts retained by the company to study ways of diversification and growth for CBS. Another CBS monitor not on the air carried the hearings, and it added to the frustration that it was our director who was calling the shots that NBC was using.

As Ambassador Kennan talked about the relations between Red China and the Soviet Union, Lucille Ball mugged, and the young efficiency expert asked me about the difference between "image orthicon" and newsreel film cameras. In the midst of this, one of our most distinguished correspondents called to ask, "Why the hell aren't we on the air?"

At 10:30 on the NBC screen Kennan was being questioned by Senator John Sparkman of Alabama while CBS was broadcasting a rerun of *The Real McCoys;* at the same time my guest was asking me to explain how CBS film was distributed to the BBC and other foreign broadcasters, while Bill Small was calling from Washington to ask what the chances were of doing a special that night summarizing the highlights of the hearings.

At 11 A.M. *Andy of Mayberry*—the rerun title of *The Andy Griffith Show*—was playing on CBS, and Andy and his fishing pole were marching across my monitor as Senator Hickenlooper began cross-examining Mr. Kennan. Simultaneously the young man wanted to know about the overseas syndication of *CBS Reports* and *Twentieth Century*. Parenthetically he asked, "Why aren't you carrying those hearings from Washington, by the way?"

At one point a CBS correspondent and an editor came into my office to protest, and one of them, after getting nothing but a corporate stiff upper lip from me, said, "What do they think they're doing across the city, mining the wasteland?" And the other looked up at *Love of Life* on the monitor and added, "Strip-mining it."

In the midst of all this I called Jack Schneider. "Jack, this is extremely good stuff. Have you been watching?"

"Watching what?"

"George Kennan's testimony. These are the most useful hearings so far."

"No, Fred, things are too hectic over here. I haven't been able to watch."

"Well, I wish you'd take a look. We've missed the boat this morning, but Small is editing the hearings on video tape in Washington and we could do a damn good hour or thirty-minute special tonight. Everyone over here recommends it."

"I'll call you back, Fred."

It was the last time I ever talked to Jack Schneider.

At noon on February 10, with Kennan still in the witness chair, I walked into William Paley's office. As I told him how pleased I was that he was going to stay on past his sixty-fifth birthday, it occurred to me that I sounded like all organization men talking to all chairmen of the board. But I meant every word. Murrow and all the other original members of the CBS news department in the late thirties and early forties—Collingwood, Sevareid, Trout—knew that the first important strides in news had been made when Paley was in command and giving full attention to broadcast operations, and he was still the news division's most loyal and acute critic.

I began our discussion by reminding the chairman of the conditions under which I had taken the presidency of CBS News in March 1964. Now, almost two years later, a new chain of decision-making had been established, and I wanted clarification.

Paley pointed out that since he had been away then, the terms of my appointment had been discussed with Stanton, but that organizations do change and that no individual can expect to report to the same two executives forever. I acknowledged this, and hastened to say that though I might not object to reporting to Schneider on budget and staff matters, the editing and scheduling of news was based on professional competence, and that for all his administrative and sales ability, it seemed to me that Schneider should not be put in the position of making the ultimate decisions on vital news judgments.

Paley retorted that our new relationship would work precisely because Schneider was *not* a newsman or a journalist. "He has little or no national news experience. He's young and bright and he learns fast, Fred. I mean what I say. He'll depend on you for news judgments more than Frank and I ever would have, just wait and see."

"Bill, if you had given me that argument yesterday I would

have bought it, or at least tried it for six months or a year. But within thirty minutes of Jack's appointment we all had a chance to see how it would work." I then gave the chairman chapter and verse on the argument over the Kennan testimony between the group vice-president and the president of CBS News, and how Schneider had summarily ended the debate. "It was not simply my recommendation, but the unanimous recommendation of everyone in the news division, including several of the correspondents, that we carry all of the hearings—particularly Kennan's. Events have already proved Schneider wrong; Kennan has been a great witness and he's still testifying." I added that I had a recommendation before Schneider at that very moment for a summary of the hearings that evening and was still awaiting word. (Word never came, and instead of doing a special program that night we had to content ourselves with six minutes on the Cronkite program.)

Paley said, "Fred, I don't want to judge this one decision. In this case he could be wrong or right, but he's new at the job and he'll learn."

"Bill, I love this job and I want to stay with it. I'm quite prepared to work with Jack, but there has to be some method by which the final appeal on scheduling and time is made by the highest authority in the company." Then I asked that the Tuesday news committee meetings be continued in some form, so that when such special events as the Senate hearings, the Pope's visit, the space program, Vietnam debates or Presidential summit meetings occurred, the head of the news division would have the same access to the management as Ed Klauber, Paul White, Ed Murrow, Dick Salant or I'd had in my own first two years.

Paley said that in a kind of "loose way" this arrangement would continue because Schneider would always have access to him and Stanton. But he pointed out that he was sixty-four and that Stanton was fifty-seven; delegation of the day-to-day running of the company had to go to someone younger, "and Jack will be the boss."

"If there is no appeal," I said, "then I don't think that I can do this job any longer, and I would like you and Frank to think of a way by which I can give up these duties."

Paley answered that over the years many executives of CBS had resigned and that he had always taken them at their word, but that in this case he hoped I wouldn't leave. He spoke of the accomplishments of the news division over the past two years, said that we had achieved in that short time what he had thought would take five years, that CBS News was now back in first place, and that he hoped I would stay on.

I wanted to stay, I said; I was, in fact, pleading to stay if the decision-making apparatus could remain the same.

Our meeting ended on that indecisive note. Paley walked me to the door, held both of my hands and urged me to discuss the matter with Stanton. "After all, it was he who hired you, he's better than anyone at working out things like this, and if in the end we can't agree he'll know how to make all the proper arrangements. But let me give you some advice. Whatever you do, don't talk about it. Sometimes you have a habit of confiding matters to other executives who are not as discreet as you think they are going to be."

The advice was warranted. "I'll be silent," I said, "but please make sure that everyone else keeps the lid on this, inside and outside the company."

Paley's last words indicated that in one way or another a compromise could be found. "You and Frank work this out" was his farewell.

This was my last face-to-face conversation with the chairman, and as I look back on it, I realize that I failed to set the proper tone for the dispute. What should have been accented was not the organization chart or Jack Schneider or me, but the radically novel concept that news judgments, historically made in the news division or at the very top, would now be exercised by an intermediate echelon. Certainly CBS News knew it could never have an open-end claim on air time with no constraints; this was why we had cut back on unlimited space coverage and adopted the "space alert" system. If Schneider had said, "If you feel so strongly about the Vietnam hearings, go ahead, but you may have to cut down on other coverage or special programs later in the year," I think I would have had no reason to protest. But what had happened here was the equivalent of the advertising department of a daily newspaper saying to its editor, "No, you can't have four pages for a Supreme Court story on civil rights, because there aren't enough ads in this issue to pay for it." Of course, the truth was that if we'd had a sponsor willing to pick up the bill for the Vietnam hearings or if the soap operas' sponsors had agreed to stay with us, there would have been no problem. I believe now that this, together with the fact that we had stayed on until long past midnight for President Johnson's return from Hawaii, was the real reason for the new policy, and I failed to make this the issue in my final meeting with Paley.

I stopped by Stanton's office after leaving Paley, but he was at lunch. By the time he called me at five o'clock I was on a shuttle plane for Washington to attend the White House Radio-Television Correspondents dinner. I called him back from the capital to say that I was taking the midnight plane back and could see him the next morning. Again I agreed not to air our dispute publicly—no easy task at the dinner, where our failure to cover the hearings that day had cast a pall on the CBS staff and was the subject of sardonic comments by our competitors.

After the dinner our Washington bureau gave a reception, during which I received two phone calls. The first was from Kidder Meade, the information officer for CBS, who told me that according to the early-morning editions of the New York papers, NBC was spreading the rumor that I had resigned and was going to be in charge of all documentaries at NBC. I said that the rumor was ridiculous, that I hadn't talked to anyone except Paley and Stanton, and that I had made no plans beyond meeting with the latter the next morning.

The next call was from Ben Kubasik, the information chief of the news division, who read me a long interview with Jack Schneider in the next day's *New York Times.* In it the newly appointed group vice-president explained that he, not the news division, had made the decision not to carry the Thursday hearings; he thought relatively few persons sat at home for the prolonged hearings, he said, and a majority of the country's opinion-makers were busy at work. A spokesman for Schneider had also told Barbara Delatiner of *Newsday,* in an interview which appeared the next day, that the decision was "not motivated by commercial considerations . . . Loss of advertising . . . did not enter into the decision." He admitted that the news division felt otherwise, but that it had been Schneider's decision to make.

The interviews also mentioned Schneider's belief that summaries on the evening news were the proper place for edited segments of the hearings, and according to the New York *Post,* he felt that full coverage "could have resulted in 'obfuscating' and 'confusing' the issues." The *Herald Tribune*'s story added that Mr. Schneider had not decided whether to carry next week's hearings of Rusk and Taylor, but that again the decision would be his to make.

The next morning, Friday, February 11, with CBS being battered by newspapers from coast to coast for not televising Kennan, I sat down with Stanton feeling that I was back where I had started on Wednesday—except that now our dispute was public. The fact that Schneider had chosen to ventilate the matter in the press seemed to me only to compound his bad judgment in not carrying the hearings. Stanton observed that both decisions "might or might not have been errors," but that they had been made in good faith and that we ought to use the time to try to figure out a solution that would accommodate both sides.

We talked for the better part of two hours and got nowhere. Finally Stanton asked me to postpone any decision until Monday. Schneider was on his way to Palm Beach for a business meeting, Paley was leaving the next day for Nassau, and Stanton had not had an opportunity to talk to either of them yet. I agreed to wait.

Over the weekend I had no direct contact with the management, but pressure was continuously applied through well-meaning third parties. Three vice-presidents in other divisions called—one to say that though he hoped I would not do anything drastic, he agreed with me completely about the hearings. Several press officers from other parts of the company called to beg me not to rock the boat "at this time," and mutual friends outside CBS also called to offer advice or moral support. Within the news division, I had never felt greater unanimity. One veteran bureau chief said, "It's a historic thing you're trying to get across. Stay with it." The heads of two affiliated stations phoned, one to advise me to forget the hearings, that they were a bore; the other to urge me to stick to my guns.

On Monday morning when I attended the weekly staff meeting, the news division was treated very deferentially. Stanton praised the Sunday Vietnam-debate broadcast as being almost as effective as the one with Stennis and Morse, and everyone was pleased by Maxwell Taylor's appearance on *Face the Nation.* When I had called General Taylor immediately after the broadcast to congratulate him on how well he had handled himself, he remarked that it had been a good rehearsal for his meeting with Senator Fulbright's committee on Thursday, "which I suppose you'll be televising."

By midday on Monday I thought I detected a slight change in positions. John Reynolds, who had succeeded Schneider as president of the television network, called me from Palm Beach, where, with Schneider, he was attending a meeting with National Football League officials to sign a new contract. When he asked for my recommendations about televising the remainder of the hearings, I told him that Taylor was to appear on Thursday, Rusk on Friday, and that the news division recommended complete live coverage. I also suggested that we do a special summary of the Taylor, Rusk and Kennan testimonies, on Friday night at 10 P.M. Previously Reynolds had indicated that this was a soft spot both in the ratings and in advertising income, and that if we ever needed the time period we could probably have it. Now I had the impression that he was about to agree, but when he did not, I asked him to try to let us know by the end of the working day. NBC had already announced their live coverage, and I urged a favorable and early decision so that we could promote our broadcast on news programs, or even run an ad for it. Reynolds said that he would call me back, but he never did.

I was back in Stanton's office at a quarter to five. Naïvely, I was hoping that perhaps he was going to tell me that Schneider and Reynolds were accepting my recommendation to televise the Taylor-Rusk hearings as an indication of their good faith. I was wrong again. The first half-hour of our meeting was spent on everything but the problem at issue—a technique this gifted negotiator employed effectively on all executives at moments of tension. Fueling his pipe methodically, Stanton would clear the air by a wry recital of his own "crisis of the day." On this occasion he spoke of the exasperations of decorating the thirty-fifth floor of the new building, and of his frustration over a lack of progress in the company's attempts to diversify. As always, by the time we got to my problem, I was so involved and impressed with the difficulties of his job that I was actually uncomfortable about discussing my troubles with him.

When we finally did get down to the matter at hand, Stanton was quite willing to discuss the new organizational plan, why he thought it would work and why I should not resign, but he refused to talk about the future hearings. "Anything such as that will have to be worked out with Schneider and Reynolds." When I brought up the weekly Vietnam report, which had originally been his suggestion and which had meant so much to the news division, I ran into a polite wall of silence. He was making it clear to me that the news division's direct access to Paley and Stanton—the right of appeal to the management —would be blocked in the future. I said again that this was unacceptable to me, just as it would have been to my predecessors.

What I did not say but what I believed then—and still do—was that the group vice-president's role had been created as a buffer so that Paley and Stanton could avoid the embarrassment of having to say no to CBS News on matters of news judgment. Perhaps I had been unreasonable in forcing them to take such stands in the past; certainly it was unpleasant for such superior men as Paley and Stanton to have to be negative when the only reason was that it would affect earnings. Never for a moment have I believed that the decision not to televise the Kennan hearings was Schneider's alone—not on his first day on the job. The system had made the decision; Schneider was merely in charge of the stop light. He would not always say no, but when that answer had to be given for financial reasons, he would be the villain to the news division, the press and the public.

I also believe that the job of group vice-president had been created at the recommendation of the efficiency experts the company had hired. Stanton volunteered that the idea had been considered during Aubrey's tenure, but that the management had realized he and I would not get along. "With Jack Schneider, we thought you'd feel differently." I said that I thought I might have if it had not been for the disastrous decisions of the past few days, along with Jack's public pronouncements and the implications as to who had the final say about news programs.

"Look, Fred," Stanton said, "we want you to stay, but I am afraid that you're painting yourself into a corner."

I agreed but said I felt that it was for a fundmental principle.

Stanton continued, "You and the news division have accomplished so much in these twenty-four months; why not compromise on this one issue?"

"Because, Frank, this one issue is Vietnam. We are going to be judged by the way we cover Vietnam." I pointed out that though I had continuously pushed for more information on Vietnam, it was not because I was dove or a hawk. "I happen to believe that the President has little choice but the one he is pursuing. But I am convinced that one of the reasons there is such uneasiness about the war is that the debate has been so bottled up. These hearings and our Sunday shows give us a chance to ventilate the struggle. It might even prevent the war from escalating any further and give the President ammunition against his critics. I want us to use television to illuminate, to stimulate debates. The fact that we are on during the day with hearings that may bore some housewives will alert the nation that broadcasting isn't doing business as usual. That's why we should have been on the air both days of the U.N. debates. That's what reporting the news is all about, and that's why Jack Schneider, who has never been a journalist, cannot be expected to make the right decisions."

"Fred, you underestimate Jack, but in any case the chairman and I will still be around. I urge you to make this one compromise."

"But it *isn't* just this one compromise," I replied. "The news division has been compromising constantly. We compromised when I let Schneider twist my arm about inserting a fifth commercial minute on the Cronkite program. Now he's trying to force me to move that extra minute into the news section of the broadcast. With his new authority, he'll probably order us to do it, and that will cause another bitter showdown. I compromised when, strictly for money reasons, I let Schneider talk me into moving the Mike Wallace morning news program from 10 A.M., where it had an audience all its own, to 7:05 A.M., where it could not possibly compete against the two-hour *Today Show.* We'll be still further compromised if Schneider makes us put a sports announcer on the Cronkite program because the sponsor wants it. I'll compromise, but not over Vietnam or what we cover or who makes the editing decisions, and I can't believe you'd really want me to. I'd no longer be the man you hired. If I keep compromising over important matters, I won't be Fred Friendly at all—I'll be a flabby mutation."

Stanton laughed, said that there was little chance of that happening, and that he and Paley wanted me to remain the irritant I was. "But, Fred," he repeated, "you're painting yourself into a corner."

"Frank, if I see any movement toward a settlement I'll stay, and you know that."

"Well," Stanton said, "perhaps we can reinstate the CBS News executive committee meetings." Paley, Stanton and the presidents of all the affected divisions were supposed to attend these meetings, which were often called off at the last minute. When we did meet, the agenda concerned itself with such important "policy" matters as whether news film should be sold to political parties or whether correspondents should be forced to plug an advertiser's product. (We had won that battle for television, but we were under great pressure to change it for radio news.)

I answered that this might be a solution if the meetings were reinstated on a regular weekly basis, and if both he and the chairman attended. I suggested that Paley be the chairman of such a committee and that the president of the news division be in charge of the agenda. This would be precisely what the Tuesday news meetings had once been, on a more formal basis, and it would preclude Schneider from having absolute power over news judgments.

Stanton did not respond to my suggestion. Instead, he asked if I would be willing to meet with Jack Schneider if he could arrange it. I said that I would be prepared to, if it was understood that the purpose of the meeting was to discuss specific proposals for a working arrangement. Clearly there was no point in putting us alone in a room together and letting us argue over the mistakes of the past few days.

I never heard another word about a meeting with Schneider. Perhaps I should have made more suggestions for solutions, but I thought that they would be regarded as ultimatums, and I also believed that the matter really could be settled only by Paley or Stanton.

Now Stanton asked me again if we could defer any decision for one more day; again I agreed. As I was leaving he showed me the draft of a resignation announcement, "should all efforts fail tomorrow." In turn I read him a brief paragraph from my letter of resignation. I asked him whether he would like to have my proposed letter to read overnight, but he said that he preferred not to see it until there was "no other way out." I told him that his announcement was satisfactory except for the fact that it referred only to my objections over reorganization, whereas I thought it should also mention the dispute over the Vietnam hearings. He made a note about this, and we agreed to meet again the next morning after he had talked to Schneider.

When Stanton finally called me the next day, Tuesday, February 15, it was about twelve-thirty; Sevareid and Cronkite were in my office, and I asked if I might call back in ten minutes. When I did I was invited to come over "as soon as convenient."

"I assume we have our regular Tuesday lunch," I said.

There was an ever-so-slight hesitation, and then Stanton said, "No, I'm afraid I have an engagement."

When I walked into the president's office some ten minutes later I noticed Tad Myers, a CBS press officer, in the outside office. In a few minutes I knew why Myers was waiting. Stanton again spoke of "painting yourself into a corner." I said that I had still not heard from Schneider or Reynolds about anything, including the Taylor-Rusk hearings. Stanton indicated he had been in great anguish over the entire matter, that he had not slept all night, but that he saw no way out. "If I can't dissuade you," he said, "I guess we'll have to put out this announcement." He handed me a revised release, which read:

> It is with deep regret that I accept the resignation of Fred W. Friendly as President of the CBS News Division. Mr. Friendly feels that he is unable to continue in his post as a result of a decision made by the recently appointed Group Vice-President, Broadcasting, John A. Schneider, not to schedule live television coverage of the testimony of George F. Kennan before the Senate Foreign Relations Committee last week.
>
> Fred Friendly has been an outstanding leader of broadcast journalism. His contributions to the public, to his profession and to CBS have been great indeed. My associates, his colleagues and I will miss him.

As I began to read it I reached into my pocket and handed Stanton my letter. "While I'm reading yours," I said, "you ought to read mine."

At that moment Stanton's secretary came into the office

and said that General Eisenhower was calling from Palm Desert and wished to speak to Mr. Friendly. I believe Stanton thought that the General was calling about our crisis; so did I. The General was a good friend both of Paley and myself, and it was conceivable that some mutual friend had asked him to be a peacemaker. Stanton excused himself so that I could talk privately, which gave him five or six minutes in which to read my letter.

The undramatic fact is that the General was unaware of our crisis and had called about a projected Abilene broadcast that we had discussed a month earlier at Gettysburg. I told him that I would call him later and described briefly what was happening. He was embarrassed, but both on the phone and in a long, sensitive letter that arrived the next day, he told me that he sympathized with the principle I was fighting for, even though he did not agree with all the senators and witnesses at the hearings. A few weeks later he told me that he thought the hearings had been divisive for the country.

When Stanton returned he asked me if I was going to release my letter. I said that I was not sure, but that I would certainly have to say something because I did not want to risk a lot of off-the-cuff telephone interviews in which my position might be obscured.

Stanton said that he would personally handle the terms of my separation. On his desk was one of the bronze letters of the company name on the old 485 Madison Avenue building, and he told me that he was going to send me the letter "E" as a memento of my sixteen years at CBS. I said that I was sorry to leave and that I thought they were making a mistake. My last words were: "Someday you may ask me back." With more emotion than I had seen from him in a long time, Stanton said, "Perhaps we will, Fred."

As I started toward the elevators I saw Myers entering

Stanton's office. There was no doubt in my mind that this final "mediation session" had only been the epilogue to a decision made by others the night before.

By the time I returned to my office in the Broadcast Center, less than ten minutes away, the CBS announcement was already on the wires and Myers had called our own news information director to tell him that the company had accepted my resignation. A few minutes later I released my letter, which read as follows:

Dear Bill and Frank:

This is the third time since last Thursday that I have asked you to accept my resignation as President of CBS News, and this time you have an obligation to accept it.

It is important that you and my colleagues in the News Division know that I am not motivated by pique or change of status in a table of organization, or lack of respect for Jack Schneider. He is, as you have both recalled, someone I had asked to join the News Division in an administrative role more than a year ago, when he was Station Manager of WCAU-TV.

I am resigning because CBS News did not carry the Senate Foreign Relations Committee hearings last Thursday, when former Ambassador George Kennan testified on Vietnam. It was the considered news judgment of every executive in CND that we carry these Vietnam hearings as we had those of the other witnesses. I am convinced that the decision not to carry them was a business, not a news, judgment.

I am resigning because the decision not to carry the hearings makes a mockery of the Paley-Stanton CND crusade of many years that demands broadest access to congressional debate. Only last year, in a most eloquent letter, you petitioned the Chief Justice for the right to televise live sessions of the Supreme Court. We cannot, in our public utterances, demand such access and then, in one of the crucial debates of our time, abdicate that responsibility. What happens to that sense of fairness and balance so close to both of you, when one day's hearings, and perhaps the most comprehensive, are omitted? How can we return on Thursday and Friday of this week without denying Schneider's argument that "the housewife isn't interested"? Why were NBC's housewives interested? What would have happened to those housewives if the Supreme Court had said "Yes" to your plea for live coverage? Where would broadcast journalism have been last Thursday if NBC had elected not to carry the U.S. Senate hearings on the war?

When last Thursday morning at ten o'clock I looked at the monitors in my office and saw the hearings on Channel 4 (pool production, by the way, via CBS News crews) and saw a fifth rerun of *Lucy,* then followed by an eighth rerun of *The Real McCoys,* I wanted to order up an announcement that said: "Due to circumstances beyond our control the broadcast originally intended for this time will not be seen." It was not within CND's control because the journalistic judgment had been, by a sudden organizational act, transferred to a single executive. Mr. Schneider, because of his absolute power, would have more authority than William Paley or Frank Stanton have exercised in the past two years. This in spite of the fact that Mr. Schneider's news credentials were limited in the past to local station operations, with little experience in national or international affairs.

The concept of an autonomous news organization responsible only to the Chairman and the President was not a creation of mine. It is a concept almost as old as CBS News, and is a tradition nurtured by the Ed Klaubers, the Ed Murrows, the Paul Whites, and rigidly enforced by both of you. The dramatic change in that concept is, to my mind and that of my colleagues, a form of emasculation.

Actually, it is the second step of the emasculation that began when CBS News was shorn of its responsibility in the news operation at WCBS-TV here in New York. Had I been in my current position at the time of this change, I should have resisted it as I do the current weakening. It denied CBS News a highly professional outlet in New York, a competitive position with the other networks, and the training apparatus for the Sevareids, the Cronkites, the Reasoners of the future.

My departure is a matter of conscience. At the end of the day it is the viewer and the listener who have the biggest stake in all this. Perhaps my action will be understood by them. I know it will be understood by my colleagues in news and I know Ed Murrow would have understood. A speech he delivered to the Radio-Television News Directors Association in 1958 spelled it all out:

"One of the basic troubles with radio and television news is that both instruments have grown up as an incompatible combination of show business, advertising, and news. Each of the three is a rather bizarre and demanding profession. And when you get all three under one roof, the dust never settles. The top management of the networks, with a few notable exceptions, has been trained in advertising, research, sales, or show business. But, by the nature of the corporate structure, they also make the final and crucial decisions having to do with news and public affairs.

"Frequently they have neither the time nor the competence to do this. It is not easy for the same small group of men to decide whether to buy a new station for millions of dollars, build a new building, alter the rate card, buy a new Western, sell a soap opera, decide what defensive line to take in connection with the latest congressional inquiry, how much money to spend on promoting a new program, what additions or deletions should be made in the existing covey or clutch of vice-presidents and, at the same time—frequently on the same long day—to give mature, thoughtful consideration to the manifold problems that confront those who are charged with the responsibility for news and public affairs."

Such a day was last Thursday when a non-news judgment was made on the Kennan broadcast.

Murrow went on to say:

"Upon occasion, economics and editorial judgment are in conflict. And there is no law which says that dollars will be defeated by duty. Not so long ago the President of the United States delivered a televisicn address to the nation. He was discoursing on the possibility or probability of war between this nation and the Soviet Union and Communist China—a reasonably compelling subject. Two networks—CBS and NBC—delayed that broadcast for an hour and fifteen minutes. If this decision was dictated by anything other than financial reasons, the networks didn't deign to explain those reasons. That hour-and-fifteen-minute delay, by the way, is about twice the time required for an ICBM to travel from the Soviet Union to major targets in the United States. It is difficult to believe that this decision was made by men who love, respect and understand news."

In that speech Ed also said:

"There is no suggestion here that networks or individual stations should operate as philanthropies. But I can find nothing in the Bill of Rights or the Communications Act which says that they must increase their net profits each year, lest the Republic collapse."

I now leave CBS News convinced that the last two years have shown some improvement, and convinced, ironically, that my leaving will help insure the integrity and independence of the news operation. I believe that the Senate hearings next Thursday and Friday will be televised live because of circumstances within the control of the man you choose to succeed me. For the kind of news executive who would warrant the trust of the two recipients of this letter would insist upon such a mandate. Senator George Norris, quoted in John F. Kennedy's *Profiles in Courage* says, "Whatever use I have been has been accomplished in the things *I failed* to do rather than in the things I actually did do."

I now leave CBS News after 16 years, believing that the finest broadcast journalists anywhere will yet have the kind of leadership they deserve. I know that I take with me their respect and affection as, indeed, I hope I do yours.

Faithfully,

F. F.

Mr. William S. Paley
Chairman
Dr. Frank Stanton
President
Columbia Broadcasting System
51 West 52nd Street
New York, New York

February 15, 1966

Around two o'clock a colleague suggested that I should have called Paley, who was in Nassau, and personally read my letter to him over the phone. When I called Stanton to ask him if he had read my letter to the chairman, he said that he had just done so, and that Paley wanted me to call him. When I did, Paley wanted to know only if I had released my letter; when I told him that I had, all useful communication ceased. "You volunteered to me last week that you would not make a public announcement," he said.

"Mr. Paley, that was on Thursday before Jack Schneider had ventilated the entire matter in the press." The truth is that it was unrealistic of me to have made such a promise and the public furor caused by my dispute with Schneider required an explanation in my own terms. Nonetheless I should have made certain Paley knew of my letter before it was released.

The last thing the chairman said to me was: "Well, if you hadn't put out that letter, maybe we could still have done something." I answered that my letter was "after the fact, long after."

At ten minutes to three I walked into the news room to talk to the assembled personnel. I asked for the continuity of news operations, and said that the most effective way to support my action was by sustaining the CBS News tradition, particularly in our Vietnam coverage. The large room was crowded with reporters, editors, producers, writers, desk assistants, cameramen, secretaries and engineers. I could see Ned Calmer about to begin the 3 P.M. news; Doug Edwards, in the studio preparing his 3:25 report, came out to listen. The atmosphere was emotional and charged.

Most of the previous departures from CBS News—Murrow, Mickelson, Smith, Salant—had come when the news division was operating from various parts of the city and had no central headquarters at which everyone could gather. Now all of the anguish, disappointment and doubt about CBS's commitment to serious news was bottled up within the four walls of one news room. The response that greeted me and that lingered after I had left was a release rather than a tribute, a burst of sorrow not so much that any one person was leaving, but that CBS had faltered under pressure. As a senior correspondent wrote me later: "I am sorry, because you had gotten this unwieldy organization off dead center and moving. It was a herculean task because when they put it together they didn't include a self-starter. You got it out of the rut and moving fast enough for the engine to catch . . . Sometimes I'm tortured by the doubt that they don't want it rolling too fast."

Later that afternoon I flew down to Washington. At our news room there I spoke to the staff of Richard Salant's role as the custodian and guardian of CBS News, of the faith that so many of us had in him, and that he could be counted on. I had strong reason to believe that the news executive at CBS who would be invited to take the job would respectfully reject it out of principle, and that the management would turn once again to Salant.

At precisely three o'clock the next day Stanton called me at home to ask if my office could be prepared for Salant; Schneider and Dick, he said, were on their way to the news room to announce that the latter was being appointed acting president of the news division.

On the night of Wednesday, February 23, there was a small episode involving the President of the United States which was a more fitting postscript to the whole incident than all the editorials, news stories and cartoons combined. Mr. Johnson was to speak on Vietnam at a Freedom House dinner in New York, where he would receive its annual award. Originally CBS and NBC had planned to show a video tape of this important address at 11:15 P.M., but at the last minute CBS changed its plan and announced that the speech would be carried live, in place of *The Dick Van Dyke Show* at 9:30. Just four minutes before air time, when the President was informed of this, he remarked, according to two White House aides, "I suppose we have to credit this to the courtesy of Fred Friendly."

In this context, there was much press speculation at the time and a few letters from senators hinting that the President might have killed CBS's coverage of the hearings by putting pressure on his friend Stanton; a few even came close to making this accusation on the Senate floor. On February 16, the day after my resignation, Senator Ernst Gruening of Alaska told the Senate: "The question remains: What lies behind this attempt to keep from the American television audiences the true facts about our involvement in Vietnam? What were the pressures—if any—exerted on CBS to cause it initially to decide that its viewers should not see a live broadcast of the testimony by

Mr. Kennan before the Senate Foreign Relations Committee?"

In a colloquy with Gruening, Senator Albert Gore of Tennessee, a member of the Foreign Relations Committee, called the Vietnam hearings the most important in the last twenty years, and asked: "If the American people are not entitled to the fullest information on such an issue as this, the issue of war and peace, then for what purpose should the government permit the use of the airwaves? Let us never forget that every single television station operates at the license of the government. The wavelengths belong to all the people of the country."

Other senators and congressmen inquired about White House pressure on CBS, and several prominent journalists wrote pieces stating that there had been phone calls from Washington to the company, but these charges were never substantiated and most of the articles never appeared. There seems to be no point in indulging in such speculation because there has been no evidence to support these rumors, and I have said so publicly. I do not think that I am being naïve in my belief that the decision was clearly one of business over journalism, of dollar-editing over the professional judgment of an entire news organization.

It is true that in spite of his public statements, Stanton was apprehensive about some of our Vietnam coverage and resisted the idea of our "Vietnam Perspective" debates, but I believe that his personal feelings played little or no part in what happened. Several officials of the Administration, particularly Arthur Sylvester, the Assistant Secretary of Defense for Public Affairs and the high priest of the policy of news-managing, were constantly complaining to the networks about their coverage and the reliability of their correspondents, but I know of no attempt actually to censor coverage of an important event.

". . . a tempest in a TV-pot," as *Time* dismissed my resignation, the "hair-triggery" act of an otherwise able man, was a far bigger story than CBS or I had expected it to be. The Aubrey dismissal made news too, but that was at least partially because Aubrey was a show-business personality, and the gossip and notoriety about him made good copy. In this case CBS simply misjudged the reaction to my resignation, just as they had consistently miscalculated the public response to television family squabbles. The morning after Walter Cronkite had been removed from his convention role Paley told a man he shared a taxi with, "I never thought it would cause such a clamor." The company's surprise at the outcry about its purchase of the New York Yankees is another example. But I too miscalculated the news value of my exit because I had believed the public was so jaded by the recent flurry of television exits that I underestimated its interest in the issue.

Today the reason for the clamor seems to me very simple: three crucial elements—Vietnam policy, the public airwaves and corporate profits—had all collided, and on live television at that. "The big switch," as the *New York Times* had described the control of air time when I was appointed, had become the ultimate button on the machine that now literally possessed the men who had built and operated it for so long. Given their choice as responsible citizens, Paley, Stanton, Schneider and every member of the board from Robert Lovett, former Secretary of Defense, to Millicent McIntosh, former president of Barnard, would have elected to broadcast the hearings. But a system designed to produce profits to respond to the stock market, which in turn responds to ratings, was governed more by concern for growth and earnings than for news responsibility.

Many of the almost four thousand letters I received after my resignation were from stockholders, and one of them said: "I own several thousand shares of stock. How do I register the fact that I would settle for less profits in return for more responsibility?" I couldn't answer the question, because the corporate moneymaking machine has no input for such a command. Maximum profit is the only signal it hears loud and clear.

"The big switch," which used to be on Paley's desk when tough, swift, forget-the-budget decisions made CBS a national asset, now consisted of many smaller switches on other desks, all requiring a consensus of approval. I had violated that system, short-circuiting the machine by appealing directly to the news judgment of Paley and Stanton.

The new *modus operandi* went into effect one hour after Schneider had been appointed, and when the damage was assessed, Paley is reported to have said, "It never should have been permitted to happen," Stanton called it "a tragedy," the news division was numb, and the public's right to know had been jeopardized again. But the new gadget on the machine had worked; keeping the Kennan testimony off the air for that one day alone had saved the company $250,000, and the affiliated stations perhaps as much again. This single decision had paid the fee of the efficiency experts who had recommended the creation of the job called "group vice-president."

As always in times of crises, it was Stanton who had to straighten out the mess. In part, this meant commissioning a public-opinion poll—not yet released—and a sober, honest letter from Stanton to troubled stockholders and viewers. One, to Mr. T. Thacher Robinson, Urbana, Illinois, was released to the press, and it was printed in the CBS house organ:

> Dear Mr. Robinson:
>
> I fully understand the concern which led you to write me about the events involving CBS News last week. Having consistently taken a serious view of the responsibility of broadcast journalism to the American people during the twenty years I have been President of CBS, I must respond at some length to your comments.
>
> The CBS Group Vice-President, Broadcasting, John A. Schneider, made an administrative decision not to broadcast

live, on the CBS Television Network, the full testimony of another witness, Professor George Kennan (6 hours), a former ambassador to the Soviet Union. CBS News did keep its crews and equipment at the hearings and, in accordance with a prior agreement with the other network news organizations, originated the coverage which was carried by NBC. Mr. Friendly disagreed with the decision not to broadcast the Kennan testimony in its entirety on CBS and insisted upon our accepting his resignation.

The decision not to broadcast Professor Kennan's testimony in full may seem to you the wrong one. But it was neither a cynical nor an impulsive one. Decisions of this kind in broadcasting often have to be made before the full impact of the event is known. They must also be made in a context that cannot always be wholly clear to the public. Factors governing such decisions include the television viewing habits of the public, the newsworthiness of the event concerned, and of the participants in it, the likelihood of time having to be made available for more significant future phases of the same event, the possibility of the specific matter of the broadcast's being handled with more meaning to more people in a later news broadcast or special summary, the announced intention of other broadcasting organizations to cover the event in its entirety, and other considerations.

Among the latter—but of no more weight than any other factor—is the necessity to maintain a sound and viable economy within the company. The cost of maintaining television and radio news organizations is enormous, and the major part of it must be borne by income from entertainment programing. The specific cost incurred by the CBS Television Network in covering the four days of the Vietnam hearings, for example, amounted to just under $1 million, and the loss in income for the stations which make up the Network is estimated to be over $1 million, in addition. Obviously, since CBS News cannot be self-supporting, we must pay some attention to the economics of broadcasting in making decisions involving such costs.

First of all, I want to assure you that CBS has believed—and continues to believe—that it has an obligation to report the Vietnam war and the issues surrounding it as fully, as revealingly, and as ably as it can. We believe that we have been conscientious and effective in trying to meet this obligation. In addition to daily reports from the battlefronts and the Vietnam countryside, CBS has also broadcast in peak viewing time many hours of special reports presenting the views of the Administration and of its critics both at home and abroad. Among those appearing on such reports have been Cabinet members, college professors and students, foreign statesmen, United Nations officials, and authors and journalists.

Seven weeks before they commenced, CBS urged the Chairman of the Senate Committee on Foreign Relations to permit live television coverage of the hearings on Vietnam that were the subject of the controversy that prompted your letter. We were aware that the hearings would constitute, on the whole, a valuable forum for enlightening the American people on our involvement in Vietnam, the forces that brought it about, and the implications to which it gives rise. On January 30, five days before the hearings opened, the CBS Television Network pre-empted an hour and a half for a special report, "Vietnam Perspective: The Congress and the War," presented live from Washington and marking the first major use of coast-to-coast television by congressional leaders to deliberate publicly America's conduct of the war. The CBS Television Network, thereafter, broadcast, in their entirety, the testimony of David Bell, Director of the Agency for International Development (7 hours, 12 minutes), General Gavin (5 hours, 11 minutes), who had gained widespread attention for his views on our military policy in Vietnam, General Taylor (6 hours, 33 minutes), military advisor to the President, who defended it, and of the Secretary of State, Mr. Rusk (6 hours, 3 minutes). In addition, the CBS Television Network pre-empted two hours of prime time for special reports summarizing and analyzing the hearings and their background, 10–11 PM, February 8 and 18.

With regard to the Vietnam hearings, it was CBS's conclusion, rightly or wrongly, that the testimony of Professor Kennan, who had not been recently and prominently associated, as General Gavin had been, with criticism of U.S. policy and who holds no official position, as do Director Bell, General Taylor and Secretary Rusk, would not be of sufficiently general public interest or of sufficiently determining significance to justify pre-empting the some six hours of television time necessary to broadcast it in its entirety, but that the testimony could be best handled in the form of a succinct summary and important excerpts in later news and special broadcasts.

Decisions of this kind all too frequently involve borderline cases. The CBS Television Network broadcasts events that the other networks do not carry and sometimes omits those that another network may carry. We have been condemned as often and as severely by audiences for interrupting regular programing for such broadcasts as we have been for deciding not to do so.

I hope that, while you may fault us on a decision with which you may not agree, you will consider our overall coverage of the Vietnam war and our overall record in electronic journalism. I hope, too, that you will reserve judgment until you have seen our future contributions to public knowledge and understanding of the war and of all other significant news developments. I can, in return, assure you that CBS News has no intention of relinquishing its position of leadership in its field and that Columbia Broadcasting System, Inc. has every intention of continuing to give the News Division its full support, and encouraging it to do an even better job in the future than it has in the past.

With all good wishes.

Sincerely,
Frank Stanton

February 25, 1966

Because it represents CBS's official position, the letter deserves analysis.

Stanton says that Group Vice-President Schneider made an administrative decision not to broadcast the hearings, and cites as one of the reasons the high cost. But Schneider's official spokesman was quoted as stating: "We were not motivated by commercial considerations. The loss of advertising revenue did not enter into the decision."

More important, however, is the content of a study made by James Boylan, editor of the *Columbia Journalism Review*, in the Spring 1966 issue. Because there are many large cities where all three networks do not have outlets, a major event on any one of them is missed by much of the nation. Boylan points out that seventy-one markets did not have access to the full Senate hearings on Vietnam. When Jack Schneider pulled the switch on February 10, he literally blacked out full coverage in sixteen metropolitan areas—including WCIA, the station in Champaign, Illinois, which is the only one Mr. Robinson, in Urbana, could have watched. The NBC station in Springfield carried only part of the Kennan testimony.

In other words, Stanton inadvertently chose to write his letter to a citizen who had had no opportunity to watch Kennan after 1 P.M. on February 10. Other major cities which missed Kennan's testimony either because they are one-station markets or because the local NBC station chose not to run the broadcast include Baltimore, Cincinnati, Grand Rapids, Kalamazoo, Flint, Lansing, Cedar Rapids, Salinas-Monterey-Santa Cruz (California), Manchester (New Hampshire), most of Vermont, western Kentucky and southern Missouri, and the Austin station which services, among other towns, Johnson City, Texas. (The Austin UHF station did carry part of the hearings.)

Thus, those people who lived in these and many other areas could not depend upon NBC for coverage. For the woman in Macon with a husband in Vietnam, or an editor in Baltimore, the plea that NBC was carrying the hearings was as ironic as it was for the man from Urbana. As for CBS News' competitive position in those areas and in the country as a whole, the concession inherent in this position is clear.

Stanton also points out that a week after the Kennan hearing, CBS carried in full the testimony of General Taylor and Secretary Rusk—an admirable decision, but one in direct conflict to Schneider's conviction that full coverage of Kennan could result in "obfuscating" and "confusing" the issues. It seems to me at least a possibility that without my resignation these hearings might not have been scheduled.

In his letter Stanton gives the other witnesses impressive credentials but dimisses Kennan merely as "a former ambassador to the Soviet Union," without referring to his role as the principal author of the so-called containment policy, or as the witness that many observers thought was the most lucid and provocative of them all. "Decisions of this kind," he adds, ". . . often have to be made before the full impact of the event is known." But the news division had no doubt that Kennan would be an outstanding witness, and said so repeatedly.

Stanton's figures, broken down to a single day, show a cost of $500,000 for a six-hour session, or an average yield of over $41,000 per half-hour—much higher than the sales department's forecast at that time. This day-time air rate indicates the huge profits being realized from the use of the miracle of television as a transmission belt for retread serials, soap operas, game shows and the like. The yield from the detergent, deodorant, bleach or food advertisers who possess the day-time schedule (whose annual expenditures, according to Stanton's arithmetic—$250,000 for network sales, $250,000 to the local stations—multiplied by two hundred and sixty weekdays, totals some $130,000,000 annually) is the principal reason why no serious programing can be sustained for any length of time during those hours. This is why Mike Wallace's morning news program had to be moved from 10 A.M. In that time period it was almost sold out and attracting a loyal and informed audience, but the 10:30 advertisers did not want it there; more important, a sales study indicated that by inserting *I Love Lucy* reruns in that spot the company's revenue would increase by $1,000,000 a year. The "sold out" sign and the $500,000 per six-hour day is a far cry from Paley's 1934 testimony that the number of commercial hours on the CBS schedule would be limited.

In his letter Stanton also talks of the high cost of maintaining television and news organizations. One cannot deny this, but the fact is that television and radio news at both CBS and NBC produce revenues from time sales almost equal to their expenses.

I am glad to be able to agree with much of what Stanton says in the last paragraph of his letter to Mr. Robinson. Any fair observer would agree that CBS has been more than holding its own with the other two networks in general coverage of Vietnam, and that it has been far ahead in interpretation. Since my departure there have been a series of special programs on Vietnam policy and on China's role, and there was one remarkable half-hour experiment in which Eric Sevareid was permitted to present news analysis as a result of his six-week visit to Vietnam. Carried both on television and radio, it was in many ways a breakthrough for the broadcasting of interpretative journalism.

So ended my sixteen years at CBS, where, to paraphrase another man at another leave-taking, "I left some of my youth and too much of my heart." I had neither the inclination nor the energy to join one of the company's competitors, or to accept a BBC invitation and work abroad, and today I still cheer CBS's victories, weep at their frustrations, and keep an eye on the Yankees' standing. There are members of the government, Supreme Court judges, FCC commissioners, senators, congressmen and journalists in other media who applauded my decision; there are a few, including one in particular whose judgment I respect, who think that I will live to regret my departure, and that it was impulsive and ill-advised.

It is true that I still hear fire bells in the night when a Surveyor is seconds away from the moon, or when a wire service reports erroneously that James Meredith is dead on a Mississippi highway, or when a major battle is raging in Vietnam, but for the most part I sleep better than I have in years. Whatever bitterness I feel over my departure is toward the system that keeps such unremitting pressure on men like Paley and Stanton that they must react more to financial pressure than to their own taste and sense of responsibility. Possibly if I were in their jobs I would have behaved as they did. I would like to believe otherwise, but I must confess that in my almost two years as the head of CBS News I tempered my news judgment and tailored my conscience more than once. Perhaps it was this, as much as the dispute over the Vietnam hearings, that prompted me to get out while I still could.

The fact that I am not sure what I would have done in these circumstances, had I been chairman or president of CBS, perhaps tells more clearly than anything else what is so disastrous about the mercantile advertising system that controls television, and why it must be changed. For this medium remains a more important story than any it covers except for Vietnam and the urban disgrace. Television may not yet be the nation's schoolhouse, but it is more a place for learning and spreading of new ideas than a grind house for C movies, and if I can't tend the big switch, perhaps I can carry a spear or write a pamphlet or stoke a fire.

10 *Common Stock vs. the Commonwe*

> The FCC for over thirty years has an all but unblemished record of misconceiving both the problems and the available remedies in broadcasting. That they have done so with the best of intentions and (except for a few sordid interludes) with high standards of integrity, is a real source of scandal.
>
> PETER O. STEINER, professor of economics at the University of Wisconsin, in the *American Economic Review*, May 1966

The rocket named television has lost its course. Carl Sandburg wrote: "When a nation goes down . . . [or] a society perishes, one condition may always be found. They forget where they came from. They lost sight of what had brought them along." In the case of broadcasting, we have not only forgotten where we came from but where we are going.

David Sarnoff understood the challenge in the twenties when he suggested no commercials. Bill Paley understood it in the mid-thirties: "Nor does Columbia appear here [before the FCC] primarily as a business organization, except to the extent that economics are a necessary means to any social end. Surely any stress of economics as an end in themselves would betray a lack of understanding of the vital role which broadcasting plays on every plane of American life . . ."

I believe Paley and Stanton would still have subscribed to that statement in the late forties when the second stage of broadcasting began with television. Even though some of Stanton's 1959 speeches may have been conditioned by the quiz scandals, I am sure that he believed it when he said: "In the long view of history, television can be regarded . . . as one of the landmarks that has characterized that slow democratization of culture which has been one of the mainsprings of Western civilization . . . Socially, it is another and perhaps more vivid example of the intense interaction that must go on between a mass medium and the total society of which it is part, if it is to be truly a mass medium serving everyone."

In the same speech Stanton remarked that television "live[s] in a mercantile society [and] we must expect expressionism to be supported to a great extent—though not controlled by—mercantilism . . ." I suggest that television has now been captured by the mercantile structure. As Lippmann wrote in 1959: "While television is supposed to be 'free,' it has in fact become the creature, the servant and indeed the prostitute of merchandising."

In the earlier chapters of this book I was in my own element when writing about news and documentaries. Now, as I presume to broaden the base of my thesis to the economics which drive and regulate the machine, I am entering what is for me the unfamiliar ground of management doctrine and social systems.

Max Weber, the German socioeconomist, called business bureaucracy a social machine, "like a modern judge who is a vending machine into which the pleadings are inserted together with the fee, and which then disgorges the judgment together with its reasons mechanically derived from the code." I believe that such a vending-machine bureaucracy, controlled by its own economics and not just supported by it, has captured broadcasting. For example, the "time-outs" for commercials and station identification—the latter a financial windfall provided by antiquated FCC rules—are the most sacrosanct elements on television. Even on big entertainment shows, instructions to the news division were that if we had to interrupt the program for a news bulletin, deletion of a commercial should be the last resort. The standard order of procedure was to sacrifice the plot but not the revenue.

What built CBS was the drive of creative men who knew the techniques of radio and early television from the bottom up; if required, they could walk into a control room or a news room and take charge. In those days programs and their content were the first concern of Paley, Klauber, Bill Lewis, Paul White, Davidson Taylor and Hubbell Robinson, and the staff had such imaginative men as Norman Corwin, Irving Reis, Robert Louis Shayon and Worthington Miner. Today, in the tall gray building that houses the management group, there are buyers and sellers; few, if any, know how to put a television show together.

I would be quite content to see network schedules which would satisfy the taste and intellectual standards of a Bill Paley or Frank Stanton, but the inventory is no longer under their control. The choice of programs is delegated to a staff of buyers and taste followers with a unique ability to select those shows which are going to capture the attention of a jury of some twelve hundred families; the viewing habits of this small group are accepted as the projection of what nearly fifty-five million other homes are watching. Aubrey was a past master at sensing what would make those twelve hundred sets respond, and when he lost his touch, the task passed on to a group of rating specialists who could predict the Nielsen ratings of any given program or evening with extraordinary accuracy.

I never knew anyone at CBS who thought much of the Nielsen sample. There were constant attempts to have it improved, but the standard answer to any protest about it was: "Don't knock it; the advertisers take it as their bible and the advertising rates are established by it." And when it came to predicting what program those twelve hundred sets would be turned to, the CBS buyers were wizards. Whatever the knack is, the other networks have now developed similar extrasensory perception, and the difference in the ratings between the three networks at certain hours or even for the week's average is sometimes less than a point.

A. C. Nielsen, Sr., with whom I once discussed the power of his sample, defends the survey as reasonably accurate, though not to be construed as a finite measurement of the viewing habits of millions. What the networks do with his figures is their business, he says, but it was not his idea that they should be the basis for choosing all of the broadcast schedule. Independent specialists in the field of sampling are convinced that a television and radio industry whose revenues total $2,750,000,000 a year and spends so little on audience research as to afford only a survey of the Nielsen proportions, is in the position of gauging space-age tolerances with the kind of dip stick used to measure the amount of gas in a Model T.

Regardless of the accuracy or distortion of Nielsen's projections, they are fed into that vending-machine bureaucracy and are the final arbiter. There are exceptions, but in general the staple diet of television is cued to the taste of those twelve hundred homes. The fact that the popularity of programs is based on a sliding scale makes this barometer no less pernicious. Programs like *F Troop* and *Gilligan's Island* are on the air because they are in the middle range of ratings, but if some exciting new gimmick appeared and dropped them in the comparative standings they would be in trouble, even if their Nielsen ratings remained constant. As soon as the system realizes that there is a larger potential audience to be found in another format, a weaker program will disappear, for what television now demands is the largest possible audience. Testifying before the FCC, Frank Stanton as much as defined it in these terms: ". . . to appeal to most of the people most of the time . . ."

When Paley suggested that CBS's troubles may have begun when it went public, he was referring to the fact that Wall Street had discovered broadcast stocks. The tragedy was that they also discovered Nielsen and the ratings, and soon a strange formula became the determining factor of what went on the air. The stock market watched the ratings and, in turn, their effect on advertising sales, expected earnings, the amount of news and serious programing, and eventually the price of the stock. Thus was the broadcast diet of the American people determined.

A graphic analysis of the impact of ratings on Wall Street was made on *CBS Reports* in July 1965 by a highly respected Wall Street analyst, Gerald M. Loeb of E. F. Hutton and Company:

LOEB: There's a direct connection, a very direct connection, because it goes: programs, ratings, earnings, market price.

REPORTER: Do you know, on Wall Street, whether these ratings are accurate or inaccurate?

LOEB: We don't know whether the ratings are accurate or not. We read the papers and the trade papers and talk to people in the industry and to advertising people. We know the controversy of whether they are or whether they aren't [accurate], but they seem to be effective. Advertising people base the amount of money they spend, and so forth and so on, and I think they affect viewers too. If viewers hear about this, they tune in more . . . Whether they're right or wrong, they seem to work out.

REPORTER: Now, if the rating goes up one week and then goes down the next week and then goes up the third week, is that reflected in the market?

LOEB: Not that closely. It was, at the beginning. And of course now the Wall Street people are going in even deeper. They look at the ratings, and then they try to be experts in all fields and they start to say, "Well, what time of day, and what about the nighttime programing, and who is ahead this day of the week and what about the sectors which are the busiest sectors," and they get into a lot of complications. But it's the real broad trend. And there's been a change . . . in that one network has come up and become competitive with the others and its stock has come up and its earnings have come up and this is what has stimulated it.

This unholy equation is not the complete formula; there are serious but limited efforts to balance the schedule, not only to keep the FCC and the critics content, but because the managements of the three networks *do* want programs like *Death of a Salesman, The Glass Menagerie*, the *Hallmark* dramatic series on NBC, and the Tuesday night *News Hour* on CBS. There is also the new phenomenon of super box-office movies like *The Bridge on the River Kwai,* which was such a success, both critically and in its ratings, in the fall of 1966. But these are occasional high-rise projects in a ghetto of high-return tenements, and though there is promise that for all its pot-boilers, the 1966–67 season will have some exalted moments, they will only help to demonstrate the magic of which this medium is capable.

Thomas Moore, the plain-speaking president of ABC Television, has stated that the battle for prestige is now beginning to influence executive decisions: "ABC, NBC and CBS are all on a virtual binge. Each of us is trying to outdo the others . . . expanding areas of concentration . . . increasing the amount of quality programing . . ." Evidently drama is this year's prestige ornament, just as documentaries were after the quiz scandals. But the eternal problem is that once the new ornament gets taken for granted, the raves turn to tarnished indifference and the schedule reverts to bread-and-butter staples that merely make money.

Some secure place between the two extremes of the rating game and the one-upmanship of prestige must be found, for the simple basic motivation that you do your best because it's the right thing to do. Sam Goldwyn, who made a good thing out of excellence and doing what comes naturally, once said to me, "Tell 'em not to make the mistakes Hollywood made . . . Don't start making shows better after the people have stopped coming . . ."

The criteria by which the standard fare on television is selected depend on the amount of pressure the management corps associates with each item as they come to work every morning. The order of priority is something like this:

1. The ratings. The overnight figures carry some weight, but it is the biweekly Nielsen sample that is really important.
2. The effect of these ratings on advertisers.
3. The effect of these ratings on the company's expected earnings, and their effect on the stock market.
4. The company's corporate image as reflected in the press, by the leadership of the community and at the FCC—in that order.
5. Responsibility for true public service and personal taste in entertainment and cultural programs.

There was a time when CBS and NBC executives read that list in the reverse order. By the time ABC became a force in television, in the mid-fifties, the priorities had been inverted, and because of the new network's initial problems of survival it was the worst offender. In the early days of television, both Paley and Stanton read that list in the proper order, and they would today were it not for a series of circumstances beyond their control.

Television's downfall is that it discovered a direct circuit between its box office and its production centers. The box office abhors empty seats, and it was discovered that by lowering the common denominator, television could reduce the percentage of vacant seats out there—not just in prime time, but all day—in the twelve hundred homes whose viewing habits the electronic turnstile was tabulating. If *I Love Lucy* reruns meant an increase in the ratings over the CBS morning news at 10, then the news was moved to 7:05 A.M.

It is true that factors other than ratings occasionally are responsible for the choice of entertainment programs, but I know of no factor other than ratings for a show's *removal* by the management, with the exception of the quiz shows. It is an oversimplification to suggest that ratings alone are always decisive. An expensive program such as *The Danny Kaye Show,* which has only a fair rating of, say, 15 percent (approximately eight million homes), is in trouble, whereas a low-budget and seemingly indestructible show like *What's My Line?* will stay on the air with the same rating because the advertiser has a better bargain in the cost per thousand viewers.

The trouble with the entertainment shows on television today is that they aren't television. What is broadcast most of the time on most of the stations is a movie-tailored product that can be distributed electronically at an extremely low cost. Hollywood, which in the late forties and early fifties was so apprehensive about the threat of the medium, not only permitted itself to be captured by television—it *became* television. The dream of a theater without walls for instant communication, culture for millions and news in depth envisioned by the Sarnoffs and Paleys and Stantons is now a grind house for inferior Hollywood movies of half-hour and one-hour lengths. The live-image orthicon camera, which is the true magic of television whether focused on the moon or the halls of Congress, has become a reel of film fabricated by the Music Corporation of America or Desilu Productions, parading interchangeable situation comedies or Westerns or crime shows.

There is a place for such shows on television, but as the dominant fare at a time when an enlightened, informed, intellectually stimulated America may mean the difference between survival and extinction, this programing is substituting escapism for insight. To turn a movie theater into a burlesque house may be an owner's prerogative, but a civilized society cannot afford to let a land-grant university or a civic center be so transformed.

As this mediocrity, which in the short term is economically profitable, fills the air, it creates appetites; it styles the nation's taste just as advertising influences what we eat, smoke and drive. The stock answer of network apologists for the current television schedules is, "We give the people what they want," but what has actually happened is that those viewers who have been brainwashed select their own brand of popcorn, while those of more discerning tastes simply give up watching or listening. If you condition an audience to expect *The McCoys* or *Leave It To Beaver,* of course it will reject the Vietnam hearings or a McNamara news conference when it is broadcast in their place. A Walter Lippmann interview in the weekly time period of *Petticoat Junction* would be greeted with just as much outrage as he would receive if you asked him to lecture between the double feature at any of the Forty-second Street movie houses.

Gresham's law—that the bad drives out the good—applies not only to the television schedules but to the television viewer. For the editor, producer or reporter in broadcast journalism today, much of the excitement and fulfillment is gone because the audience that used to turn to *See It Now* or *Omnibus* or *David Brinkley's Journal* is gone. The remarkable public response to our McCarthy program might not be forthcoming now; the audience attuned to the great issues of our time has been at least partly supplanted by a more superficial one in search of escape.

If that audience and its taste have declined, who is responsible? Did the dream that was going to make this the best-informed nation on earth become a fantasy? Have we attained this magical power to communicate to millions of people at the click of a switch only to find that the viewers all this was built for, and who need it more than ever before, have disappeared or stopped looking, while those we have made addicts of mediocrity have become the nation's taste makers?

The real paradox of television is that if by some miracle the network shareholders and officers suddenly determined to use only good taste, good judgment and their conscience to guide their choice of programing, the power of the local stations would overrule them. Moreover, a network operating with an unbridled sense of responsibility would soon see its affiliates seceding to another network, perhaps even a new one, that traveled the low road to ratings and revenues. The harsh fact is that most affiliates are too profitable under present circumstances; mining gold from the ether as they are, they have no incentive to tamper with the magic results of "giving the people what they want."

A case record of profits with which I am familiar is the television station in Providence. In 1955 the owners of the Cherry and Webb Department Store, who were the operators of radio station WPRO, went on the air for an original investment, financed by radio profits, of a little more than $1,000,000. Channel 12 in Providence, a city of two hundred thousand people, serves a state with a population of some eight hundred thousand, and parts of nearby Massachusetts and Connecticut. Still, because the Boston stations also carry to Rhode Island and because Providence has had difficulties with its economy, WPRO-TV cannot, comparatively speaking, be called a bonanza. Yet in 1959 the Cherry and Webb interests sold their radio and television stations to Capital Cities Broadcasting Corporation for $6,500,000, and today, its president told me, the franchise could not be purchased for $12,000,000.

WPRO-TV's annual profit, something over $1,250,000, earns the 1959 purchasers more than 19 percent a year on their equity. But WPRO-TV is below average; the median revenue of profitable VHF stations in 1965 was $1,490,433.

The actual physical property of many television stations is only a fraction of their net annual profit; in some cases it is as low as 20 percent. The four hundred and seventy-three independently owned VHF stations operating in 1965 averaged a 45 percent rate of return on original investment in broadcast property, and a better than 90 percent rate of return on the undepreciated portion of this property. The true equity is the government franchise, which comes up for renewal every three years and "need not be renewed," according to the Communications Act of 1934. But because there is so much trafficking in licenses—some stations have changed hands several times, often for millions more than the previous sale—the new owner's investment in his electronic medallion is so heavy that he cannot afford any diminution in earnings or rate of growth. Hence the pressure on the station manager to show an ever-larger rate of return; those who cannot increase profits do not survive for long.

A producer of merchandise can improve his earnings by manufacturing and selling more of his product while spreading his fixed costs and thus reducing his unit costs up to a point. A newspaper or magazine can increase its news pages and advertising. But the television station manager, who has only a certain number of hours a day to sell, can only reap more profits by raising rates, selling more commercials, holding program costs down and giving up no more time to network unscheduled news events than his budget for this contingency allows. Therefore, a decision to pre-empt a whole day for Churchill's funeral, or to cancel all night-time programs when the Gemini VIII astronauts lost control after their docking operation, affected local revenues so much that station managers complained that their monthly earnings had sagged because of a decision made in New York. In contrast, the newspaper that adds four or eight pages for an important story loses little or nothing in advertising revenues.

For this reason, a public-spirited station manager must sometimes turn down a news special or a documentary series if he is running behind his projected sales. Even when sponsored, a network-public affairs broadcast costs that manager as much as 70 percent of his hourly rate; if he sells the same time locally or to a national advertiser who desires exposure in his area, he keeps all but the agency and spot-sales commission.

Though many individual stations are locally owned by banks, newspapers, merchants or entrepreneurs, some national corporations own the legal limit of five VHF channels. Multiple owners such as Metromedia, Capital Cities, Time-Life Broadcast, Post-Newsweek, Cowles, Storer Broadcasting Company (which made so much money out of broadcasting that it bought Northeast Airlines), Cox, Taft, Westinghouse and General Electric, control lucrative stations in major markets. For years the Corinthian Broadcasting Company, Jock Whitney's holding company for five television and four radio stations, helped support the losses of the New York *Herald Tribune*.

The multiple-owner companies are constantly attempting to horse-trade their five franchises into larger markets. Moreover, the country's tax system is an incentive for the trustee of a station to liquidate his stewardship for a handsome capital gain. It's like the game of Monopoly, in which you sell off lesser properties and buy "Boardwalk" or "Park Place" to put up rent-producing houses or hotels. For example, Capital Cities might be prepared to sell off Albany or Providence in order to buy a station in Cleveland or Los Angeles. And Corinthian might want to give up Houston to obtain a franchise in New York or Chicago.

In 1954, because of the five-VHF-station limit, CBS gave up its part-ownership in Washington and Minneapolis, enabling it eventually to purchase a station in a richer market, WCAU-TV and radio station WCAU in Philadelphia, for $20,000,000. This clearly served CBS's revenue needs, but it was a tremendous handicap to the news department, which could no longer control what news events could be seen in the nation's capital. The embarrassment of having a Presidential press conference blacked out of the news center of the world was sometimes difficult to explain to the White House. John Hayes, who formerly ran the broadcast stations for the Graham family and the Post-Newsweek interests, was an enlightened manager, but there were times when I literally had to plead with him to carry certain events. Several times the Washington *Post*'s diligent television critic, Larry Laurent, chided CBS for not carrying an event which we had on the network but which had not been carried by his employer's station.

The fact that all three networks are multiple-station owners in the richest markets means that there is an automatic conflict of interest between the operation of the network as a whole and its station division. The manager of, say, CBS's owned and operated station in St. Louis knows that he will be judged by his figures, and the one-minute sale he is able to make to a local brewer will dramatically increase his profits as compared to the sale of a similar commercial for a national brewery when it is channeled through the television network during a news report.

The inauguration of the CBS Saturday evening news program, an aspiration of Paley's and mine, was delayed for more than a year because the company's owned and operated stations did not want the television network to sell that time nationally. The disagreement was never argued on those terms —it was always put on the basis that "the local needs of the community require regional news"—but when a cost study established that the parent company would make more profits out of a national sale than the five owned and operated stations would lose, the program was finally given a place on the schedule.

Although the words "local" or "regional" have a kind of small-town ring to them, economically there is nothing small-time about these stations. Network-time sales account for only 35 percent of total television-time sales, whereas ten years ago they amounted to 45 percent. But although the stations are the rich relations, the three networks have concentrated their ownership in the largest markets—New York City, Los Angeles, Chicago, Philadelphia and San Francisco. There are thirty stations in these five cities—approximately 5 percent of the country's total—and they accounted for 28 percent of all station revenues in 1965.

In the same year the three networks and their fifteen owned and operated stations had profits of $161,600,000 before taxes, or very slightly over a 100 percent rate of return on broadcasting property, and 165 percent on the undepreciated part of tangible broadcast property. But while the networks showed profits of $59,400,000 before taxes, their owned and operated stations produced profits of $102,200,000.

The stations are obviously where the money is. At an FCC hearing in Chicago in 1962 the manager of ABC's owned and operated station in Chicago was quoted as saying, "The networks that own us need our profits, must have our profits and must continuously nudge us for more profits. This city [Chicago] is not their creative zone. This is their vital money zone . . ." Although the FCC has traditionally tried to free affiliated stations from what is called "network domination," its desire to encourage local live programing has in many cases worked in reverse, giving the local station an excuse to carry more lucrative local news instead of national network news and documentaries. Few stations have exploited this loophole more than some of the network owned and operated stations. (In an excellent cover story on Walter Cronkite in October of 1966, *Time,* whose parent corporation happens to own five lucrative television stations, reported: ". . . no local stations want a network news program at 11 P.M.—which is where Cronkite would like to be—because they can make twice the money at that time with local spot ads on their own local news show . . .")

Thus, the CBS Television Network and its supplier, CBS

News, on which most of the responsibility for the reporting of national and world affairs rests, in effect have no local outlets; these channels are under the control of the autonomous station division where the expanding profits are. In other words, all divisions are autonomous, but the hand closest to the big money—the final point of sale—is more autonomous.

When Jack Schneider, a product of the CBS national sales organization and manager of WCAU-TV, Philadelphia, and WCBS-TV, New York City, became president of the CBS Television Network in 1965, it meant that the point of view of the stations would be better represented at the network level. When he was appointed group vice-president (he is now president) in charge of all the CBS broadcast divisions, the philosophy of the station managers asserted itself over all divisions. It was hardly surprising that a lifetime of conditioning at the station level prevailed when it became Schneider's responsibility to adjudicate the conflict over the Vietnam hearings.

In 1958, in his speech warning the affiliates that it would be very difficult for the network to maintain its profits, Stanton pointed out that "eight or nine of our largest affiliates again exceeded the total net profits of the network." In an accounting sense, Stanton was proven correct; the growth through 1965 had increased pre-tax profits of the networks and their stations by 110 percent, and of the other VHF stations by 195 percent.

The profit-and-growth rate of the television industry from 1958 through 1964 has been extraordinary. CBS points with pride to the fact that its stockholders' equity increased by 250 percent in the past decade, and 485 percent since 1951. (The corresponding statistics of NBC are not meaningful, because television is a comparatively small part of its parent corporation, RCA, but there might be a relevant analogy in ABC's figures prior to its merger with IT&T. Like NBC, CBS is also diversified, but to a far lesser degree, and net income galloped at this same high rate as stockholders' equity.) That is, net income grew at the amazing average rate of 18 percent per annum, and the revenues from the owned and operated stations and the television network itself were the main source of these earnings. As a basis for comparison, the Securities and Exchange Commission reports that only two industries in the entire economy had a higher profit ratio in 1964 than CBS and the television industry as a whole: motor vehicles (19.5 percent) and drugs (20.3 percent). But even those returns were below CBS's 1964 figures, and it is worth noting that neither the drug nor the automobile industry operates under a grant chartered by a government agency in the public interest.

Words like "grant" or "the public's air" now seem to be rejected as a misconception of the networks' responsibility. Yet as late as 1954 Paley said: "A grant of opportunities has been offered to us of this industry, wholly unlike, in range and scope, any grant of opportunities to any other group of modern men. And it happened in a democracy! Which must make us eternally wary of abusing it . . ."

Even a 1943 Supreme Court ruling asserting the FCC's responsibility for what goes on the air ("The facilities . . . are limited . . . Congress acted upon the knowledge that if . . . radio was not to be wasted, regulation was essential") is not accepted as the law of the land. In the same decision, the Court also ruled: "But the [Communications] Act does not restrict the Commission merely to supervision of the traffic. It puts upon the Commission the burden of determining the composition of that traffic." In spite of such rulings our society has never really established who owns broadcasting's franchises; the argument as to whether they are the public's or the investors' has never been settled because we have never delineated a philosophy of broadcast law. By default we have permitted the investors' equity to control what is basically a public-service industry. Broadcasting has been treated as though it was some kind of nineteenth-century mercantile enterprise in which property alone meant ownership. But in our times, power no longer derives solely from property, and particularly in broadcasting it is not derived from property ownership. Television's and radio's influence is derived from a formula of property plus technology plus education plus a government franchise; without the last three there would be no television.

There are those who insist that television is like any other industry in the free-enterprise system, and that it is entitled to make as much return on its investment as possible. I cannot agree. CBS and NBC have little in common with an automobile manufacturer or the cosmetic industry. Property, venture capital, creative management and patents internally provided give these companies their power, and if they don't make unsafe products or abuse the antitrust laws, they are free to compete in the marketplace and make as much profit as the traffic will bear. But each time that the FCC grants a radio or television license, those to whom it is awarded walk out with a medallion symbolizing service to all the people their station can reach over the airwaves.

It is true that networks are not licensed, but the five owned and operated individual stations—"the five jewels in our crown," a high officer of CBS once described them—*are* franchises. As long as the stations keep their licenses—and so far none has been revoked—and as long as the stations' share of a $2,000,000,000 industry continues to be the biggest portion, rising every year, the investor in most VHF stations is in effect part owner of an enterprise as safe as and more profitable than the Golden Gate Bridge. Of course there is public ownership of bridges and tunnels, but usually this is in the form of 4 or 5 percent tax-free bonds with limited returns. The bridge authority is accountable to regulatory supervision; it is not free to raise its rates without higher public authority, and the bondholder does not expect higher returns on his investment each year.

Many distinguished economists believe that television is a public utility, but the Communications Act says it isn't. True, but neither is it Kellogg's Corn Flakes or Disneyland. A television station is better compared to a land-grant college, which has certain obligations not to turn itself into a beauticians' school for the sake of higher profits, or to the operator of a lodge in a national park who has a responsibility to the public and must follow prescribed rules about rates, operating standards and advertising signs. The concessionaire at the Statue of Liberty doesn't have the freedom to sell whatever he might like, or to price it at the markup he might prefer. Broadcasting is something in between a public utility and purely private enterprise, and because it is so vital a social force, it cannot be permitted to drift on in its decaying course.

The industry resents this talk about public equity, which, it maintains, leads to government intrusion, thence to dangerous control of entertainment and news, and eventually to government enterprise. But is this true? The Sherman Antitrust Act was government intrusion; so were the Wagner Act and the Federal Reserve Act. Yet the industries that they affected continued to survive and even to prosper notwithstanding the humanizing constraints this legislation imposed on them.

An argument used by the late Secretary of Labor James Mitchell in an interview for our "Harvest of Shame" broadcast has some relevance to the dilemma of television today. In 1911 the garment industry in New York employed thousands of children, but every attempt to stop this practice failed because each manufacturer claimed that if he stopped using low-cost sweatshop labor, his competitors would undersell him and put him out of business. Then the Triangle shirtwaist factory fire occurred, and a shocked community demanded the passage of child-labor laws. Secretary Mitchell pointed out that in 1960 his wife could buy blouses much more economically than her mother could have in 1911, that the manufacturer made more money than ever, and that child labor no longer existed.

If one applies this argument to television and radio—and no invidious comparison is intended—it seems to me reasonable to propose that there be some kind of federal broadcasting authority which would make it impossible for one network or station to do its worst, and most profitable, while others did their best, which occasionally would be unprofitable. Some industry critics will pounce on this with the argument that it would be tantamount to government regulation over programing, that it would make the federal government a censor, and that such a step would be a violation of the First Amendment.

Just as I am no economist, I am no lawyer. But I *am* enough of a journalist to know that the broadcaster who wraps himself in the First Amendment while clutching his franchise to his bosom is asking to have his Constitution two ways. The applicable part of the First Amendment says that "Congress shall make no law . . . abridging the freedom of speech, or of the press." But the instant that a station wins a license to occupy a frequency to the exclusion of all other applicants, and if all other channels in that community are assigned, then the First Amendment is limiting the rights of every other citizen; the law calls this "prior restraint." A publisher in, say, Washington with sufficient capital, courage, skill and energy can compete at the newsstand with the Washington *Post*, *Star* or *News*, but it is impossible for even the wealthiest, most creative and most public-spirited broadcaster to go into effective competition with the *Post*'s or NBC's or Metromedia's or the *Evening Star*'s television station—unless he can persuade one of them to sell its franchise.

Throughout my career in broadcasting I have resisted any form of censorship or indirect pressure as to subject, manner of reporting or production. But it would be cynical for anyone in the business end of broadcasting to use the First Amendment as a shield. The Bill of Rights still flies high; it just doesn't happen to have much to do with the profits of a government-granted monopoly.

Some say that it isn't the FCC's job to exert its influence, and certainly we can't expect the franchise holder, who is subject to all the pressures of the stock market demanding larger earnings, and of the advertiser demanding larger audiences, to police himself. Therefore some new kind of philosophy of joint management that acknowledges both public good and private need is required.

The great malfeasances against the people of our country, whether Teapot Dome, the quiz scandals, Joe McCarthy or Billie Sol Estes, are much more an indictment of the society that permitted them to happen than of the individual rogues who committed the frauds. In the case of television, it isn't a question of scoundrels or frauds; rather, an indifferent society has given away more than it was ever entitled to, like an executor who permitted the trust in his care to be squandered.

Writing in the *Yale Law Journal* of April 1964 about "The New Property," Professor Charles Reich says that the granting of public property for private rights "depends not on where [the] property came from but on what job it should be expected to perform." The key sentence in Professor Reich's article reads: "Thus, in the case of government largess nothing turns on the fact that it originated in government. The real issue is how it functions and how it should function."

How does broadcasting function and how should it function? Certainly it does not function in the way Secretary of Commerce Herbert Hoover anticipated in 1922 when he said that it was "inconceivable that we should allow so great a possibility for service, for news, for entertainment, for education and for vital commercial purposes to be drowned in advertising chatter," or in the way that David Sarnoff envisioned NBC as a nonprofit organization from which all advertising was to be excluded; RCA would make its profits by manufacturing radio sets. (Carl Dreher, a radio pioneer, mentioned in a recent article in the *Atlantic Monthly* that Sarnoff appointed an NBC advisory council consisting of such men as Charles Evans Hughes, John W. Davis and Elihu Root.)

Nor does broadcasting operate as Paley suggested in 1934 in defining radio as a cultural force. At that time he talked of not just giving the public what it wanted to hear, but of "the second axiom: to reserve some program space to offer what the program director believes people would like if only they had an opportunity to know about it. In these periods, for instance, go cultural programs, primarily supported in the beginning by minorities—with a view to educating majorities to wider appreciation of their excellence . . ."

Four years earlier, in testimony before the Senate Committee on Interstate Commerce, Paley had said: "We have found ourselves able to devote approximately seventy-five percent of our time on the air to service as contrasted with sponsored programs." Pleading against "legislation . . . which will prevent us from continuing on a sound business basis," he gave assurances that radio advertising would be restricted to "the briefest announcement of sponsorship." With the permission of the committee chairman, Paley placed CBS's "credo" on record:

1. No announcement of prices and no direct selling.
2. No false, unwarranted, exaggerated, doubtful or superlative claims.
3. No statements ambiguous in meaning that may be misleading.
4. No reflections on competitors or competitive goods.
5. No infringement of another advertiser's rights through plagiarism or imitation of copy slant.

6. No medical advertising that makes remedial or curative claims, either directly or by inference, not justified by the facts or common experience.
7. No advertising of a speculative nature through recommendations for purchase of specific securities, commodities, or real property for the purpose of realizing on the appreciation of values.
8. No announcements that are vulgar, repulsive, or offensive, either in theme or in treatment.
9. No inclusion of mention by any advertiser of another generally advertised company or product; this includes mentions by artists of recordings, theatrical engagements or music publishing houses.
10. No details of prize contests; mention may only be made that a contest is in progress and information given as to where details may be obtained.
11. No overloading of a program with advertising matter, either through announcements that are too long, or by too frequent mentions of a trade name or product.
12. No other advertising matter that may cause a loss of confidence in the Columbia Broadcasting System, or in honest advertising and reputable business, or that is generally unfit for broadcast advertising.

When a senator on the committee asked Paley how much advertising matter appeared in an hour of broadcasting, he replied, "Well, that varies . . . I do not know how many minutes during an hour we actually give for the advertising time, but a few weeks ago our research department told me that of all the time used on the air during a particular week, the actual time taken for advertising mention was seven-tenths of one percent of all of our time."

In 1966 one can count as many as twenty-five commercials or announcements per hour on radio and television. In a recent monitoring exercise at the Columbia University Graduate School of Journalism, every network weekday broadcast was found to have commercial sponsorship. More than 17 percent of the time on the three New York network television stations in an eighteen-hour day (September 19, 1966) was advertising matter; when grouped with announcements for program promotion, the interruptions represented 21 percent of air time. The day-time average was 24 percent, with a commercial interruption or network promotional plug at an average rate of twenty times per hour. Even in the time devoted to news, network and local, the average commercial time was 23.8 percent.

Of course, Paley's credo was written in 1930 and was intended for sound broadcasting, but radio has always been accepted as the matrix on which television law and promise were based. And in all fairness, it should be pointed out that some of the policies in Paley's credo are still enforced.

In his scholarly history of early radio, *A Tower in Babel,* Erik Barnouw explains how those standards were lowered:

> In 1931, although the air was crammed with loud, insistent announcements, NBC still did not mention prices and prided itself on decorum; it had long lists of taboo words.
>
> As CBS fought for business, George Washington Hill found that he could say what he wanted on CBS about his Cremo cigars: that they cost five cents and were not made with spit. "There is no spit in Cremo!" the announcers shouted. The next year William Paley was quoted as saying that the art of advertising by radio was developing rapidly. He added, like one tracing an aesthetic movement: "Our specific contribution toward this end is the permitting of price mention."
>
> Not long afterward President [Merlin] Aylesworth of NBC [who had also told Congress that he was opposed to any direct advertising on the air] was telling his Advisory Council of distinguished citizens about a policy change:
>
> "We believe that the interests of the listener, the client and the broadcaster are best served under our American system of broadcasting by frankly recognizing the part that

each plays in its development. With this thought in mind, and after long consideration, the company has decided to alter its policy with reference to the mention of price in commercial announcements."

What happened to the dream? What softened the promise and hardened the sell? Newton Minow, for over two years an FCC chairman who cared, said in 1963: ". . . bureaucracy has failed to keep up with the technological changes in the broadcasting industry. When broadcasting began, the concepts were based on a radio system to be operated by many small local stations. Networks were nonexistent. When the law governing broadcasting was passed, networks were either just beginning or too weak to matter. Now networking is indispensable to broadcasting and has profoundly changed and improved it. But the government grinds on inexorably, doing the same things in the same ways, asking the same tired questions, applying the same passé techniques to different conditions. The rules remain the same, but they are being applied to a dramatically different game . . ."

The FCC, an administrative never-never land, as Chairman Minow wrote President Kennedy at the time of his resignation, consists of seven commissioners, each of whom serves as judge, legislator and administrator. "I do not believe it is possible," said Minow, "to be a good judge on Monday and Tuesday, a good legislator on Wednesday and Thursday and a good administrator on Friday." Minow favored a single administrator; this may be a step in the right direction, but no chairman without a new charter could be anything more than a public scold. A description of the FCC that many of its commissioners, past and present, would recognize, came from Professor R. H. Coase: "The regulation of the broadcast industry . . . resembles a professional wrestling match . . . The grunts and groans resound through the land, but no permanent injury seems to result."

In 1960 James M. Landis, former dean of Harvard Law School, was asked by President-elect Kennedy to prepare a study on the regulatory agencies. Landis accused the FCC of having "drifted, vacillated and stalled in almost every major area." Regarding its procedure for granting licenses to applicants, Landis said: ". . . programing proposed by applicants is of high-sounding moral and ethical content in order to establish that their operation of a radio and television station would be in the public interest. The actual programing bears no reasonable similitude to the programing proposed. The Commission knows this but ignores these differentiations at . . . renewal of licenses . . . [continuing] with its Alice-in-Wonderland procedures."

The FCC, which, according to Minow, spends six times as much of its time on radio as on television, is immobilized by the giant broadcasting industry. With the possible exception of the Federal Power Commission, it is the most overworked, understaffed regulatory agency in history. At this moment it is frenetically conducting a three-year study of the telephone company, while the colossus which is television goes virtually unattended in its efforts to brainwash the American consumer. The FCC has a budget of $17,500,000 to enforce, among others, the $2,000,000,000 television industry—and the broadcast license is free. By contrast, in most states and cities, drivers and peddlers are required to help pay the expenses of the authority that licenses them.

The vagueness of the Communications Act of 1934 has been described by one of its original drafters, Senator Clarence Dill, in Newton Minow's book *Equal Time:* "He [Dill] told me that the draftsmen of the legislation reached an impasse in attempting to define a regulatory standard for broadcasting . . . at that time . . . new, uncharted and risky. The government wanted to encourage people to invest in the construction of stations without fear of rate regulations as a public utility or ceiling on profits for their risk taking. At the same time, Senator Dill reminisced, the government knew that a firm measure of public control was needed."

The original radio station licensees never dreamed that their franchises would become profit centers in themselves. Many of them were owners of newspapers or department stores; some were even automobile dealers who were investing in good will and advertising. None of them foresaw that broadcasting's profits would one day dwarf the rest of their business. The legislation governing the field was equally short-sighted, for its drafters could not know what they were giving away. Because the Interstate Commerce Act had used the words "public interest, convenience and necessity," the same regulatory definitions were applied to radio stations, and later to television stations. As Minow points out, the Federal Communications Act states that broadcasting is not a public utility; yet the legislative language historically employed for the regulation of public utilities is used.

Therefore, today, when broadcast risks are minimal and profit opportunities unlimited, there is no philosophy of law defining either satisfactory public service or equitable private gain in this industry. (In 1960 Frank Stanton told the FCC: ". . . a program in which a large part of the audience is interested is by that very fact . . . in the public interest . . ." By this criterion, *Peyton Place* and *Batman* are in the public interest.)

Though it is undoubtedly true that a variety of private individuals can operate television and radio stations in the public interest more effectively than the government could, the disclaimer that television is not a public utility left the Communications Act toothless at birth. But in spite of the weasel wording of the act, the Supreme Court has little doubt about the power of the FCC to determine just what "public interest, convenience and necessity" means. In 1943 Supreme Court Justice Felix Frankfurter wrote for the majority: "Congress was acting in a field of regulation which was both new and dynamic . . . In the context of the developing problems to which it was directed, the Act gave the Commission not niggardly but expansive powers." More recently the U.S. Court of Appeals in the District of Columbia declared: "In performing its functions under the Act, the Commission is given broad discretion. The statute contemplates that the Commission will take the lead in exploring the possibilities of radio, and we think it unlikely that Congress had in mind a particular method to this end . . . The purpose of Congress in establishing the Commission was to set up an expert agency capable of coping with the ever-changing and constantly increasing problems of a blooming industry."

Is it unreasonable that a station which, when originally franchised, was not expected to make much money and now makes $5,000,000 or $10,000,000 a year, should have its public charter amended because of changing circumstances? Should a license received originally for little or no outlay become a legacy worth $20,000,000 or $30,000,000 without the people who granted it retaining some equity in it? The Communications Act as defined by the Supreme Court clearly states: "The policy . . . is clear that no person is to have anything in the nature of a property right as a result of the granting of a license. Licenses are limited to a maximum of three years' duration . . . and need not be renewed." Yet no major TV license has *ever* gone unrenewed, and if Henry Luce or Mike Cowles, who run much better magazines than television stations, were suddenly told to show cause why they should continue to operate their channels because the gap between their private profits and their public service was too vast, cries of government interference and violation of the First Amendment would sound throughout the country.

. . .

For all of broadcasting's occasional achievements, forty years of industry "self-discipline" have provided us with a record which cannot be ignored or justified. To feed the additional largess of communications satellites and all they portend into this laissez-faire system is to defy the lessons of history. If indifference and naïveté caused us to give away our electronic inheritance when the industry was in its untested infancy, to do so again now with the stakes so high would be little short of cultural suicide.

Why can't legislation be drafted that provides for the safekeeping of some public resources that even the wealthiest nation cannot afford to fritter away? Future generations will hold us accountable for the long-range fallout from television, as they will for other forms of radioactivity and pollution of the atmosphere. We ask eminent legal scholars to draft laws governing outer space, while television is regulated by the same words, "public interest, convenience and necessity," which were originally intended for steam locomotives, grain elevators and paddlewheel steamers. In an age of $60,000 minutes, when fortunes are swapped on the sale of a license, when pictures are bounced off publicly subsidized antennas twenty-two thousand miles up in space, when the news room and the classroom draw closer together, "public interest, convenience and necessity" can mean as much or as little as convenient.

One of the problems of broadcasting is that the economic literature is so scanty, and that most of what does exist has been written by special-interest parties in order to create a climate for favorable congressional or FCC action. It is no longer news to talk about the "vast wasteland" or the "intellectual ghetto"—and it is usually unproductive. What is needed is a dialogue and a literature concerned with the political, intellectual and economic environment that allows commercial television to be a $2,000,000,000 industry while noncommercial television is forced to get by on less than $80,000,000 a year. Even those figures don't reveal the whole story of the plight of noncommercial television. There are only one hundred and eight educational stations in the country; many major markets have none at all, and many have UHF stations, which a vast part of the audience cannot receive on their sets without a special adapter. Furthermore, most of the educational channels have to use a major part of their budgets merely to stay on the air, and this leaves perhaps only $20,000,000, or even less, for programing.

At lunch one day Walter Lippmann put the plight of television today into dramatic perspective by saying, "It's as though this nation had three mighty printing presses. *Only three*. What would we do with them? How would we use them?" The fact that some parts of the nation have only one or two printing presses makes the analogy even more sobering. At this moment all three "presses" are producing advertising matter much of the time, or else spewing out a comic-book, pulp-magazine concoction that will provide the right aura for the sales messages.

Suppose that in 1776 there had only been three printing presses? Suppose that there were only three today; what would we print on them? Texts, books of general interest, newspapers, magazines, comic books, catalogues, advertising matter? Ideally, all of them, but surely there would be some order of priority. Television's defenders would claim that it dispenses all of these items. This is true, but the order is almost exactly the reverse of the above; the amount of time devoted to illuminating, teaching and informing is dwarfed by the amount of hours spent on entertainment and advertising.

Three soap companies—Procter & Gamble, which spends $161,000,000 per year on television advertising, Colgate-Palmolive, which spends $71,000,000 per year, and Lever Brothers,

$58,000,000—account for about 15 percent of the nation's total television sales. This is one reason why Americans know more about detergents and bleaches than they do about Vietnam or Watts. The three great printing presses in their seven-day-a-week continuous runs are so oriented to advertising and merchandise that after a single day of viewing television, a visitor from another planet could only infer that we are bent on producing a generation of semiliterate consumers.

Obviously, if only three powerful printing presses existed, a special commission would be set up to assure the nation that they would be used in the public interest. In fact, the Communications Act of 1934 provides for such a commission—but the sales managers of the three networks and various soap-company vice-presidents have much more to do with the state of television than the chairman of the FCC.

If television can make so much profit for its stockholders by pursuing the maximum audience most of the time and cannot afford to pursue excellence more than a little of the time, what is it that demands this proportion, and is the public equity and need sufficiently represented in this formula? If the law has not changed since 1934 but the economics have, and if a money machine rather than an intellectual and social one drives television, don't these new circumstances demand a change? Obviously the spirit of the original law has been breached by simple indifference and laissez faire. If we are a nation of laws, if the FCC can't enforce its regulations without violating the First and Fifth amendments and the concepts of free speech and free enterprise, if the network and station operators can't do their best because of the pressure for profit—then we must either write television off as one more resource squandered, or else provide safeguards which will encourage the medium to do its best and penalize it for doing its worst.

Once again there is an automatic rebuttal: "What is the worst and what is the best programing, and who is to determine what is good and what is bad?" I would like to propose a not-altogether-facetious experiment. If the chairman of the board and the president of each of the three networks were to sit before three television monitors showing each company's scheduled programing from 7 A.M. until midnight for just one day, with a television camera focused on them to record their reactions, I think that their pride and sense of judgment would soon establish a sense of what is good and what is bad. If the mere idea of making a Sarnoff or a Paley or a Goldenson watch his programing in public all day sounds offensive, that in itself is a commentary, for the head of General Motors or even Procter & Gamble would proudly spend a day displaying his complete line of wares.

Economic proposals have been made to alter the behavior pattern of television. In 1959 it was suggested that stations be charged rent for this valuable public resource, just as a hydroelectric plant pays rent for its public site, or a concessionaire on the New York Thruway pays rent for his. Jack Fischer, editor of *Harper's Magazine,* proposed that the money "be turned over to a national broadcasting authority—a public body chartered by Congress but insulated from politics," and charged with producing public-service programs. A year later Congressman Henry Reuss reiterated this idea of rental income in a bill (HR 9549) which he introduced on January 12, 1960, but which never emerged from committee. Under his scheme the commercial stations would carry public-service programs (which Reuss actually defined) for one-fifth of their broadcast day, but the rental income would be used to support nonprofit broadcasting stations. Writing in the *Georgetown Law Journal* in 1961, Professor Harvey Levin summed up this proposal as a halfway house between patching up what we now have and a far more "radical, sweeping innovation . . . one last attempt to place our regulatory house in order, short of still more drastic remedies . . ."

Somehow we need to find a way to harness the profit motive without destroying it. Perhaps the FCC, through the Treasury Department, should impose a steep tax on all broadcasters' profits over a reasonable rate of return but give tax rebates for broadcasting time devoted to public-service programing. Profit-rate regulation of the sort that governs AT&T clearly has not prevented the Bell System from becoming the envy of the world.

Other plans have been suggested for a special tax over and above the normal capital-gains tax every time a station is sold at a profit. In addition, some senators have suggested public revelation of revenues, profits, cost of programing and ownership.

Scholars attempting to write serious tracts on the inner workings of broadcast economics run into a blank wall when they try to base them on accurate figures. The FCC's secrecy on the stations' and networks' financial reports is as impregnable as a personal income tax form. Even the annual figures for a single-station market and a one-station state are a secret, thus protecting the monopoly station. The ostensible reason for this is to protect station operators and networks from their competition, and yet the enterprises are so similar that an experienced operator can sketch his rivals' finances as accurately as he can predict ratings. If broadcasters were common carriers who had no shroud of secrecy, their rates, costs, rate of return and investments would all be available to lawmakers, economists and broadcast scholars. But the secrecy that conceals profits makes it impossible to determine how much public-service programing is reasonable.

As for public identification of ownership, it might dispel claims that many congressmen benefit directly from an industry which they regulate, and that this affects their votes. There are reports that as many as 25 percent of the members of Congress own interests in radio and television stations, but *Broadcasting* magazine reported in May 1965 that only nine senators and fourteen representatives and their families had such investments.

None of the above remedies is presented as a recommendation, but simply to indicate that there is nothing inviolate about the status quo. The economics of television, which make it what it is today, need not *always* be what they are today, and they can be changed as much or as little as the society that gives the industry its mandate wishes them changed. Those who resisted the Federal Reserve System most strongly were the bankers who eventually benefited the most from it. Similarly, any change in broadcasting economics will be resisted by an array of lobbyists, public relations pleaders and outraged owners. In the end, television will gain the most if it is given a less profit-minded base; instead, its health would be guaranteed by the nation's intellectual well-being, which it must help develop in order for both the country and the medium to survive.

In the year 1966, when satellites promise to change television as much as television altered radio, when the education boom is about to do for our economy what the industrial revolution did for the nineteenth century and what the automobile did for the first half of the twentieth century, the challenge to reorder our television circuits and to establish a Magna Carta of broadcasting is an opportunity that must be exercised now, or perhaps never.

Of television's unique economics, Newton Minow has said: "Never have so few owed so much to so many." There is no accurate way of knowing how many public investors hold broadcast stock because the broadcast interest is often a small part of a giant electronic or other industrial complex, but it is doubtful that it is more than 1 or 2 percent of our population. If the pressure of the forty-one thousand stockholders of CBS—a minuscule percentage of the population—is responsible for producing a $50,000,000-a-year profit, while denying one hundred and ninety million citizens the kind of television they deserve, who is to blame—the few or the many?

In the *Yale Law Journal* Professor Charles Reich wrote about the plight of the industrial nations which have been forced to develop centralized planning and allocation of resources in a complex society: "In the United States the political and economic tradition inherited from the nineteenth century was dead-set against planning and allocation . . . This tradition did not, however, enable the United States to resist the inevitable. It merely affected the way in which the inevitable arrived . . . Businessmen were the active forces of collectivism and planning in the United States. In time they forced the hand of government . . . Government regulation, such as the Sherman Act and the Interstate Commerce Act, was designed to place some degree of public control on private systems of planning and allocation. To this end private business was, wherever possible, given jobs to do that which government might have carried out itself. Hence private entrepreneurs were permitted to fly the nation's air routes, broadcast over the government-owned airways and control much of the hydroelectric power of the nation's rivers. A compromise has been worked out in which such private enterprise operates public service for profit, but in 'the public interest.'"

But as it has worked out, we as a nation have permitted "public planning" and "socialism" to be construed as having virtually the same meaning; broadcasters rebel at the thought of government or anyone but themselves defining "public interest." The FCC doesn't plan; it has very limited funds for research. "In my tenure here," FCC Commissioner Robert E. Lee has said, "we have not anticipated problems but have necessarily had to wait until the problem is here." The commission is at best a referee, and at its worst is only a sounding board for special pleaders. With the notable exceptions of a few of its members, it has made a virtue and a credo out of abdication of its responsibilities. In regulating a natural resource of vision, sound and imagination, it is blind, deaf and unimaginative.

If too many of our commercial planes crashed, or the passenger rates were too high, we would blame the Civil Aeronautics Board; if our national parks became eyesores we would impeach the Secretary of the Interior and get rid of the head of the National Park Service. But when television fails us we turn it off and curse the darkness. Or we blame the networks' managements, who in turn plead that they must get the stockholders a fair return on their investment.

I accuse the Federal Communications Commission of failure to plan and failure to understand the true meaning of television. And because the FCC *is,* as Speaker Sam Rayburn once told one of its chairmen, "an arm of the Congress," the buck stops there.

Someday the Congress, which transformed the Tennessee Valley from an eroded disaster area into a safe and fertile valley, and which is now passing legislation to make our waters and air fit for human consumption, will realize that perhaps the potentially most rewarding reclamation of all will begin when one of its members stands up and says, "Mr. President, I ask for the floor in order to speak for television . . ."

1 *The Beginning: Circumstances Within Our Control*

The final chapter of this book has become a prologue. A theoretical concept whose aim was to create a second service has now become an idea in motion. Thirty days after what was to have been the last sentence of this book, the phenomenon of a United States senator rising to speak for television occurred. John O. Pastore, Democratic senator from Rhode Island and chairman of the communications subcommittee of the Senate Commerce Committee, looked out over a crowded hearing room and said:

> Now the question resolves itself . . . how does the United States of America want to go in developing educational television? And where is it going to get the money to do it[?] . . . this [Ford Foundation] proposal . . . has almost been a bombshell . . . and I hope out of it all, the public interest will be served. I don't think we are quarreling with anyone—with Comsat, with the law, [the] Ford Foundation, AT&T, or . . . with anybody else. But . . . this is the point of challenge. This is the time when the executive and the legislative [branches] have to put their heads and shoulders together to develop something that is going to be permanently good. We have made these mistakes before. We have allowed this thing to just go along . . . until [we] . . . couldn't retreat or retract, and that was bad . . . [There] were the [broadcast] pioneers. They pre-empted the field

> . . . You could no more take power away from a station today without a big contest going right up to the Supreme Court.
>
> And the point is to [take action] now. I think America has to decide . . . what it is going to do about these satellites, what it is going to do about educational television . . . As Mr. Bundy said, "I don't care how you do it, but do it and do it right."

On February 16 McGeorge Bundy was leaving the White House as Presidential Assistant on National Security, I was out of a job, educational television was short of money, and a satellite twenty-two thousand miles over the equator, smaller than a bass drum and with less power than a 50-watt bulb was casting its shadow on all of us. What brought a former dean of the Harvard faculty who knew little about television to call a former television producer who knew little about education or the intellectual, scientific, legal and economic complications of the task ahead, can be traced to the fine Italian hand of Walter Lippmann.

The first call I took the morning after my resignation was from McGeorge Bundy at the White House. He told me that he was going to become president of the Ford Foundation, which had spent some $100,000,000 on educational television with doubtful results, and that when he came to New York the following week he'd like to have dinner with me. He also said the Lippmann had "planted the seed that you might have some ideas about noncommercial television," and had given him my phone number.

Bundy and I had met occasionally because of the Presidential "conversations" and the Vietnam debates. Also, in 1948 I had read the memoirs of that remarkable statesman, Henry L. Stimson, which Bundy, then a Harvard junior fellow, had coauthored. I had always remembered Stimson's last sentence: "The only deadly sin I know is cynicism."

Our first dinner lasted for five hours, and at the end of it we agreed to meet again. Bundy is a brilliant conversationalist and a good listener, who has an instant impatience with the obvious. Our talks distilled down to the essence of the dilemma. With its $2,000,000,000 revenue, commercial television has the resources and professional talent to do all the things that television should be doing, but because of its stockholders, it does not feel that it can often afford to appeal to excellence. Inversely, noncommercial, or educational, television, which has the time and the impetus to pursue excellence, does not have the technical, economic and professional resources to provide it.

How could these elements be brought into proper balance? To help find a way, Bundy invited me to become part-time adviser to the Foundation on television matters, and I quickly accepted. My first assignment was to read a series of papers that had been commissioned from some impressive broadcasting figures—among them Ed Murrow, Newton Minow, Irving Gitlin, Louis Cowan and John White, president of National Educational Television. Their plans were imaginative and ingenious, but they all had one thing in common: none of them offered any suggestions as to how to finance noncommercial broadcasting. The Ford Foundation had been supplying funds at the rate of about $10,000,000 a year, for more than ten years, but its new president and the board of trustees felt that this was only a crutch which was in effect preventing educational television from finding a financially secure base of its own. The Ford Foundation's philosophy is to supply ideas and "seed money" to help various organizations grow and find their own economic way; its philanthropy is not intended to be the sole or major support of any cause, no matter how worthy.

Of course, there were other sources of funds for noncommercial television—enough to allow it to exist, but not enough to enable it to grow above the malnutrition level. Along with matching state funds, the Educational Television Facilities Act of 1962 has provided for some $50,000,000 to educational television over a three-year period, but this has furnished only a fraction of the minimum estimate of $100,000,000 needed annually. Some local stations, notably Boston's WGBH, San Francisco's KQED, and recently New York's WNDT, have worked heroically to raise money in their communities. But men like Hartford Gunn, of WGBH, have to spend too much of their time as fund-raisers and too little of their energies on programing. Yet WGBH is relatively well off; most educational channels, like the minister in a distressed town, are dependent on hand-me-downs—obsolete cameras and studio equipment for which the local commercial station has no further use—though the three networks, notably CBS, and some individual stations, have been as generous to the educational stations as their stockholders would allow.

But money is not the only commodity in short supply in noncommercial television. Though some talented and dedicated craftsmen have ventured into the field, educational television has not attracted enough first-class broadcasters. Even those producers and reporters willing to work for less than the commercial scale are justifiably apprehensive about achieving first-class results with third-class budgets and facilities. At times CBS had suggested that perhaps I should help in the production of educational television, but I and others like me did not feel that there were sufficient craftsmen and equipment available to do the kind of job expected of us. I admire those who made the jump, but the fact is that many of them left the commercial world reluctantly and would return if they could.

The personnel of noncommercial television can't be *almost* as good as their commercial colleagues; they must be *better*, because the challenge and the opportunities are greater. If both kinds of television were to start afresh and from scratch, priorities and goals would be set and decisions made to allocate our resources where they belong, but in a country which spends more than twice as much money advertising cat and dog food on television ($40,700,000) as it does on educational television program production, the economics of a new order come hard. In 1957 the launching of Sputnik shook us out of our complacency enough to make it possible to pay a Nobel laureate professor almost as much as the football coach, but educational television has never benefited from such a scare. Commercial television did have a bad moment in 1959 because of the quiz scandals, but this was palliated by the passage of time and by promises to behave. No one had any suggestions for the rehabilitation of the medium other than Congressman Reuss, Walter Lippman and Jack Fischer, who wanted the networks and stations to pay rent. But this was an idea rather than a plan, and little attention was paid to it.

There is another economic obstacle to noncommercial television: the high cost of long lines. This expense is shared with the networks, but with their huge revenues they are able to afford it. A network cannot exist without a chain of cable, or microwave, relays between stations. Without these lines, stations would be isolated from one another and from the networks. In the early days of radio, Sarnoff and AT&T fought bitter battles for the control of the early long-line chain that tied the pioneer NBC network together, and Paley can still remember the days when the phone company insisted on cash in advance before providing service. But the price paid for what is known as "interconnection" is enormous; the three networks spend approximately $50,000,000 a year to the long-line division of AT&T under tariffs approved and protected by the FCC.

The cost of long lines is so high that often television fails to take advantage of one of its greatest assets: mobility. The expense of switching from New York or Washington to, say,

San Francisco is based on a formula of $1.15 per mile with a minimum charge of one hour's usage; a two-minute feed in these cases costs more than $3,000.

Such excessive charges discourage competition and are responsible for the networks' use of the "pool" system on space stories and other big news events. Just a few weeks before the 1964 Democratic Convention, the telephone company announced that the bill for the special lines it had constructed to Atlantic City would be over $2,000,000, which the networks had to absorb. Since AT&T is continuously adding lines to its system, and such construction is amortized over many years, some believe that the true broadcast cost of lines like these might be startlingly less; unfortunately, the company does not share its accounting system with its customers. Privately the networks complain bitterly, but any serious effort to protest is discouraged by the fear that if broadcasters attempted to regulate or reduce rates for a carrier, a precedent might be established for regulating their own rates.

For educational television, the high cost of interconnection is so overwhelming that until very recently it was not even seriously discussed. Yet a network without interconnection is not a network at all but only a film syndicate. Aside from the obvious fact that news or special-events programs cannot be syndicated because of the time element, lack of interconnection cripples promotion and exploitation. National news services and syndicated newspaper critics are sometimes reluctant to devote space to broadcasts which are scheduled at various times in different cities.

Moreover, educational television's burden of distributing films and tapes by mail is prohibitive. For a network's situation comedy, only one print and an extra safety copy are required; interconnection simultaneously sends the program to two hundred stations with the speed of light. But National Educational Television, the noncommercial broadcasters' nearest equivalent to a network, has to go through the expensive, time-consuming process of duplicating programs. A visit to the reproduction facilities of NET at Ann Arbor, Michigan, proves just how valuable interconnection is. There, banks of videotape machines work around the clock seven days a week, grinding out copies of broadcasts which are then mailed to NET's eighty stations. The cost of this copying center is more than $1,000,000 a year—one-sixth of NET's total budget—but the price of leasing an interconnected network would be $8,000,000 a year for an eight-hour daily schedule.

In sum, the commercial networks exist thanks to interconnection, and NET is not worthy of the name without it.

In 1965 the American Broadcasting Company, troubled by the high cost of interconnection and aware of the promise of communications satellites, petitioned the FCC for permission to launch one of its own, and offered to provide free service to educational television. The FCC asked for technical clarification and resubmission of the application at a later date, but it did then send out a notice of inquiry to interested users, for a domestic satellite service.

Satellites are not a new subject to broadcasters. For years they have held out their promise to all, but their economic application heretofore has been disappointing. In the late fifties I watched flaming, twisting rockets and their tiny satellites tumble and fall out of control into the Banana River near Cape Canaveral, and I wondered where the vast expenditure of money on this humiliation would lead us. My hopes and those of everyone in the industry soared with the orbiting of Telstar, whose inaugural broadcast I produced for the three United States networks. But our expectations were dashed by the international ground station's red tape and bureaucracy—particularly that of the French—which crippled its usefulness. In addition, Telstar, a low-level random-orbit bird, spent most of its time out of range of the Andover, Maine, ground station, and this presented scheduling problems. It was not always possible to make historic events occur during Telstar passes over this country, although Telstar II did perform miracles during the Kennedy and Churchill funerals.

The breakthrough came with the Syncom concept of a synchronous satellite in a fixed orbit over the equator. When I saw those first live, brilliant Syncom pictures from the Tokyo Olympics, at 1 A.M. on October 10, 1964, I gasped, and engineers watching it in the West Coast control center told me that the transmission there was even more dazzling.

In 1965 I traveled to London with the news chiefs of the other two networks to meet with our European counterparts and plan the inaugural broadcast and help establish the rates of Early Bird. Comsat officials had invited us to attend the meeting presided over by the British Post Office, which controls all telephonic and satellite operations in the United Kingdom. Those of us particularly interested in broadcast journalism pleaded for rates which would enable us to use this magnificent instrument; we hoped that the price would be no more than the $1.15 per mile per hour that we paid in the United States for domestic landlines. But once the inaugural broadcast was over and regular service had begun, the cost of using Early Bird turned out to be excessive—more than twice what we paid for domestic long lines. For this reason the $1,000,000 that CBS News had budgeted for Early Bird's use was hardly touched, and in its annual report for 1965, the company broke precedent by being publicly critical of a government-regulated company's tariff.

In short, I had learned about satellites the hard way, and so in the spring of 1966 it was natural that the concept of using synchronous satellites to rescue noncommercial television would enter my mind. It was clear that communications satellites were going to cause a revolution. The AT&T system of long lines, a network of many hundreds of line-of-sight microwave relays which passes video pictures and sound from one hilltop to another, is an outmoded electronic bucket brigade that could soon be replaced by "stationary" satellites which can spray their input down to broadcast stations. Satellites would also be far more economical. In 1965 the cost of television and radio's long lines was $65,000,000. AT&T estimates that this figure will have to jump to $84,700,000 in 1967 to provide a fair return on its investment. A fourth network, Overmyer, will begin operations next year, so by 1968 the cost of long lines may be as much as $80,000,000. Yet the day the first satellites go into use, most of this same job will be done for considerably less money, perhaps for as little as $25,000,000 to $30,000,000.

Who should be the beneficiary of this by-product of our $25,000,000,000 space program? Should it be Comsat? The Communications Satellite Act of 1962 had already given this corporation a privileged position; their stockholders have more than doubled their investment. Should the beneficiary be the networks and stations, as ABC and subsequently NBC have implied? If the satellites were given to the broadcast industry, they might save some $20,000,000 or more, and the carriers might earn a similar sum, though the figure would be obscured by these companies' systems of cost accounting and amortization.

Why not funnel these savings into noncommercial, educational television? Most pragmatists would reject the idea because the most formidable array of communications corporations, called carriers or carriers' carriers—AT&T, Comsat, Western Union, IT&T, among others, and individual stations—would mobilize against the concept immediately. On the other hand, perhaps the networks themselves would back the plan because of the savings involved.

. . .

When I mentioned to Bundy the idea of a constellation of satellites serving all broadcasters and operated by a nonprofit corporation, the profits themselves to be used in helping found an educational network, he asked dozens of questions, even the first of which—"Is it technically feasible?"—I could not answer.

It so happened that my family and I were going to California during the spring vacation, and I volunteered to spend some time with Dr. Harold Rosen, the brilliant physicist who had willed the synchronous satellite into being and who worked for the Hughes Aircraft Company. So a few weeks later, while Andy, Lisa and David Friendly climbed the Matterhorn at Disneyland and played golf in Palm Desert, I met with Rosen and Paul Visher, also of Hughes, to learn about such matters as power flux density, free space propagation and effective radiated power.

Two weeks later Rosen came to New York to meet Bundy, and what came to be known as the Ford Foundation plan was under way. The facts are that my major contribution to this project began and ended with the basic idea. Bundy sparked to the concept, and with his customary vitality and appetite for leadership, he organized the scientific, legal and economic expertise that was required. This is not the time to write the history of our proposal, but the marshaling of the necessary information and intellects could hardly have been accomplished better than by a former dean who had learned how to get things done from Henry Stimson, and who had behind him the prestige and $2,500,000,000 of the Ford Foundation.

Bundy was convinced that David Ginsburg, of Washington, was the ablest lawyer in the country for the particular task that lay before us. Ginsburg was in the midst of several government assignments for the White House, but Bundy persuaded him to enlist in our cause. With him Ginsburg brought Lee Marks, a former counsel on communications for the State Department. To tell us whether Rosen and Hughes's estimate of the capability and cost of our proposed satellite was accurate, Bundy drew on the services of Eugene Fubini, former Deputy Secretary of Defense and now chief scientist for IBM.

The first phase of the project was to make sure that the plan was feasible and to build a model. The submission of our proposal to the FCC had to be made by August 1 lest complete control of the satellites be given away to other interested parties (Comsat) without proper regard for noncommercial television. We were anxious that there be no leaks about the plan because for maximum effect its fresh approach had to be a complete surprise. There was no doubt in our minds that satellites could be the instrument by which all broadcasting, even the new community antenna system of cable connections, and someday satellites-to-home television, would eventually be transmitted, but this would be impossible in, say, 1975 if the proprietorship of these instruments was given away in 1966.

In the thirty days prior to our submission, the eleventh floor of the Ford Foundation looked more like a news room just before election than a philanthropic institution. On the weekend before August 1 there was little time for sleep, and the janitors in the building were stunned by the processions of executives and waves of secretaries entering and leaving at all hours. The esprit de corps was miraculous.

With minor support from his new television consultant, Bundy had briefed his board of trustees about our plan, and they had given their consent to its submission. As the model developed and the legal brief took form, Bundy personally wrote and rewrote entire sections of the document to be presented to the FCC. In addition, he reworked his letter to Rosel Hyde, the chairman of the FCC, over and over again.

At ten-thirty on August 1, copies of our submission were delivered to the chairman and commissioners of the FCC in Washington. At eleven o'clock Bundy walked into the Foundation's conference room in New York, where there were assembled some fifty or sixty reporters, who had been alerted by telegram over the weekend about our press conference. Standing at the back of the room, I was immediately conscious of the intense interest that this story would attract.

Bundy began by reading his letter. Because it is one of the most significant documents I have been associated with, and because I believe it will be remembered someday as the charter for a new era of television, I quote it in its entirety:

> Dear Mr. Chairman:
>
> I have the honor to submit herewith a statement from the Ford Foundation which responds to the invitation of the Federal Communications Commission for "the views and comments of interested parties" on "proposals for the construction and operation of communications satellite facilities" by others than recognized common carriers. I am also addressing this same letter to each of the other Commissioners.
>
> In this covering letter I want to summarize our conclusions—and also to explain informally the deep concern which moved us to make the studies which have led to this submission.
>
> First, I note that the Ford Foundation has no commercial interest and no operating interest in this matter. We exist for the purpose of giving money away—as wisely and constructively as we can. This is the source of our deep interest in the present question.
>
> We have a wider and longer experience of the effort to establish effective noncommercial television than any other single institution in the country. We have been by far the largest single source of funds for this effort. We have fifteen years of experience. We have made grants, directly and indirectly, of more than a hundred million dollars; currently we are making additional grants at the rate of more than ten million dollars a year.

From this experience we have learned three lessons:

(1) The first and most important lesson is that noncommercial television has unlimited potential, for human welfare and for the quality of American life. The best achievements of the best existing stations are proof enough—but there is still more powerful evidence in the best achievements of the best services abroad. And the most powerful evidence of all is in the all-but-unanimous conviction of the ablest men in American television today: that nothing is more needed—for television itself as well as for the country—than a first-rate national noncommercial service.

(2) The second lesson is that existing services, and existing means of support, cannot hope to develop more than a fraction of this potential. The existing systems are much better than nothing. Compared to what this country deserves, they are a depressing failure. This is not the fault of the talented and dedicated men who have worked their hearts out for noncommercial television. It is the fault of all of us—in that we have not yet found a way to give this work the resources it needs. It can well be argued that we at the Ford Foundation have contributed to this failure. When we give $6,000,000 a year to the National Educational Television and Radio Center (NET), we seem to have done a lot. And for us it *is* a lot—it is our largest continuing annual grant. But the brutal fact is that our big gift is much too small.

(3) The third lesson follows from the first two: it is that the nation must find a way to a wholly new level of action in this field—one which will release for our whole people all the enlightenment and engagement, all the immediacy and freedom of experience which are inherent in this extraordinary medium and which commercial services—as they freely admit—cannot bring out alone.

These three general conclusions are broadly shared, I believe, among all who have studied this problem—by leaders in the Congress, by the members and staff of your Commission, and by independent experts. They underlie the establishment last year of a distinguished Commission of private citizens to study the future of noncommercial television, under a charge from the

Carnegie Corporation and with encouragement from President Johnson. Under the chairmanship of Dr. James Killian that Commission is working hard to produce a prompt and constructive report. It will be good if we can avoid major decisions affecting the future of educational television until we have the benefit of the Carnegie report. A decision limiting the ownership and operation of communications satellites would be such a decision—and *on this ground alone* the Commission would do well to avoid any ruling of this sort at this time.

But there are legitimate and important interests which are pressing for early decisions. The Ford Foundation can well understand the forces that could lead some to argue that great commercial questions should not be delayed for months while everyone waits for "one more report" on the future of educational television. Because the Carnegie Commission is still at work, it is not in a position today to contest this point in detail. Yet it has seemed to us a matter of high importance that the public interest in the future of noncommercial television be fully and properly represented in the pleadings before your Commission. This is what our submission aims to do. Our right to present this view is the right of any element in our society to be heard. Our duty to do it grows from experience, expenditure, and the terms of our Foundation's charter.

This right and this duty are made doubly urgent because of the promise that satellite communications may permit a revolution both in the technology and in the economics of television. Intensive exploratory studies have convinced us at the Ford Foundation that these revolutionary possibilities offer the promise of building a cost-free highway system for multiplied regional and national noncommercial services—and also of providing a large part of the new funds which are desperately needed for noncommercial programing at every level.

The model we present is *one* way, not the *only* way. We are sure it can be improved by public study and comment. The state of the art is changing so fast—and we have had so much to learn since March 2—that we are sure our present design can be improved by criticism. For this reason alone we would welcome hearings on this whole subject. And on wider grounds we are sure that any major restrictive action taken without hearings would be offensive to the public sense of fairness.

While the financial needs of educational television are widely recognized, the sources of the needed funds have been elusive. With the shining exception of the Educational Television Facilities Act of 1962, the Federal Government as a whole has stood to one side (and the Act of 1962, with all its generosity and foresight, carries a total appropriation which is lower than the funds spent by the Ford Foundation alone in the years since the Act was passed). Moreover, Americans are understandably cautious about direct Federal financing of channels of communication to the public. A number of additional remedies have been suggested, and we must hope for more light on this from the Carnegie Commission, but the hard fact is that up to now no remotely adequate solution has been found. We all want educational television to be properly funded. We do not want the Government to "pay the piper and call the tune." We are looking for an answer.

And that is what makes the possibilities of satellites so extraordinarily important. Noncommercial television has two great needs: first, to become a true national network, at a cost it can afford—and second, to have money for programing, at a wholly new level of excellence. Properly used, a television satellite can meet both needs. By its natural economic advantage over long landlines, it can effectively eliminate long-distance charges as a determining element in network choices—commercial and noncommercial alike. And if in the case of commercial networks a major share of these savings is passed on to the noncommercial programers, then both problems are on the road to solution, and everyone is better off than he was before. This is not magic, or sleight-of-hand. It is a people's dividend, earned by the American nation from its enormous investment in space.

We are far from contending that a portion of the savings of the commercial users will pay for every possible program tomorrow.

In our formal submission we estimate that such a system might produce $30 million a year for ETV programing almost at once, and perhaps twice that much within ten years. This is more than enough to start the revolution we seek—and there would be still more in the future.

And all this, our analysis suggests, should be accompanied also by a wholly new level of investment—public and private—in the programs of live *instruction* that the satellite system invites. The satellite, used in the right way, can make the desert bloom for whole new areas of television. We do not claim that our way of doing it is the best. We do believe the best way must be found.

One cause of questioning may be the initial human effort of establishing a service of the sort that we suggest. Where can we find the first-rate men for a new nonprofit venture? We have considered this question, and we have asked a number of the best professionals for their opinion. Their verdict is unanimous. We are talking here about a vision of excellence for the life of all Americans. Good men will want to work for it. We are convinced the signal of approval for a system like this one would release a rush of talent for the leaders of the new enterprise.

There is also a question of money. Once it is started, the enterprise will surely pay for itself and for much good besides. But who has the money to get it off the ground? That is a fair question, but we are convinced that there are good answers—in the resources of the commercial networks, in the lending power of those who know a sure success when they see it, and in the resources of those who hold the view that money which helps to turn this corner will be money well used for the quality of American life. Our own commitment to this general purpose is clear.

We fully recognize the legitimate and reasonable needs of others who are concerned with satellite communications. We are convinced that our proposal does no significant harm to the legitimate and recognized interests of Comsat or the common carriers. With or without added responsibility for domestic television, Comsat will remain an unusually privileged commercial enterprise—a prime and protected investment with exclusive chartered rights in international satellite service. Comsat faces international horizons which can engage its full energies for decades to come. The prosperity of *all* does not require for *any* a monopoly of the space communications available to the American people. And for the common carriers the revenue presently at issue is less than 1% of a business which grows by more than that in every season of every year.

For all these reasons, we believe the door to a new and separate broadcast satellite service must not be closed. We do not now present a formal application. We think it right to wait for the report of the Carnegie Commission, and we also believe that the Ford Foundation should not undertake alone the framing of a formal application in a matter which relates to the interests and concerns of all Americans. What we have done initially is to develop one possible model of a solution. We have tested it for technical feasibility with the professional counsel of Dr. Eugene Fubini of the International Business Machines Corporation. We have tested it against the laws with the help of Mr. David Ginsburg of Washington. We have tested its economic validity with the advice of Dr. Paul MacAvoy of the Massachusetts Institute of Technology. We have tested it against the realities of television programing with the help of Mr. Fred Friendly, our Advisor on Television. We have tested it against our own experience in the philanthropic support of noncommercial television. We think this model is sound against all these tests. But our purpose in presenting it is not to ask the Commission to grant a license now, to us or to anyone else. Our immediate purpose is rather to urge the Commission to take no action now that would foreclose these possibilities.

We think the Commission should invite a more formal proposal from the widest possible public. We think such a proposal would be forthcoming. We think it would be compelling. We would be glad to join with others to present it. All that we feel it right to do today is to enter the strongest possible argument against any action that would close the door to this new hope for all Americans.

In summary, our underlying purpose is not to press for a particular solution, and still less to interfere in any way with the legitimate interests of others. Our purpose is to stress four fundamental propositions:

(1) the critical importance to American life of properly designed domestic communications satellite systems;

(2) the very great—and largely unstudied—potential of such systems for noncommercial television and for education in its widest sense;

(3) the possibility that the management of this new national resource and the rates charged for its use can be arranged in such a way as to provide adequate resources for a wholly new level of service to the American people; and

(4) the desirability of most careful deliberation before national decisions are reached with regard to the assignment of responsibility in this area.

This is a time for due process, and for greatness.

Sincerely,
McGeorge Bundy

The Honorable Rosel H. Hyde
Chairman, Federal Communications Commission
Washington, D. C.

As examples of what could be done, Bundy then outlined two possible solutions for a domestic satellite system, each of which would supply at least ten times the number of interconnections as the existing grid of landlines currently used for broadcast distribution. If either of these solutions, or an equivalent, were adopted, the elaborate, time-consuming and costly system of microwave switching and construction could be obsolete.

In addition, the reporters were supplied with a legal brief prepared by David Ginsburg, setting forth the constitutional arguments involved and citing the fact that the Satellite Act of

1962, which established Comsat, clearly stated that "it is not the intent of Congress . . . to preclude the creation of additional communications satellite systems, if required to meet unique government needs or if otherwise required in the national interest . . ."

If the launching of the "Bundy Bird," as it was unfortunately nicknamed, was startling, the public reaction to it was even more electric. This is not just a concept "whose time has come"; clearly it is an idea which for years has been waiting to be discovered, like one-way streets, the graduated income tax or birth control. This is not to say that the Ford plan was universally praised; many people were intrigued by it but were skeptical of its details. But the excited reaction was due simply to implicit recognition that the status quo of television was not frozen, and that an examination of its dilemma was under way at last.

The editors of the *New York Times* considered the Ford Foundation proposal a major event, and their front-page coverage and a comprehensive series of stories filling more than a page set the standard for other media. Jack Gould wrote that August 1, 1966, "will undoubtedly stand as a historic occasion in the evolution of broadcasting." The Washington *Post* stated: "Now is the moment, when the whole television and communications industries are embarking upon a period of massive expansion, to set aside a fraction of this new wealth for the public interest." The St. Louis *Post-Dispatch* called Bundy's vision of excellence "a historic new watershed," and *The Christian Science Monitor* proclaimed: "May the new Ford Foundation proposal . . . fly high, wide, and handsome. It is perhaps the most exciting and encouraging suggestion for improving television . . ." Altogether there were more than fifty editorials in newspapers across the country in the next few days, virtually all of them favorable.

The commercial networks expressed immediate but cautious

approval. Jack Schneider of CBS called it "an imaginative approach to a very vexatious problem." Leonard Goldenson, president of ABC, was perhaps most enthusiastic; he stated that the Ford plan "appeared to expand upon ABC's earlier suggestion in the same area," which indeed it did. Julian Goodman, president of NBC, declared his company in favor of a domestic satellite because it could "provide the public, the stations and the networks with real benefits . . . and very substantial reductions in costs . . . To the extent that the Ford Foundation proposal promises these advantages, we heartily support it in principle." John F. White, president of NET, endorsed the proposal wholeheartedly.

In its proposal filed the same day as ours, Comsat challenged the Ford plan without even mentioning it by name; the corporation insisted that it alone was authorized by Congress to establish a domestic satellite system, and it proposed to set up one of its own for all forms of communication. American Telephone and Telegraph also opposed any "privately operated" system and said that the satellites should be run by the authorized carriers. Not surprisingly, it favored Comsat, on whose board AT&T has four directors, and of which it is the dominant stockholder.

In mid-August, when Senator Pastore's subcommittee called hearings of interested parties, Bundy and I, the first witnesses, did little more than amplify our submission of August 1. Then James McCormack, a former Air Force general and M.I.T. vice-president who is the chairman of the board of Comsat, testified, stating that his corporation could do the job better and that it was the only entity authorized by Congress to operate a domestic satellite. Still, it was obvious that the general was very much in favor of the goals of the Bundy proposal, and he was generous enough to say so. Privately he hinted that he and Joseph Charyk, president of Comsat, were working on a proposal of their own to assist educational television; when urged by Pastore's committee to produce an alternative plan, however, McCormack was silent.

Next, AT&T and the other carriers criticized our economics, our engineering and our knowledge of law. But when they asserted that our arithmetic might be off by as much as $30,000,000, Bundy told the *New York Times,* in non-Foundation language, "They're crazy."

Witnesses for the networks were now more cautious than they had been on August 1. Nevertheless, Stanton did say that the Ford proposal might prove "a giant step forward . . . if the apparent problems are ironed out," and on another occasion he stated that the Foundation "should be thanked and blessed for having brought this thing to attention at this particular time." NBC and ABC were almost as generous in their language, but they also had reservations which outweighed their praise. NBC's Goodman wanted more facts and figures, but declared that "if the Ford Foundation proposal can be developed to the point of demonstrating that its charges to the networks would be generally comparable to charges under alternative approaches, and that its contribution to educational television would be substantial, we believe that it should not be penalized because its concept is unorthodox."

The networks' chief objection was that they didn't want to feel committed to the plan without "safeguards," as they put it; while some of the dividends from the satellite savings should go to noncommercial television, "substantial reductions in charges to the networks" should also be guaranteed. In the networks' board rooms the language was less euphemistic; in effect, the managements of the three corporations were worried that if they publicly agreed on the principle that they had a responsibility to support noncommercial television, what was to prevent the rates from doubling or tripling once this obligation was accepted? They had a good point.

One of the highlights of all the testimony before the committee was Stanton's remarks; cutting right to the heart of the issue, they may provide a blueprint for the plan which will eventually evolve: "If . . . the problem is to get funds for educational television and you say it has to come from the people's development, as the people's dividend, then I would submit that perhaps the basis on which it is computed should be broader than just the television networks' use of the satellite." That is, educational television needs much more support than the networks can give, even if their price of interconnection is substantially reduced, and a way to broaden the base of aid must be found.

Six days later, on August 29, in an exclusive front-page story in the *New York Times,* Jack Gould reported that Comsat had just such a plan "that would call on all commercial companies benefiting from the use of space communications facilities to help support noncommercial television." General McCormack's imaginative presentation, conceived without the knowledge or approval of AT&T, called for a multipurpose satellite system which he said would do the job better than the Foundation's proposal. As Gould described it, in what was clearly a story authorized by Comsat, it "would spread the burden of underwriting educational television among all domestic communications carriers and major users, including telephone and telegraph companies and the commercial networks . . . Comsat's role would be that of a collection agency . . . Part of the savings that would otherwise be passed on in rate reductions would instead be handed over to a designated private body for use in educational programing. In addition, educational television would receive technical facilities for nationwide live service without charge."

On that same day, exactly four weeks after the Ford submission, Comsat confirmed the *Times* story; it appeared to become our first ally.

. . .

To a man who has a reputation for having puttered with broadcasts up until air time, it seems unnatural to finish a book in late October that will not be read until next spring. To volunteer prophecy in the field of broadcast politics and economics is dangerous; yet at this writing I am rash enough to believe that some satellite system benefiting noncommercial television is going to emerge in the coming months. There will be the Carnegie Commission report, and further hearings as well, but this time noncommercial television will not be denied.

The first objective has already been won; precipitous action that would have precluded the use of satellites for a nonprofit broadcast service has been blocked. Already accepted is the concept of a fourth network that will be instructional and informational. This network will be financed at least in part by the profits and savings from the use of satellites.

Noncommercial or educational television and radio will at the very least get free interconnection. At current long-line rates, this would cost NET $8,000,000, which is $2,000,000 more than its current total budget. So we will be at least $8,000,000 ahead already.

There will be other sources of revenue, perhaps a levy on broadcasters' profits, perhaps an excise tax on television sets. But whatever the means, it now seems likely that at least $100,000,000 a year will be made available for a service of excellence. As Richard Lewis, the science writer for the Chicago *Sun-Times* put it: "Of all the institutions in America, the Ford Foundation has been the first to seek the exploitation of this Promethean gift of American satellite technology for Americans themselves."

. . .

When I testified before the Pastore committee in August, I said: "The need for this kind of watershed decision now will be dwarfed by the demands of the complex, space-age society we will have in 1976 and in the year 2076; yet a proposal such as ours will come too late when those who then sit in your chairs and mine a decade from now look back to this year of opportunity and ask, 'Why didn't someone push a little harder in 1966 when there was still time to do something?' "

At one point toward the end of Bundy's and my testimonies, Senator Hugh Scott brought me up short by calling me "an emotional man." Before I could protest, the senator from Pennsylvania went on to pay me a compliment for something which I have spent a lifetime resisting: "I am glad you are an emotional man. I think this kind of mission . . . this kind of controversy you have begun, requires the dedication of emotional men. I am an emotional man too, Mr. Friendly."

All my adult life I have been denying that I am an emotional man. The McCarthy broadcast in 1954, my resignation in 1966, and a number of incidents in between, were labeled "emotional" by some observers. But as I sat in that hearing room pleading for an idea, I knew that far from making me a prisoner, my emotions had been a liberating force. I *am* emotional about television.

I am also an idealist. "Man is born a predestined idealist, for he is born to act," wrote Justice Oliver Wendell Holmes. "To act is to affirm the worth of an end, and to persist in affirming the worth of an end is to make an ideal." "Your old men shall dream dreams, and your young men shall see visions," says the Bible. Television is still young enough for visions. Its first twenty years are but a prelude to a new era which will begin when the Atlas Agena lifts the first broadcast satellite into its space station.

Said an editorial in the London *Economist:* "The Ford plan bears the Bundy stamp; like a good Harvard examination question, it will force the Federal Communications Commission to think harder than it had planned to do."

What happens next is not just a test for the FCC, but for all of us, and history will mark us by the results.

About the Author

FRED W. FRIENDLY, whom Carl Sandburg once characterized as a man who "always looks as if he had just got off a foam-flecked horse," was born in New York City in 1915. He spent much of his boyhood in Providence, Rhode Island, however, and began his broadcasting career there in 1938. After serving in the CBI Theater during World War II he came to New York, where, in 1948, he met Edward R. Murrow. Their partnership lasted for twelve years, and together they were responsible for many of television's most distinguished moments.

From 1964 to 1966 Mr. Friendly was president of CBS News. During his sixteen years at that network he received scores of awards for his work in broadcasting, and perhaps his contribution to the medium is best summed up by a 1962 Special George Foster Peabody Award, which reads, in part:

> More than any single individual, he has brought a dynamic meaning to the phrase "electronic journalism." For most men, it is enough that the broadcasts which they conceive and bring to fruition be landmarks—as Fred Friendly's have been. But television owes a debt to Fred Friendly not only for his broadcasts, but for the broadcasts by other television journalists on other networks and stations which have been stimulated by Mr. Friendly's pioneering. As a result, not only CBS News but the news organizations of other broadcasters—and the public—have been vastly enriched by the remarkable journalism of Fred Friendly.

Mr. Friendly now serves as the first Edward R. Murrow Professor of Broadcast Journalism at the Columbia Graduate School of Journalism; in addition, he is television consultant to the Ford Foundation. Married and with three children, he lives in Riverdale, New York.

DISCARDED